AF506169

The Philosophy of Art:
The Question of Definition

Bloomsbury Studies in Philosophy

Bloomsbury Studies in Philosophy presents cutting-edge scholarship in all the major areas of research and study. The wholly original arguments, perspectives and research findings in titles in this series make it an important and stimulating resource for students and academics from a range of disciplines across the humanities and social sciences.

Available in the series:

The Philosophy of Art: The Question of Definition

From Hegel to Post-Dantian Theories

Tiziana Andina

Translated by Natalia Iacobelli

B L O O M S B U R Y

LONDON · NEW DELHI · NEW YORK · SYDNEY

Bloomsbury Academic

An imprint of Bloomsbury Publishing Plc

50 Bedford Square
London
WC1B 3DP
UK

175 Fifth Avenue
New York
NY 10010
USA

www.bloomsbury.com

First published 2013

This book was first published in Italian as *Filosofie dell'arte. Da Hegel a Danto*,
copyright © 2012 by Carocci editore S.p.A., Roma.

British Library Cataloguing-in-Publication Data
A catalogue record for this book is available from the British Library.

ISBN: HB: 978-1-4411-4051-7
ePub: 978-1-4411-3651-0
ePDF: 978-1-4411-6278-6

Library of Congress Cataloging-in-Publication Data
Andina, Tiziana.
[Filosofie dell'arte. English]
The Philosophy of Art: The Question of Definition from Hegel to Post-Dantian theories/
Tiziana Andina; translated by Natalia Iacobelli.
pages cm. – (Bloomsbury studies in philosophy)
Includes bibliographical references and index.
ISBN 978-1-4411-4051-7 (hardback) – ISBN 978-1-4411-3651-0 (ebook) –
ISBN 978-1-4411-6278-6 (ebook) 1. Aesthetics. 2. Art – Philosophy. I. Title.
BH39.A53513 2013
111'.85–dc23
2012046563

Typeset by Newgen Imaging Systems Pvt Ltd, Chennai, India
Printed and bound in Great Britain

For my mother

Contents

Introduction: On the Philosophy of Art

1 Hegel or the beginning

The specialized areas of philosophy – that is, the philosophy of the mind, of language, of music, of science, of history, of law or of religion – are generally distinguished by a clear disciplinary identity. In all of the aforementioned cases, philosophy has a precise and detailed objective: history, science, music, law, language or even ourselves, insofar as we are beings gifted in mind and in thought.

The philosophy of art is no exception. If we were to ask an average cultured person, someone not particularly experienced in philosophy – a sort of ingenuous philosopher endowed with a robust common sense – what they would expect to find in a book on the philosophy of art, they would most probably answer that they would expect to read a reflection, in essay format, whose object is art and the products of art. Quite simple, really. The task of answering questions such as: 'what is art?', 'what is an artwork?', 'what is beauty?', 'what is the difference between a common object and an artwork?', and so on, would be reserved for the philosophy of art.

Let us now suppose that our cultured reader, who is minimally experienced in philosophy – we will call him Frescoditesta – must face a rather delicate task entrusted to him by an elderly uncle who himself is keen on philosophy. The eccentric and comical uncle collects works of art, the majority of which are piled up in a large warehouse together with objects of everyday use. When his uncle passes away, Frescoditesta attends the reading of his will which takes place in a climate of great sadness. The will, in which Frescoditesta is appointed universal inheritor, includes two clauses: first, in order to inherit the artworks Frescoditesta must be able to distinguish them from common objects. The artworks will remain in his possession, while the other objects will be forever destroyed. The will relates another codicil, the second provision: the young nephew will have to carry out this task without the aid of experts, availing himself solely of his intelligence and, perhaps, a few books. After performing a site inspection of the warehouse, Frescoditesta realizes the difficulty of this endeavour. His uncle's collection is remarkably extensive; it includes ancient archaeological finds – pottery, all sorts of furnishings and countless objects dating back to the most diverse civilizations – alongside paintings from all time periods, some of which are beautiful while others could be considered as junk. There are objects which can be found in any given supermarket, mingled with other truly original artefacts, and atop all of them stands a large fish which looks like a shark, conserved in formaldehyde. In addition is a collection of old LPs – Velvet Underground, The Rolling Stones, Michael Jackson and so on.

What is he to do? There is no way of getting around the testamentary provisions, and of this Frescoditesta was fully aware. The only solution is to begin studying in an attempt to find inspiration from books dedicated to the topic. The difficulty is not in separating the beautiful paintings from the ugly ones, the high-quality artworks from the poor quality; it is, rather, a matter of actually singling out the artworks, beautiful and ugly alike. In such a situation, it would be useless to consult books on art criticism; instead, it is necessary to turn to philosophy. Fully determined, Frescoditesta decides to visit an abundantly stocked library. After wandering about and browsing the shelves, he finds the section dedicated to the 'philosophy of art', and there he discovers, happily, that the history of the discipline does not date too far back, at least when compared to the general history of philosophy. The baptism of the philosophy of art took place in an exact period, from 1842 to 1843, the year of publication of the *Lectures on the Aesthetics* by George Wilhelm Friedrich Hegel, who was among the first to distinguish aesthetics from the philosophy of art:

> the present course of lectures deals with 'Aesthetic'. Their subject is the wide *realm of the beautiful,* and, more particularly, their province is *Art* – we may restrict it, indeed, to *Fine Art.* The name 'Aesthetic' in its natural sense in not quite appropriate to this subject. 'Aesthetic' means more precisely the science of sensation or feeling [. . .]. We shall, therefore, permit the name Aesthetic to stand, because it is nothing but a name, and so is indifferent to us, and, moreover, has up to a certain point passed into common language. As a name, therefore, it may be retained. The proper expression, however, for our science is the 'Philosophy of Art,' or, more definitely, the 'Philosophy of Fine Art'. (Hegel, 1842–3, Eng. trans., 3)

In Hegel's book, aesthetics is a science that concerns 'sensation and sentiment', and it pertains to art only when artworks are considered in relation to the emotions they produce in their audience: wonder, fear, compassion and enjoyment. The object of the philosophy of art, therefore, is not that which is naturally beautiful or beauty at all. Rather, it is that which arises from the hands (and from the genius) of man:

> By the above expression we at once exclude the *beauty of Nature* [...] It is true that in common life we are in the habit of speaking of beautiful colour, a beautiful sky, a beautiful river, and, moreover, of beautiful flowers [...] We may, however, begin at once by asserting that artistic beauty stands *higher* than nature. For the beauty of art is the beauty that is born – born again, that is – of the mind. (Hegel, 1842–3 Eng. trans., 4)

Frescoditesta is quick to seize the point of Hegel's discourse: the beauty of art is the fruit of the work of the mind. It is neither accidental nor random, and in this work (at least at a basic level) the truth of the Absolute Spirit is unfurled. Art, therefore, is many things; but it is, above all, the unfolding of the truth inasmuch as it is configured as the sensory manifestation of the Spirit. There are certainly more perfect exemplifications of the Spirit, yet art remains one of its necessary manifestations. According to Hegel's reasoning, a work of art is composed of at least three elements: a material and sensory body, a content (i.e. an initial manifestation of the Spirit) and the pertinence of that body and of those contents.

At this point, after reviewing Hegelian thinking, Frescoditesta encounters his first astonishing realization. His recollections of philosophy are undoubtedly scarce, at times nebulous, yet he knows he is not mistaken in comparing the Hegelian system to a marvellous Baroque cathedral where art, in just the same way as religion and philosophy, carries out a fundamental task. How are we to blame him? In Hegelian thinking, this represents one stage in the manifestation of the Absolute Spirit. Therefore, to inquire about art means to inquire about the Spirit and, thus, about the Absolute and the truth. Frescoditesta is confused: he had turned to Hegel to interrogate him of precise matters and to better understand how to distinguish a work of art from that which a work of art is not, yet he now finds himself discussing the Spirit, truth and even God. This discovery is of no use to him, and so Frescoditesta resorts to posing new questions: is the history of the Spirit in any way related to works of art? Better yet, if the Spirit (with a capital 'S') did not exist at all, what would constitute the philosophy of art? Would it still have something to do with artworks?

Special philosophies distinguish themselves from the Hegelian philosophy of art on the basis of one detail: the philosophy of language does not maintain that language is the manifestation of a recondite and more complex divine language; the philosophy of law concerns itself with our social world, not with another world; the philosophy of science devotes itself to science and to epistemology, not to the means of knowing God by way of man. After reflecting upon all of this, Frescoditesta is still confused and concludes that Hegel is not his cup of tea. No one knows precisely if the Spirit exists or not, while everyone knows for certain that artworks exist (he, for one, is sure that his uncle's warehouse is full of them). At this point, Frescoditesta abandons the prospect of expanding his horizons and considering the philosophy of art of the twentieth century from a more general point of view: he knows that there no longer exist traces of the Spirit, and that artworks are generally seen for what they are.

Frescoditesta's journey will be a long one, and we shall follow him in hopes of learning if the theories formulated by the philosophies of art help him to resolve his predicament. The reader may have noted the fact that the story of Frescoditesta is inspired by the mental experiment elaborated by William Kennick in the essay entitled *Does Traditional Aesthetics Rest on a Mistake?* and published in *Mind* in 1958 (14–27). We will discuss this essay in due course (infra, 99), but for now we might predict that Kennick would have recommended that Frescoditesta give up since, for reasons we will soon encounter, no theory can (and never will) help him in his endeavour. We shall soon discover how and why we can be more optimistic than Kennick was.

2 Works of art and definitions/depositions

The second point is purely theoretical. The example of Kennick brings with it a recurring stem from a specific assumption: the notion that one of the tasks – perhaps the principle task – of the philosophy of art is the elaboration of a definition that answers questions such as: 'What is the difference between an artwork and a simple thing?', 'What type of thing is an artwork?', 'How can I distinguish a common object from an artwork?', 'If there are differences between things and artworks, which general consensus seems to uphold, upon which conceptual bases do such differences rest?', 'How can I distinguish two artworks when the reference of one artwork by another artwork appears to be the result of plagiarism?',[1] the list goes on.

On the one hand, this way of understanding the task of the philosophy of art cannot satisfy everyone; Hegel, for example, would not have agreed with it.[2] On the other hand, it poses a problem connected to the other discipline dealing with art and artworks: aesthetics. As we have seen, Hegel maintained that the distinction between aesthetics and the philosophy of art was above all a matter of linguistic subtleties, but that the two fields more or less coincided. Throughout the course of the twentieth century, for a variety of reasons, this became more complicated, and to such a degree that aesthetics and the philosophy of art eventually developed as separate domains.

Customs officials prove to be a useful example in explaining the daily occurrences of the special philosophy committed to problems related to art and artworks. The objection made towards mental experiments such as those involving Frescoditesta, as well as the protagonist of the Kennick story, is founded upon the doubt that such cases can never be verified in reality and, therefore, to envision them would be a futile activity.[3]

Mental experiments are generally associated by a common trait: they describe a world that does not exist but, through an imagined world, allow an important problem to be brought into focus. For example, it is highly unlikely for one of us to ever find ourselves in the regrettable situation of being deceived by a spiteful genius, but by hypothesizing that it could happen we are offered the possibility to examine certain mechanisms of human knowledge. The philosophy of art under this profile is decidedly unique since, as we will see, reality has prefigured the formulation of odd mental experiments, placing us amidst matters which philosophy has been unable to avoid. The contents of the mental experiments were at hand, and the first to come to this realization were the customs officials themselves. The following three examples alone – three names and three dates – should be sufficient in defining the basic concepts of the philosophy of art: Constantin Brâncuşi 1926, Andy Warhol 1965, Dan Flavin 2010. What they have in common is their problematic relationship with customs.

Bird in Space is a sculpture by Brâncuşi that arrived in New York by sea. Upon inspecting it, customs officials challenged the idea that the strange object was a sculpture, seeing as it in no way resembled a bird. For this reason, they refused to categorize Brâncuşi's creation as a work of art, preferring to consider it a kitchen utensil. They therefore applied to it the taxation that was normally reserved for merchandise, while works of art were subject to fiscal exemption. As expected, Brâncuşi was outraged and the matter was brought to Federal court. Thus began one of the most notorious trials in the history of art: 'Brâncuşi vs. the United States'. Edward Steichen, the photographer who had bought the sculpture, explained the affair to Gertrude Vanderbilt Whitney, founder of the Whitney Museum in New York who, upon realizing that the case would become a formidable judicial precedent, offered to cover the legal fees of the trial. Six members of the jury redounded in Brâncuşi's favour: Edward Steichen, sculptor Jacop Epstein, the editor of the journal *The Arts*, the editor of *Vanity Fair*, the director of the Brooklyn Museum of Art and art critic Henry McBride. Marcus Higginbotham represented customs.

The US government had two jurors as well: sculptors Robert Aitken and Thomas Jones. The state defended the customs officials, recalling a prior case: 'United States vs. Olivotti' from 1916, in which the only artefacts that qualified as works of art were those that were recognized as imitations of objects in nature. The following are a few lines from the debate: Jude Waite asks Steichen 'What do you call this?' Steichen responds: 'I call it what the sculptor calls it, *oiseau*, which means bird'. Waite continues: 'How can you say that it is a bird if it does not resemble one?' Steichen: 'I am not saying that it is a bird, I am saying that it looks like a bird to me just as it was stylized and named by the artist'. Waite replies: 'And the only reason for which you say it is a bird is because he (the artist) called it one?' Steichen: 'Yes, your Honor'. Waite persists: 'If you had seen it on the road, would you have called it a bird? If you had seen it in the forest, would you have shot at it?'

Steichen: 'No, your Honor'.

The trial came to a close on 26 November 1928 with the acknowledgement that Brâncuşi's work, *Bird in Space*, was in fact a work of art.[4]

Same place, same problem: *Brillo Boxes*, Andy Warhol's famous sculpture exhibited in 1964 at the Stable Gallery in New York, disembarked in Canada in 1965 in the care of art merchant Jerrold Morris. Customs officials yet again classified them as products, specifically boxes from a grocery store, and applied to them the corresponding taxation. Their confusion, in reality, was understandable: grocery stores were full of Brillo boxes, containing sponges for cleaning pots and pans. An expert was therefore consulted; Mr Charles Comfort, director of the National Gallery of Canada who, having seeing Warhol's work in photographs, supported the opinion of the customs officials: *Brillo Boxes* was not a work of art.

Another example: *Icons*. These are works made with fluorescent lights symbolizing the icons of our time, and Dan Flavin, the American artist, exhibited them in some of the most prestigious museums in the world. Nevertheless, as was described by *The Guardian*, customs officials in the European Community determined that Flavin's works were light fixtures and, accordingly, would be subjected to the corresponding toll (meaning no offence to the art world).

These three cases illustrate one very simple point: it would have been enough for Kennick to look around himself in order to picture his experiment. Within this context, it would have been very odd if philosophy had not attempted to respond to a problem posed by reality: it was plain to see that the conceptualizations which were used for centuries to explain what exactly a work of art is no longer worked.

3 Questions of definition

In a study published in 1999 entitled *Philosophy of Art. A Contemporary Introduction*, American philosopher Noël Carroll indicates a theoretical point that is important and useful in understanding both the specificity and the role of the philosophy of art throughout the course of the twentieth century.[5] Carroll argues that the theoretical dimension of the philosophy of art concerns the primarily conceptual analysis and the duty of clarification which is typical of analytical philosophy, rather than the theoretical corpus which distinguishes aesthetics of Continental origin and tradition (Carroll, 1999, 3–7).[6]

This involves a separation of domains which rests upon a difference of method and research. Within this framework, the philosophy of art faces questions primarily concerning definition – such as the unique nature of the objects belonging to the class of artworks – while aesthetics, as a matter of principle, might never deal with art nor artworks and, nonetheless, still achieves its objectives.

The idea is that the domains of the philosophy of art and aesthetics ought to be separated: the class of artworks is composed of objects which the philosophy of art aims to define, while aesthetics deals with the knowledge derived perception and, more generally, from sensibility. The claim that the philosophy of art must use the findings of aesthetics in order to define its subject appropriately is up for discussion, and a good philosophy of art would find it difficult to disregard aesthetics.

It is worth noting that the philosophical research of definitions boasts ancient origins and is enlivened by the idea that basic knowledge relies upon concepts for which we have identified the necessary and sufficient conditions. Platonic dialogues demonstrate this point in a masterly fashion. Socrates's strategy often involves pointing out to the interlocutor how, in spite of ostentatious certainty, people rarely possess a definition for that which they claim to have knowledge of (which means, according to the Platonic *standard*, that they rarely possess knowledge). This might seem to be of little importance considering that we are able to get around the world relatively well even when we orient ourselves according to imprecise notions and cognitions. But this is not the case, and artworks are successful in demonstrating this as they possess a good and efficacious definition that leads to a vast consensus and allows valuable and noteworthy problems to be solved.

Everyday life is overflowing with the problems that Plato warned of. If a resurrected Plato were to ask us to define the word 'bachelor', what might we respond? Typically, those who are able to recognize a bachelor when they see one would respond by saying: 'A bachelor is an unmarried adult male.'

The definition is composed of two concepts: 'male' and 'unmarried adult'. This means, to put it simply, that in order for an individual to be a candidate for the definition of 'bachelor', he must possess certain characteristics: he must be a male, he must be an adult and, of course, he must not be married. Should these conditions not be fulfilled contemporaneously – perhaps because the candidate is a woman, a Martian or an adult male who is married – the person with whom we are dealing is not a bachelor.[7] In order for the definition of 'bachelor' to fulfil its objectives, it is necessary to determine the properties shared by all bachelors, after which it is necessary to identify the properties that distinguish bachelors from similar classes such as that of 'husbands'. The philosophy of artworks, in an analogous fashion, attempts to identify the properties shared by all works of art in order to determine the properties that distinguish artworks from classes of similar objects, such as artefacts.

Let us now turn briefly to aesthetics. According to the argument which I am proposing, 'philosophy of art' is not another way of referring to aesthetics: it does not, in fact, deal exclusively or prevalently with problems regarding sensory knowledge, perceptions of aesthetic qualities or the aesthetic experience. Furthermore, it does not elect as its privileged object of research the queen of all aesthetic qualities; that is, beauty.

4 The relationship with a close relative: Aesthetics

The task of defining aesthetics was successfully undertaken by its founder, German philosopher Alexander Gottlieb Baumgarten,[8] who, in *Aesthetica* (1750–8), affords the following definition to the discipline:

> §1. Aesthetics (the theory of the liberal arts, lower gnoseology, the art of thinking beautifully, the art of the analog of reason) is the science of sensitive cognition. (1750–8, 27)[9]

And subsequently:

> § 3. Among the principle applications of artificial aesthetics [. . .] along with natural aesthetics, are: (1) to prepare the adequate material for the sciences which are to be known primarily through the intellect, (2) to adapt scientific knowledge to common understanding, (3) to extend the life of knowledge beyond the limits of what we can know clearly, (4) to provide good principles to the most pleasing of studies and to the liberal arts, (5) in everyday life, on equal terms, to excel in conduct. (1750–8, 27)

It is not surprising, therefore, that aesthetics and the philosophy of art have so little in common. Upon closer inspection, it becomes clear that they do not even share an interest in artworks, considering that the former, as suggested both by the etymology of the word and the history of the concept,[10] should concern itself first and foremost with sensory knowledge. I will, therefore, begin with the idea developed in a seminal fashion by Maurizio Ferraris[11] who, by consolidating Baumgarten's hypothesis of aesthetics as an inferior gnoseology, treats the discipline as a part of epistemology, considering it the foundation of the architecture of our cognitive activity (Ferraris, 1997, 47).

The class of objects which fall under the domain of sensory cognition is quite vast; with the exception of imaginary, ideal or non-existent objects, the rest involve the jurisdiction of our senses. For what reason, therefore, should aesthetics concern itself primarily with artworks? It might be noted that the senses play a pre-eminent role in the understanding of artworks and, therefore, aesthetics should have something legitimate to say in regards to them if it is in fact true that in order to appreciate the aesthetic qualities of a Tintoretto we make use primarily of our sight, while *La Traviata* involves, fundamentally, our hearing. Yet, it is not difficult to imagine a counterexample: what about *Wuthering Heights*? Which one of our senses do we engage in the story of Catherine, of Heathcliff and of their impossible love? It is hard to say.

The philosophy of art is launched from this very realization: as we will observe extensively, one idea that is central to the philosophy of art is that it is not sufficient to consider the relationship between our senses and works of art in order to get to the heart of the question of definition. Ever since art expressed its wish to give up its mimetic vocation, especially throughout the course of the twentieth century, it has not been easy to identify artworks based solely upon perception. If we reflect momentarily on the fact that many objects exhibit aesthetic properties despite their not being artworks (Apple products, for example, are beautiful: elegant and sophisticated in their design), we are able to understand the nature of the problem. 'What is an artwork?' Plato asked himself in the tenth book of the *Republic*, meaning that to identify the exact ontological position of objects which fall under the category of 'artworks' was certainly not a banal matter. Nevertheless, if we can identify a constant beyond the variations, it would be the idea that the primary function of art is the imitation of reality. As beautiful or ugly as reality may be, art depends on it; not only because art is part of reality, but also because it too often describes it, reflects it and, at times, embellishes it.

On the other hand, theories in philosophy often serve to explain the parts of reality that surround us. When the nature of the facts that surround us undergo a profound change, following an historical discontinuity for instance, theories may favour a necessary and radical renewal as they find themselves unable to explain the facts of the new world. This is what occurred at the very moment in which the twentieth century began producing artworks that not only did not imitate parts of the world, but that also were themselves pieces of the world that perhaps other artworks had already imitated.

It has been noted[12] that according a considerable theoretical weight to the avant-garde could be an error of judgement, as if we wished to understand health through a disease. And yet, if we were able to avoid confusion or, in continuing with the metaphor, if the cases having to do with disease would distinguish themselves from those that convey good health, I would not believe this to be a serious problem. It is not a matter of reducing all art to the *ready-made* model or to the avant-garde. It is, rather, a matter of emphasizing how the avant-gardes posed a specific philosophical problem that would eventually manifest itself as a specific historical moment.[13] Hence the urgency to return to questions related to definition.

It is certainly true that artworks such as the *ready-mades (et similia)* are eccentric when compared to the corpus of the 'history of Western art'; and yet, if we were to follow the line of reasoning of those who make this objection (whom we will conveniently define as 'classicists'), we feel a certain degree of discomfort towards the artistic production of the past century. We end up not knowing how to consider most of the 'art' produced in the twentieth century, given that traditional definitions do not struggle solely with *ready-mades*, but also with the products of the avant-garde. The typical classicist reaction would be to suggest how an explanation is not necessary, as it would ultimately be a marginal feat.

Rather than considering the problem from an extensional point of view, by developing a definition which incorporates everything that falls under the category of artworks, philosophers like Peter Kivy (1997) and Nick Zangwill (2007) suggest a change in perspective, proposing that what we actually need is not an extensional criterion, but, rather, an explicatory one. An explanation of the phenomena of the consumption and production of artworks and perhaps even an explanation of the interests related to their protection and conservation would be of tremendous use.[14] Philosophy might call on sociology, in some cases economics, and even jurisprudence:

> Suppose that the project that is being pursued is the analysis of the concept of art, and this concept is assumed to include painting, sculpture, architecture, literature and music. Then at least the following four issues arise [. . .]: (1) The project assumes that there *is* a concept of art that it is in good order and that awaits

analysis [...]. (2) There may be quite a few concepts of art that we might analyze. But if there are competing notions, it raises the question of which concept we *ought* to deploy [...]. (3) The fact that we have a certain concept, even if it is universally shared, does not mean that the concept succeeds in including a range of objects that share a common nature. It may or may not do so [...]. (4) Even if there were a concept of art that is in good order and that did pick out a range of things that share a common nature, it is not clear that explanatory issues can be addressed given only a grasp of the concept of art. (Zangwill, 2007, 389–90)

Zangwill's objections are therefore, paradigmatically, made up of two types. The first is 'of law': to set as an objective the definition of a concept means to assume that there exists a concept which is suitable to that which we intend to define (something Zangwill does not seem to be convinced of). The second type is 'of fact': the result of the analysis may not be guaranteed.

Concerning the second point, we might mention that those are the risks of the trade, and Zangwill should be aware of this. In regards to the substantial objection that involves the concept of art and, specifically, the observation that there may not even be a concept to begin an analysis of, we might put forward a reflection which seems to me to be of importance. In his indisputable masterpiece *The Lives of the Most Excellent Painters, Sculptors and Architects*, Vasari develops a striking narrative that assures the possibility of telling the story of a concept – the concept of 'art' – which encompasses objects that display important similarities: these objects are artworks. General consensus has already welcomed and embraced the Vasarian notion that should we support a different idea, we would have to be accountable for the philosophical reasons that compel us. In other words, in order to commit to a thesis that maintains that things are different, we cannot prescind from a philosophical analysis of the concepts of art and artworks, whatever the result may be.

That said, there is nothing else to do but to choose which path to follow. We will begin by dealing briefly with prior events; that is, with the first important narrative in Western philosophical thought to have taken an interest in art: the mimetic theory of Plato. The heart of the theory is expressed in the tenth book of the *Republic* (X, 595–621) and is well known. It attests to the intrinsically imitative character of art. Art is the imperfect imitation of reality; in short, a copy of a copy. Plato voluntarily poses his question on art within the domain of ontology (and not of aesthetics, it should be noted), as the core of the concept that motivates him has to do with an obviousness that, though certain, philosophers tend to underestimate. Whatever our objective may be – to know, or even transform the world – we must pre-emptively identify the structure, and accordingly the ontology, of what we are dealing with.

5 Prejudice in favour of beauty

In the beginning, then, there was the idea that art was a sort of mirror of reality. Beginning in the middle of the eighteenth century, the relationship between aesthetic thought and art was marked by a powerful prejudice that, by referring to a similar prejudice pointed out by Alexius Meinong, I will define as 'prejudice in favour of Beauty'. Though we will encounter different versions of this prejudice, for now it will suffice to illustrate it in its eminent form.

As we have seen, in Baumgarten's definition, which is attested by the etymological root of the Greek term αἴσθησις, aesthetics is the science of the knowledge derived from the senses. It qualifies as a theory of the liberal arts and of free thinking, as an inferior gnoseology and as the art of the *analogon rationis*. It is, therefore, a discipline which is strongly tied to sensibility and its various dimensions, including, obviously, its cognitive dimension. The transition has been quite smooth from this to the point of binding sensibility to the study of beauty, associating knowledge through the senses with the knowledge of beautiful things and, therefore, of artworks that are (or should be) mimetic representations of beautiful things, as attested in the following annotation by Polish philosopher Władysław Tatarkiewicz:

> *Cognitio aesthetica.* In the early centuries, even those interested in the aesthetic experience did not call it that: the term is later, and considerably so, than the concept itself. [. . .] The adjective 'aesthetic' is evidently of Greek origin. The Greeks used the word αἴσθησις, meaning sensory impressions, coupling it with νόησις, meaning thought. Both these terms were also used in adjectival form, αἰσθητικός and νοητικός, meaning sensitive and intellectual respectively. In Latin, especially in mediaeval Latin, their equivalents were *sensatio* and *intellectus*, *sensitivus* and *intellectivus*; and sensitivus was sometimes called, after the Greek fashion, *aestheticus*. All these terms were used in the philosophy of antiquity and of the Middle Ages; however, only in theoretical philosophy; in discussions of beauty, art and the experiences associated with these, the term 'aesthetic' was not used. [. . .] It was in the middle of the 18th century, in Germany, that one of the philosophers of the school of Leibniz and Wolff, Alexander Baumgarten, while retaining the ancient distinction between intellectual and sensitive cognition, *cognitio intellectiva* and *sensitiva*, gave it a startling new interpretation: he

identified *cognitio sensitiva*, sensitive cognition, with the cognition of beauty and gave to the study of the cognition of beauty the Graeco-Latin name *cognitio aesthetica*, or *aesthetica* for short. (Tatarkiewicz, 1975, Eng. trans., 311)

As Tatarkiewicz notes, the distinction between sensible and intellectual knowledge is age-old, yet Baumgarten's interpretation of it is 'new' and 'surprising'. It is from this very interpretation that 'the prejudice in favour of Beauty' emerges.

Tatarkiewicz has explained a theoretical logic that bases itself upon two assumptions: the first is the idea that art is mimesis, and the other is that art is the beautiful mimesis of beautiful things. Indeed, what is more beautiful than the objects that reproduce reality after their authors have had the chance to eliminate all defects and imperfections that unrelentingly scar it? This is why the mind (at least Baumgarten's mind) had to turn to art or, better yet, to the visual arts, since literature, for instance, seems to save itself from this cliché despite the Platonic admonition made to the poetic arts (*Republic*, 598–608). Clearly, the idea that it is necessary to reproduce reality in order to improve it is associated with the conviction that the image of a mitigated, perfected and improved reality responds to a typically pedagogical purpose: by showing examples of virtue, minds become bred in virtue; a description of courageous actions leads to courage; a representation of what is beautiful in reality prompts the realization of beautiful things. Baumgarten's predecessors had summarized this well before him and with delightful concision.

It is widely known, however, that perfection and beauty do not represent the predominant qualities of this world. A Nazi, while observing *Guernica*, asked Pablo Picasso if he had 'made it', to which the artist replied that the painting was not his, but 'theirs' (i.e. the Nazis'). The moral of the anecdote is that there is nothing beautiful to be found in a painting meant to signify the horror and anguish experienced by all those who came to know what had occurred in Guernica, the Spanish Basque town where, after three hours of mad bombardment on 26 April 1937, more than 1,600 people were atrociously killed in the midst of a civil war. Guernica is not '*beautiful*', at least not in the traditional sense of the word, and it certainly does not represent good things. And yet, it is one of the universal symbols put forth by humanity, deploring the barbaric acts of war. It is art, therefore, in a sublime sense.

Giovanni Lanfranco's *Crucifixion*, on the other hand, is what we would call a beautiful painting, despite the fact that it depicts neither good nor beautiful things – in this work, as in the former, the subject matter of the painting is assassination. Of course, there are also paintings that succeed in expressing beautiful things that, at times, are also good things. This involves a different conceptual undertone: in this case, it is not a matter of beauty in and of itself but, rather, of the internal beauty of the depicted subject. The question covers the matter from time to time (infra, 86 ff.), but the point concerns the distinction between the representation of a beautiful object and a well-made representation of an object that is not beautiful.

Beauty is not a necessary condition of art and this understanding, from the time of Karl Rosenkrantz's *Aesthetics* (1853), has been expressed with vigour by the philosophy of art of the twentieth century. In this sense, the twentieth century was fundamentally a departure from two ancient and deeply rooted prejudices; one in favour of mimesis and the other of beauty. Perhaps, more simply, it is a matter of distancing oneself from the 'prejudice towards Plato'. In the next chapter, we will begin our reflection from this very point, from one of the most powerful theories ever produced by the philosophy of art: the imitative theory. Before we consider this direct confrontation with Plato, we ought to examine the second prejudice that burdens the way we understand art and works of art. We shall call this the prejudice in favour of truth.

6 Prejudice in favour of truth

It is widely known that the Greeks were of the idea that there existed a bond between goodness and beauty, between ethics and aesthetics. Truth, they believed, was something separate. Plato maintained that art was the imitation of appearances, and that this was contrary to truth:

> Then consider this very point: What does painting do in each case? Does it imitate that which is as it is, or does it imitate that which appears as it appears? Is it an imitation of appearances or of truth? – Of appearances. – Then imitation is far removed from the truth, for it touches only a small part of each thing and a part that is itself only an image. And that, it seems, is why it can produce everything. For example, we say that a painter can paint a cobbler, a carpenter, or any other craftsman, even though he knows nothing about these crafts. Nevertheless, if he is a good painter and displays his painting of a carpenter at a distance, he can deceive children and foolish people into thinking that it is truly a carpenter. (*Republic*, X, 268–9)

He therefore denied that a positive relationship existed between art and truth: a painter is a good painter when they are able to deceive us with their mastery[15] and this was the essence of the matter. Pliny the Elder's *Natural History* is another famous work regarding the topic:

> In a contest between Zeuxis and Parrhasius, Zeuxis produced so successful a representation of grapes that birds flew up to the stage-buildings where it was hung. Then Parrhasius produced such a successful *trompe-l'oeil* of a curtain that Zeuxis, puffed up with pride at the judgment of the birds, asked that the curtain be drawn aside and the picture revealed. When he realized his mistake, with an unaffected modesty he conceded the prize, saying that whereas he had deceived birds, Parrhasius had deceived him, an artist. (xxxv, 330)

Art deceives, and it does so purposefully. And that's not all: the perfection of the deceit is proportional to the skill of the painter. Art thus creates a specific space in which the rules of fiction are fair game, which means that it is in no way expected to express things that are true. The point is that while from a Platonic perspective this becomes a potential hazard to the state, for Aristotle it is simply a matter of fact, given that art is an autonomous sphere of reality for which the rules of morality are not valid. Indeed, the object of the tragedy is not truth, but rather verisimilitude; there would be no sense in searching around the world for a mother named Medea in order to ask her the reasons for which she committed infanticide, while it would make sense to study that 'type' of human who in the tragic representation is named Medea, in order to better understand the psychological structure of all characters like Medea, for example. Therefore, in one case (the Platonic theory) art has to do with truth only to deny it, while in the other (the Aristotelian theory) its objective is verisimilitude and the universal – not historical truth, but, rather, supra-historical and structural truth.

Getting back to Frescoditesta, he is still busy unearthing books and theories that might help him resolve the problem posed by his uncle's will. Let us suppose that during his quest he stumbles upon the two most influential art philosophers of the hermeneutic school of thought: Martin Heidegger and Hans Georg Gadamer. 'What is an artwork?', Martin Heidegger asks himself (1950, Eng. trans., 2). This question, so precise and so clear, must have seemed wonderful to Frescoditesta, as it in some way foretold his predicament:

> If we regard works in their pristine reality and do not deceive ourselves, the following becomes evident: works are as naturally present as things. The picture hangs on the wall like a hunting weapon or a hat. A painting – for example van Gogh's portrayal of a pair of peasant shoes – travels from one exhibition to another. Works are shipped like coal from the Ruhr or logs from the Black Forest. (Heidegger, 1950, Eng. trans., 2–3)

The point that was so close to Frescoditesta's heart was, undoubtedly, very clear to Heidegger: the year was 1935 and, by writing *The Origin of the Work of Art*, Heidegger expressed that he realized that deep changes were taking place around him. Those in the avant-garde were wreaking havoc and artworks were being treated more and more often as ordinary objects or, conversely, ordinary objects were being treated as artworks – 'works of art are shipped like coal from the Ruhr and logs from the Black Forest'. In reality, if we were to take a closer look, the situation was far worse, considering that a man by the name of Marcel Duchamp had had the audacity to put on display a urinal as if it were Donatello's *David*. As he looked around himself, Heidegger noticed that something important was occurring in the circuit of art and that classic definitions were becoming increasingly problematic. Thus far, Heidegger's theoretical operation fosters valid arguments. However, as we will see, his argument is problematic in general, and particularly where it concerns the relationship between art and truth.

Heidegger approaches the question in a unique way: he does not identify the necessary and sufficient conditions in order to develop the best definition. Instead, he poses the problem of origin so that, in this way, the eminently philosophical problem of essence is addressed. Heidegger claims that an artwork and its artist are inescapably related and that philosophical analysis is meant to respect this inextricable relationship that, oddly, he does not consider problematic:

> The artist is the origin of the work. The work is the origin of the artist. Neither is without the other. Nonetheless, neither is the sole support of the other. Artist and work *are* each, in themselves and in their reciprocal relation, on account of a third thing, which is prior to both; on account, that is, of that from which both artist and artwork take their names, on account of art. [...] What the work is we can only find out from the nature of art. It is easy to see that we are moving in a circle. The usual understanding demands that this circle be avoided as an offense against logic. [...] The collecting of characteristics from what exists, however, and the derivation from fundamental principles are impossible in exactly the same way and, where practiced, are a self-delusion. So we must move in a circle. (Heidegger, 1950, Eng. trans., 2)

Heidegger's position is curious considering that common sense does not have a problem with loops or with fallacies. Rather, philosophical thought should try to avoid them, which is, by definition, an argumentative thought. Heidegger begins his inquiry by considering the proximity between things and artworks, the very aspect that had alerted him to the fact that artworks are not easily distinguished from mere things.

Works of art are things insofar as they are artefacts, material objects produced by human beings. It would be worthwhile, therefore, to first pose the ontological question regarding things, and in order to reach a suitable response, the question on the realm of the belonging of the subject must be addressed. Let us make an observation: Heidegger asks his readers to remain within the circle, but he himself leaves it almost immediately and argues not about art, about artworks, nor the world of art, but rather about things. The question must be resolved by first considering the materiality of the artwork. Given that the artwork is a material object (in other words, a 'thing'), a good starting point would be to clarify the concept of 'thing' in order to then define the concept of 'artwork', which it will likely depend on. In this case, once again, the method is genetic: to retrace traditional doctrines regarding an entity or a thing and to prove their insufficiency. An artwork cannot be truly understood by referring to the concept of 'thing' as foundation or substance, nor can it be understood as the synthesis of a multiplicity of sensory perceptions, nor as a union of material and form (Heidegger, 1950, Eng. trans., 9–12). Heidegger insists that to forgo the conceptual pair 'material-form' means to forgo the 'classic conceptual scheme of each art theory and of all aesthetics', which has constituted the pillar of art reflection from Plato to Hegel and beyond, and upon which the key concepts of aesthetics were based, among them the concepts of creation and of imitation.

At this point in our analysis, the subject already developed in Heidegger's *Being and Time* (1927, 15) comes into play, in a context in which a 'thing' is principally considered an instrument. In existential analysis (1927, 14 ff.), the distinction between natural objects and things is founded upon the very idea that the latter can be useful. Things, as opposed to natural objects, are artefactual in nature; they are all useful in that they fulfil a purpose, are usable and execute the objective for which their author created them. In order to find the solution to the problem, Heidegger uses the same manoeuvre that will be adopted, in another context, by the artefactual theory (infra, 73 ff.): he distinguishes between mere things (natural objects) and utensils (artefacts). Natural objects do not refer to anything but themselves. A block of granite, for instance, is an object whose particular form is not predisposed to any specific purpose. Artefacts are clearly different. Since a work of art falls into the category of things, rather than mere things, particular as it is, it is also an artefact. It is not needed for practical purposes; it would be silly to use a painting in order to cover an imperfection on the wall, or to use a book in order to stabilize a wobbly table. Paintings and books were conceptualized and created for a more complex purpose, one that has to do with truth.

In order to illustrate this point, Heidegger uses a painting by Van Gogh whose object is a pair of shoes.[16] Whether those shoes were really a depiction of a farmer's shoes, as Heidegger maintains, or the shoes of Van Gogh himself, as argued by Mayer Shapiro,[17] the salient theoretical point resides in the fact that their intrinsic nature emerges with clarity in the representation, more so than in their actual counterpart:

> Van Gogh's painting is the disclosure of what the equipment, the pair of peasant shoes, *is* in truth. This entity emerges into the unconcealedness of its being. The Greeks called the unconcealedness of beings *aletheia*. We say 'truth' and think little enough in using this word. If there occurs in the work a disclosure of a particular being, disclosing what and how it is, then there is here an occurring, a happening of truth at work. (Heidegger, 1950, Eng. trans., 35)

And thus, to reach a definition: 'in a work of art the truth of a being is a happening of truth at work' (Heidegger, 1950, Eng. trans., 35). This point is particularly important: art has a privileged relationship with truth and this does not occur within a fictional space, but, rather, in the real world. Truth – the kind that interested Plato – is more in an artwork than in the world. As a result, in order to comprehend what the shoes authentically are, it would be useful to study them in Van Gogh's painting more than it would be to wear them. The intrinsic truth, which has little or nothing to do with the depiction of the shoes, is unfurled within the artwork. While it is evident that art does not have a mimetic duty, the idea of truth which Heidegger affiliates to it is less patent: an artwork does not depict the real state of things (i.e. how things are out there in the world), but rather it expresses to us an approximate truth that is more true than the corresponding 'banal' truth. The authentic significance of the world of relationships, history and meanings lives in an artwork and it is there, more than anywhere, where it finds its finest expression. Within this framework, Heidegger's theory could be read in two ways: if he intends to demonstrate that an artwork expresses the artist's vision of the world and their cultural context, this is certainly and trivially true. If, instead, he intends to demonstrate that truth is created in an artwork (the stronger, yet more problematic, theory), Heidegger's idea of truth must be less ambiguous:

> In the light of the delineation of the essence of the work we have reached, according to which the happening of truth is at work in the work, we can characterize creation as the allowing of something to come forth in what has been brought forth. The work's becoming a work is a mode of the becoming and happening of truth. [...] What, however, is truth for it to be the case that it

has to happen in something like a creation? [. . .] Truth is un-truth. (Heidegger,
1950, Eng. trans., 35–6)

All things considered, everything becomes confused: an artwork stands for
something else – the truth – which is hard to understand since it is also its
opposite. If we were to interpret Heidegger's position with a bit of common
sense, we would find that it leaves itself open to at least two objections. The
first concerns the concept of truth used in this book: truth as conformity is of
no importance in a work of art but, more radically, a different kind of truth is
found in it. This truth is even more 'true', if possible, than the last; it is a truth
that reveals the authentic nature of things (their relationships, their historical
nexus) that is found only within the artwork. Thus, an artwork 'makes' truth that
otherwise would not exist:

> In the tragedy nothing is staged or displayed theatrically, but the battle of the
> new gods against the old is being fought. The linguistic work, originating in
> the speech of the people, does not refer to this battle; it transforms the people's
> saying so that now every living word fights the battle and puts up for decision
> what is holy and what unholy, what great and what small, what brave and what
> cowardly, what lofty and what flighty, what master and what slave. (Heidegger,
> 1950, Eng. trans., 42)

Thus, in a hypothetical world in which the humans who inhabit it have never
produced art or in a world in which art becomes extinct, truth would not exist.
But why?, we might ask ourselves. A world without art is possible, though it
would certainly be a less interesting world. Perhaps Heidegger has in mind a
hazier theory, and he means to say that truth expressed by artworks is something
like the spirit of time. This can be trivially true and in most cases it is; but it
should be kept in mind that artworks can also be many other things: for example,
they can foretell visions of the future world, they can summon back a bygone
mythicized Arcadia, they can imagine non-existent and fantastic worlds, they
can cite other works or even worlds that no longer exist and so on.

The second objection concerns a corollary of the principle theory, when
Heidegger argues that the materiality of an artwork vanishes at the very moment
in which the artwork is an artwork (1950, Eng. trans., 31). In this case, once again,
the theory is trivially true if it means that we do not pay attention to the ink or to
the spelling of the words that compose a page of Shakespeare, for instance, but it
is false if we were to argue that we can prescind from the materiality of the work
because what matters is solely the truth implemented by the work itself. If the
truth that Heidegger has in mind – supposing that it exists – takes shape in an

artwork rather than, let's say, in the thoughts of an artist, it is because that work has a body, unlike a thought that has a body when it is written down but that becomes an artwork only once it assumes and articulates that body.

Hans Georg Gadamer came close to understanding the thorny difficulties present in the thoughts of his teacher and, as a result, attempted to soften certain theories of his by standardizing, when possible, his philosophy of art. His *Truth and Method* (1960) takes on a precise objective: it intends to legitimize an idea of truth that is alternate to that of the natural sciences. His theory is that the notion of truth must be bipartite; on the one hand lies the truth that belongs to the domain of the natural sciences, and on the other hand lies the other truth, the one which is handled by studies in historical, philosophical and social fields. *Truth and Method* is a text that aspires to be a stronghold in literature and a rampart for its scientific legitimization, located at a historical juncture in which the sciences are progressively taking hold (1960, Eng. trans., 3–7). Within this framework, artworks exhibit (and implement, as we shall see) this second type of truth:

> Here the scholarly research pursued by the 'science of art' is aware from the start that it can neither replace nor surpass the experience of art. The fact that through a work of art a truth is experienced that we cannot attain in any other way constitutes the philosophic importance of art, which asserts itself against all attempts to rationalize it away. Hence, together with the experience of philosophy, the experience of art is the most insistent admonition to scientific consciousness to acknowledge its own limits. (Gadamer, 1960, Eng. trans., xxi–xxii)

While Heidegger theorizes that truth is created in artworks, in *Truth and Method* Gadamer similarly considers an artwork to hold a privileged position in terms of the acquisition of truth, but, at the same time, he greatly simplifies and clarifies Heidegger's theory: the truth implemented in an artwork is something intimately related to the representation of the depicted thing. The true essence of what is depicted is able to find its place very easily in an artwork: the pain of a man (*The Scream*), the despair of a mother (*Medea*), fraternal love (*Antigone*), the conflict of multiple personalities (the self-portraits of Francis Bacon), the torment of war (*Guernica*), the nature of time (*Empire*), we could continue infinitely.

> Thus the situation basic to imitation that we were discussing not only implied that what is represented is there (das Dargestellte da ist), but also that it has come into the There more authentically (eigentlicher ins Da gekommen ist). Imitation and representation are not merely a repetition, a copy, but knowledge of the

essence. Because they are not merely repetition, but a 'bringing forth,' they imply
a spectator as well. They contain in themselves an essential relation to everyone
for whom the representation exists. (Gadamer, 1960, Eng. trans., 114)

While truth is always at stake, Gadamer identifies it with precision and detracts from it some of its mystery: in an artwork we find the quintessence of what is made to be the object of a representation. Hence, Homer's Achilles is, in some way, more true than the Achilles who existed; the narrative of Achilles' character as presented in *The Odyssey* expresses a universal trait. For this reason, Aristotle was able to argue, and Gadamer was able to agree, that poetry is more philosophical than history (*Poetics*, 9, 1451 b 6). This is why, Gadamer observes, the model offered by the mimetic theory is still not sufficient: representation is constitutively selective, while mimesis is reproductive. At the moment in which a poet creates a character – a type – they select certain characteristics that distinguish that character and omits all the rest. To select certain qualities at the expense of others is useful not only in order to construct the artistic unity of the character and of the plot, but also, we might suppose, in order to favour the understanding of the particular ethical qualities related to the exemplified character: the Achilles described by Homer allows us to understand the essence of virtue, courage and strength (certain qualities, in other words, that are exemplified by that particular type of human). Thus, as a corollary of Gadamer's theory, art produces a specific understanding that has an intrinsic relationship with truth that, moreover, can only reside within the environment of the artwork (this is perhaps the most important theoretical element of the hermeneutic perspective).

Let us now try to imagine a society which does not know art, which has never produced art. One might think that the members of this society have no true experience or knowledge of the things that are generally found in artworks. For instance, would there be no human capable of understanding the feeling of affection for a brother, or respect for a god? Or, would the members of that society not know that there are multifaceted personalities and that hate (in its most devastating state) produces autodestruction, or that war barbarizes human beings to the point of making them inhumane? It would be banal to observe that passions, emotions, sentiments and ideas reside first and foremost in life and that, though the premise of Gadamer's discourse is correct, to which we will return by dealing with representation theories (infra, 132 ff.), the idea which Gadamer associates with an artwork is problematic for a variety of reasons. It is one thing to argue that human beings would not be able to live without paintings and novels, but it is entirely different to assert that without art human beings would surely live in a poorer way and, perhaps, even be worse off themselves. It is certainly possible to live without art, without philosophy and without science; it would be more difficult, perhaps impossible, to live without technique. Not because a certain mysterious truth is revealed in technique, but because without technique our life would be more complicated. If our species has produced art for millennia, there must be a reason, but it does not have to do with the elaboration of a sort of supplement to truth. If not, it would be like saying that Andy Warhol had been in need of his self-portrait in order to be the Andy Warhol he actually was, in order to *really* be Andy Warhol. Or if Guernica had really been 'Guernica' only after Picasso's painting. Artworks follow life; they do not precede it, though some artworks are able to describe the world wonderfully. All of this entails a rather challenging theoretical move: to associate the sciences of the spirit (i.e. the disciplines that are distinguished from the hard sciences) to a different type of truth that, as it is made to be understood, is likely more complicated and elusive.

What does this mean exactly? Let us consider historiography and the following scenario: we are in the year 3012, in a hypothetical world. In this world, we find an historian who is determined to write a book that describes the Second World War as it took place on planet Earth. Our historian is of the steadfast conviction that the truth of the facts will never be 'truly ascertainable': in short, his readers will never truly know the truth. This is not because it would not be possible to collect the totality of the facts that determined the 'Second World War': in a not so distant future that task might even be accomplished, insofar as what seems to be essential to the understanding of the facts is an understanding of the historical-cultural dimension that determined them. Let us suppose that the historian in the hypothetical world is interested in the attack on Pearl Harbor 7 December 1941, carried out by Japan against the United States without a declaration of pre-emptive war. The theory which they commit himself to could have two different declinations: first (the strongest and on the verge of being paradoxical), they could argue that it is not possible to separate the facts from their interpretation. Within this framework one cannot know the truth considering that interpretations are intrinsically subjective; it is a trivially false thesis since, until proved otherwise – until something different, based upon a new fact, is demonstrated – it will always be true that the attack on Pearl Harbor took place on 7 December 1941, regardless of the interpretation of the event. The second declination is perhaps more insidious and certainly no less problematic. Should our historian choose to commit themself to this second declination, they would argue that we can describe all of the facts that determined a given event, but that this operation boils down to very little when compared to what is required by the complexity of historical comprehension. History reveals itself as something different from pure and simple chronological verification of the succession of events. This is certainly true: a correct recording of events is a necessary, though insufficient, condition for obtaining a reconstruction of history. What is missing from the chronicle that prevents it from becoming history? Let us turn to the following simile for clarification: is the presence of two molecules of hydrogen and one of oxygen (given that we know the molecular constitution of hydrogen and of oxygen) enough to say that we have water? The answer is 'Yes'. Can we say that it is enough to know the sequence of the facts that we classify as 'Pearl Harbor' in order to claim that we understand the historical event of 'Pearl Harbor'? The answer is 'No'. We must, though, beware of one point: the reconstruction of the historical sequence of facts is an insufficient condition for an historical understanding, but it is obviously a necessary condition (which means that it is not possible to prescind from it). In order to establish the sequence of facts, it would be necessary to go around the world gathering evidence, consulting archives, cross-checking sources and so on. This research is similar to that which is carried out by a chemist who studies the composition of H_2O.

A rather simple observation will serve to explain the difference between history and chemistry: water will always be such as we know it, no matter what its form, as long as there will be two molecules of hydrogen and one of oxygen that unite. The totality of facts that we classify as 'Pearl Harbor', on the other hand, is only relatively stable. It is always a possibility that one day an historian could discover a conversation that took place between the ambassador Nomura and the Japanese foreign minister in which the minister orders his ambassador to deliver a declaration of war to the American secretary of state two days before the attack. In this case, a new fact would be added to those already known, influencing the historical opinion on Pearl Harbor, and the opinion would be revised.

Moreover, if things really had gone this way – if we were to discover that Japan had acted loyally and had declared war on the United States before treacherously launching the attack, but this declaration was not able to reach its destination, inflicting dual damage (to Japan in honour, and to the United States in substance) – we would be compelled to revisit the many opinions regarding not only Pearl Harbor, but also the entire Second World War. What if it were discovered that Roosevelt was aware of the attack, as some have conjectured, before it took place? In this case, historians would again have to revisit many facts. Chronicle, on the other hand, distinguishes itself from history by the complexity of the relations at stake: the description of a chronicle episode is circumstantial to that single event, but that very fact, when considered from an historical perspective, must be placed in relation to dozens of other events. Chronicle gathers all of the events of Pearl Harbor while history places them in relation to other happenings (some previous other subsequent), and based on these relations, it formulates an opinion. Facts are ascertained while the relations which we give to them depend on many factors, some of which are cultural and historical in nature. The domain of historical truth must certainly assess a greater number of variables, but this does not mean that historical opinions and history itself cannot be true or false. Yet for art, in general, things are different. Let us consider two works of history: Winston Churchill's *War Memoirs*, a masterpiece of literature, and the film *Pearl Harbor*, directed by Michael Bay. Might we expect to find in them the same type of truth?

Churchill's narrative could not be more impassioned. His main source is his memory, which is proverbially prodigious. And then there are the archives, the detailed instructions dictated during the war and the notes. The narrative reveals a series of true occurrences (that have been verified and certified) that Churchill places in relation to other events. A few of those relations could be discussed and perhaps modified, but the same cannot be said for the facts considered individually or for the structure. The link between history and truth is, therefore, a necessary link. In the case of art, on the other hand, this link is strongly attenuated. We know that *Pearl Harbor* is inspired by an event in history and, accordingly, we expect the director not to distort the narrative content of his work (though it is quite possible that the dramatization will overlook the accuracy of the details). If Michael Bay had told a story in which a Chinese general had sabotaged the delivery of the declaration of war from the Japanese ambassador to the American government, no one would have cried scandal unless, of course, Bay had argued that his narrative corresponded to historical truth; that is, to fact. Art is in no way responsible for truth; that is to say, it is not liable for the representation of things that are true, nor to a true representation (congruent with truth) of things that are true. Art, therefore, has the absolute privilege to do what it wishes.

1

The Twentieth Century and the Long History of the Imitative Theory

1 Plato, Aristotle and the duplicate world

1.1 Homer Simpson's argument

The question posed by Heidegger, considered in the introduction, persists. What does not work, however, is the solution he has proposed. Is it all the fault of works like *Brillo Box* if works of art as a class has become an indistinct nebula?

Many philosophers and artists have argued just this. Throughout the course of this work, we shall attempt to demonstrate that, in essence, works of art have always been, and remain, the same thing – using philosophical language,[1] we might say the same kind of object – despite the numerous transformations in style and taste. We shall argue that a good way to confront the question of definition is by considering artworks as objects that are similar to words; therefore, as objects that inhabit the same ontological region as language. In both cases, physical structures transmit meanings (infra, 132 ff.). Words and artworks are both 'about something', and this 'something' (the meaning) is altogether different compared to the physical structure that carries it and which, conversely, can have various forms and appearances.

We shall uphold this theory while proceeding negatively, so to speak: we shall pave a path across the philosophy of art of the twentieth century, and we shall show how this is the theory, among the manifold and diverse theories, that exhibits the most consistent advantages.

It may not seem obvious at first that a work by Caravaggio, for instance *Boy Bitten by a Lizard*, has something in common with the word 'house'. The word 'house' is composed of a certain collection of letters (h-o-u-s-e, in the English language) that bears no likeness to an ordinary depiction of a house.[2] For example, the collection of letters is not written in the shape of a house and, yet, within the conventional system of the English language, that particular grouping of letters denotes a 'house'. A similar system of conventional thinking suggests that the pictorial representation of a man who gazes at his own reflection in a watery mirror will recall the sad affair of Narcissus.

The theory that we hope to develop is this: the category of works of art exhibits the same metaphysical structure, insofar as they are objects that communicate 'something' (a meaning) that does not necessarily correspond to the material body in which this something is contained.

This peculiarity regarding words had already captured the attention of Gorgia who, polemically committed to sustaining the non-existence of a being, observed how, even if a being were to exist, it could not be spoken of because in order to speak of it we would need words. Words have a unique feature: they do not reflect things. The word 'red' clearly does not need to be written in red in order to achieve its goal. In regard to images, however, this is not so: after all, a body hanging from a cross represents a dead body, and does so by means of a direct depiction. Therefore, the word 'red' does not actually need to be red, while a depiction of the colour red ought to be.

Nevertheless, let us consider the famed painting by René Magritte, *Ceci n'est pas une pipe*. As Michel Foucault rightly notes (1973, Eng. trans., 17–49), the caption, literally speaking, describes the truth, yet most of the time we do not pay due attention to it. It is evident that Magritte's work is 'not' a pipe; Sherlock Holmes, for instance, would not be able to smoke it because it is an artwork that 'represents' a pipe.

While this might appear to be a trivial matter, it is crucial to understanding the nature of the ontological question related to art. Plato and Aristotle would have argued that the artwork 'imitates' a pipe, and this very theory is upheld by the twenty-first-century American pop icon Homer Simpson.[3] In an attempt to justify his sudden success as an avant-garde artist, Homer mocks Marge and cajoles her into thinking that he adores her paintings because they 'look like the things they look like'. Homer clearly feels guilty that Marge, who had attempted to pursue an artistic career from a young age, had struggled through art school, and who actually knew how to paint, was never able to achieve success, while he had entered the art world on a whim, and had become a star.

If the strength of a philosophical theory is measured by its concordance with our naïve ways of thinking, then the imitative theory is evidently an extremely strong theory. In fact, Homer's argument has a near-universal hold: who has never felt relieved, while roaming the contemporary art collections in a museum, upon finding a work that depicts, perhaps in a realistic way, a part of reality? In the majority of cases, contemporary art remains foreign to us, precisely because it lacks the type of understanding that Homer proves to have for Marge's art. If a red line exists that links the thought of illustrious philosophers with that of commoners, who have little to nothing to do with philosophy, or even with cartoons, it might just be that this idea suggests that common sense with regard to art has matured over the centuries.

While discussing Gorgia's argument, Aristotle noticed how he had neglected an important property of language: that words posses a semantic meaning, unlike images that 'imitate' reality. What's curious is that, despite having seized the theoretical point perfectly, Aristotle struggled to focus on it in his reflections on art and ended up endorsing Plato's stance, notwithstanding certain differences which we shall touch upon later. The two are united by the idea that art is, first and foremost, mimetic. The difference lies in their respective conclusions: Plato maintains that art is useless and damaging, while Aristotle attributes to it a specific purpose.

On these grounds I shall treat the Platonic-Aristotelian theory (which I will define 'duplicative' or, even, 'imitative' as it considers art by the same standard as it does a duplication mechanism in reality) as a single position, which prefigures the representational or neo-representational theories.

Yet, as we shall see, this powerful and long-lived theory has exhibited limits throughout the course of the twentieth century that have rendered it inefficacious.[4] It was the art of the last century that, in revealing an important ontological incongruity, accidentally displayed the inefficaciousness of the imitative theory. Let us proceed in an orderly fashion and examine first the theoretical-conceptual roots of one of the most influential theories in the history of Western philosophy.

1.2 Objects that imitate other objects: The imitative theory

If Gorgia is in fact right in supposing that the drawing of a house imitates a house, then the drawing must express truth about the house more effectively than words would. Nevertheless, Plato draws together the threads of his ontology by overturning Gorgia's perspective and articulating an important theoretical point: the drawing of a house has little value if compared to a real house which, in turn, has little value if compared to the idea of a house – that is, with the universal correspondence.

Plato therefore concludes that, all in all, it is best to do away with drawings and artistic imitations in general; in order to know we ought rather to rely directly on ideas whereas, if we are interested in actions, those regarding real things are undoubtedly more valuable than those which are objects of the fictional world. In Plato's view, the most prestigious knowledge is the knowledge that permits us to 'know' how to drive an automobile, for instance, whereas to know how to write novels that describe the accomplishments of Ascari, or to know how to paint a classic Ferrari using a superb fiery red, boils down to very little. In an attempt to establish a hierarchy, we might state the following: it is best to know how an automobile is made, after which it is important to know how to drive an automobile and, finally, in our spare time, it could be useful to learn how to paint and describe an automobile.

Art has instigated philosophical marvels since the beginning of time. Plato, in the tenth book of the *Republic*, emphasized how works of art, despite their being artefacts for all intents and purposes, exhibit particular properties that a reductionist theory is unable to account for. If it is in fact true that a painting is an artefact – in other words, a product of human intentionality, created with a purpose – an artefactualist, and therefore reductionist, position seems unable to account for certain peculiarities which, at least intuitively, are accorded to artworks: for example, we do not consider a raw canvas (an artefact) and a painting in the same way, just as we would not in the case of a bound notebook of A4 sheets and a book by Simenon.[5]

A bed carved of wood and the depiction of a bed are two different objects insofar as the former 'is' the object, while the latter is 'about the object'. That is, the former is the product of strict identity, while the latter is simple imitation: a painting of a bed 'imitates' the bed. This means that while the word 'bed' shares no property with a true bed, the mimetic representation of a bed reproduces certain properties of a bed (the shape, the width and the length, for example), on a different scale than that of a true bed. Let us now consider the theory that we defined as imitative and that, as mentioned earlier, is exemplified by Plato and, intermittently, confirmed by Aristotle.

For Plato, works of art are parts of reality just as a house, a train or even a telephone is. Yet while these objects (a house, train or telephone) reproduce universal equivalents (the ideas of a house, a train or a telephone), works of art reproduce – or, better yet, imitate – objects of the world: the houses, trains and telephones that we use every day. Artworks reproduce objects that are, in turn, imperfect and that imitate the same imperfections of reality that is reproduced, at times adding others. Let us summarize:

a. works of art are artefacts just as common artefacts are;
b. common artefacts are *tokens* of their respective *types* (ideas);

c. works of art are copies and, therefore, are *tokens* of common objects.

Plato draws two consequences from this argument, one of which ensues from the premises of the argument while the other, in effect, appears to be rather extrinsic:

d. works of art are residual products; it is more important to 'know how to conduct' an army than it is to 'know how to speak' of the conduction of an army (e.g. when writing an epic poem);
e. artists and all works of art must be banned from the ideal state.

Given the progression of Plato's argumentation, the astounding point here is 'e'. In fact, it does not surprise us that Plato judges art as if it were a waste product; this consequence derives directly from the general traits of his ontology. What is perhaps most surprising is the banishment that Plato issues towards art and artists; they must be excluded from the ideal state as their activities are at best useless, and at worst pernicious. Obviously, what is useless is not necessarily harmful, and this is why Plato's inference does not seem entirely justified.

Nevertheless, Plato's reasoning demonstrates in the negative a second property that distinguishes common artefacts from works of art: in general, works of art are not of great utility. Certain novels might be used for edifying purposes: 'do you want to be saved?', a high school teacher might ask, 'well, take note of the sins that the reprobates in Dante's Inferno were stained of and mend your ways if you truly care about the afterlife'. Yet, in essence, this is a fairly marginal kind of utility; it is, moreover, characteristic of the historical periods in which the majority of works of art reflected religious convictions.

In a similar way, we can stress the decorative function of the visual arts. Paintings can serve as an embellishment for our houses, just as music is used to distract and to calm us. Nevertheless, we know that the value of a work does not depend minimally on the way in which it fulfils this function. Certain works have tremendous value, yet we would be reluctant to place them in our homes as they are far from being decorative or enlivening, but are, rather, upsetting and bothersome.

Art in general, then, 'serves' little purpose. And yet, a world devoid of literature or music would be a very different world and certainly a more aseptic one. On these grounds, Plato rightly argued that the primary property of works was not to 'serve a purpose'.

Few things lack such a practical purpose and yet are still able to interest mankind for centuries; it would, therefore, seem logical that these objects must have a certain purpose. This must have been the reason for which Plato believed that works of art had the objective of imitating reality. We may formalize the imitative theory, in general terms, as follows:

x is a work of art only if it is an imitation.

This is the very point with which Aristotle agrees: be it the appearance of things, or the actions of man, painting and poetry, in substance, imitate and reproduce. Aristotle completes his general theory by integrating it with a theory on emotions which functions as a bridge between the subject and the works. For the time being, though, let us adhere to strictly ontological issues and take up the subject of history.

1.3 *'Ars'*: A brief history of concepts

If it is true that the most evident theoretical questions were manifested through the challenging of a few consolidated paradigms, among them the prominent theoretical question that accentuates the distinction between ordinary objects and artworks, then it is also true that the definition of the concept of art (and, accordingly, the concept of an artwork) has always encountered some difficulty. A bit of conceptual history will easily prove this point. It comes down, first and foremost, to difficulties in classifying, which is nothing but the epiphenomenon of a deeper conceptual disorder.

The categorical proximity between ordinary objects and artworks was well known in the classical world, when it was believed that the work of an artist and that of an artisan were akin. To be a good artist it was essential to have technical abilities, since to create (and to imitate) is to give form to a material and, therefore, to an object. The term 'art' is of Latin origin (*ars*) that, in turn, translates from the Greek τέχνη. In Greece, as much as in Ancient Rome, and still in the Middle Ages up until the dawn of the Modern Era, τέχνη and *ars* meant the capacity to 'make' (as in to construct materially) an array of different things: an ordinary object (from a tiny object to a building) or even a statue (therefore, *pars pro toto*, works of art in general). Those who possessed *ars* were gifted with specific abilities (leading an army, persuading an audience or staking out a property, for example).

The concept of art was, for this reason, closely tied to practical abilities that were comprised of the capacity to 'know how to make' (to build, to write, to speak, to measure, to lead) something: a house, a dress, a bed, a ship, the staking out of a property, an oration, a painting. Consequently, those who possessed artistic ability were artisans, architects, potters, surveyors, generals, farmers, orators and rhetoricians, painters, sculptors and poets. In short, all those who knew how to do something with skill, albeit while following certain rules (Tatarkiewicz, 1975, Eng. trans., 11).

Within this context, the term *ars* covers a significantly vaster field than it currently does, insofar as it includes not only the fine arts but also handicrafts. This distinction was made based on the amount of physical exertion required to produce an object, a written work or an oration. Forms of art that did not require effort were called *liberales*, while those which involved physical exertion were coined as *vulgares* (which in the Middle Ages were referred to as mechanical arts). Throughout the course of the Middle Ages, it was customary to use the term *ars* when referring exclusively to the liberal arts: grammar, rhetoric, logic, arithmetic, geometry, astronomy and music. It should be noted that painting (which was not a theoretical discipline, but required physical effort) and poetry (which was considered to be related to improvisation) were excluded from this list. Upon closer inspection, it would seem that to speak of *ars* was, oddly enough, to refer to the sciences.

This categorization was preserved, with few variations, up until the Renaissance, when a significant transformation took place: both handicraft and science were expunged from the category of art, while poetry was added to it. Following this small yet important revolution, it was increasingly understood that what remained of the arts formed a compact nucleus, a distinct 'class' that involved the products whose realization depended on specific abilities. At this juncture, it is worth making a few observations to point out continuity with the history of concepts, and therefore let us focus on the collocation of poetry. It was not a difficult task to include poetry in the catalogue of the Renaissance, especially because Aristotle had already done so centuries earlier in his *Poetics*, as he reflected upon the rules of tragedy.

Yet, the separation between fine arts and handicraft depended on two fundamental factors: first being the artists' aspiration to better their social standing, and second the economic instability that marked the Renaissance. To briefly digress, it should be pointed out that it is in this historical period that the habit of considering art a relatively safe and superior form of economic investment was developed and later consolidated. As we shall see, this is a habit that, throughout the course of the twentieth century, will structure important economic trends, which are oftentimes independent from true artistic reality. Though we will soon have the opportunity to consider this matter extensively (infra, 51 ff.), for now it will suffice to point out the origin and the salience of a field that will become central to the dynamics of artistic production of the modern world. Let us, therefore, briefly resume our discussion of history.

Art's relationship with science remains solid until the end of the Renaissance: artists such as Piero della Francesca and Leonardo made ample use of mathematics, a fundamental element in their practice. Among the first to critically examine this premise was Michelangelo when he theorized a profound separation between art and science. While the arts could have concerned things that were even more relevant than what was dealt with by the sciences, it was of essence to understand that art and science concerned distinct matters. This was the beginning of an important divarication: from this moment onwards, art and science would take different paths. Nevertheless, the idea that art founds itself upon a nucleus of (amendable and progressive) scientific knowledge will long endure throughout the history of art.

The year 1747 was important for finalizing this process. Charles Batteux published a well-received book that introduced the idea of 'fine arts'. By 'fine arts', the author referred to a particular class of objects that specifically included art painting, sculpture, music, poetry, dance, architecture and rhetoric. Therefore, as of the second half of the eighteenth century, science and handicraft were definitively excluded. During this same period of time something else took place, which is of extreme importance from our point of view: scholars began to pose the question of definition (Tatarkiewicz, 1975, Eng. trans., 21). They became aware of the fact that when speaking of art (specifically the 'fine arts'), and when speaking of works of art, they were referring to objects that were to exhibit common properties in order to be classified in the same category. It was quite natural for Batteux to designate imitation as the common property, considering that his illustrious predecessors, among them Plato and Aristotle, had done the same. The theoretical panorama remains nearly unchanged up until the twentieth century, when the unforeseeable occurs. Let us continue our reading of Tatarkiewicz:

> Looking back at the evolution of the concept of art, we will say that such
> an evolution was natural, indeed inevitable. [. . .] Yet something peculiar
> happened: The ancient-mediaeval concept of art – the point of evolutionary
> departure – had been rough but clear and had permitted of simple and
> correct definition. On the other hand, today's concept, the terminal point
> in that evolution, narrower than the latter and, it would seem, better
> defined, as in fact undefined – eludes definition. (Tatarkiewicz, 1975, Eng.
> trans., 22)

A surrender; an inconspicuous outcome. Conceptual confusion leads to the conclusion that it is impossible to reach a definition.

This is the important point: the ancient definition of art was clear, but as of a certain historical period of time it became unusable as it no longer reflected original parameters. In other words, it was no longer useful in explaining the phenomena that concerned the domain of art. And yet, subsequent definitions, including the most modern, are not clear and seem to be agreed upon less than ever. The theoretical framework becomes complicated due to the complicatedness of the artistic panorama of the twentieth century.

Imitation was no longer in practice, and this was the first true difference from the former situation: along came abstract art whose artists programmatically chose to problematize the paradigm proposed by the mimetic theory, and the invention and the diffusion of photography and cinematography were obviously of great importance to this process as well.[6]

Modernism[7] and the production of *ready-mades* only further disrupted the theoretical scene: as of 1917, the year in which Duchamp exhibited *Fountain*, there no longer existed a distinction between ordinary objects and works of art. The two classes – which in Antiquity were diligently kept separated – were now fused and confused: for each ordinary object there would be an indiscernible object that was considered a work of art, and vice versa. Whereas in 'Plato's world', artworks imitated objects while remaining different from the objects themselves (in this world, as we have noted, imitations are worth less than what is imitated), in modern times, it is not rare for daily objects to become works of art.[8] It goes without saying that the properties exhibited by ordinary objects and by works of art are one and the same. Artworks do not imitate ordinary objects, but rather they *are* those objects: boxes of detergent, bottle racks, beds and anything that has ever been imagined. To unearth the properties that characterize works of art as works of art becomes, at this point in time, a truly noteworthy endeavour. Since daily objects share (or can share) all of their properties with works of art, the distinction proposed by Plato becomes unusable, and the theoretical question must be formulated differently. We might imagine a formulation of the following nature: in the event that an ordinary object and a work of art are to be attributed the same properties (physical properties, or aesthetic and artistic properties), how would it be possible to define the class of artworks and, at the same time, distinguish it from the class of everyday objects? Is this distinction still necessary? And, if not, how are we to face the practical questions that are inevitably to arise?

1.4 A property ignored by Plato and unveiled by Aristotle

While the question of the definition of art is posed *in primis* by Plato, it is important to remember that in the third book of the *Republic* he confronts another decisive point, this time related to our experience with works of art.[9] Imitation is, once again, the fulcrum of Plato's reasoning. Painting is not the only imitative art; poetry, which reproduces the behaviours and characters of man through different modalities, is also imitative in nature. The reality that is imitated by art is not only natural, artefactual or social, but also includes the actions and behaviours of human beings.

Just as the trade of reproducing objects of the world is considered to be of scarce prestige, so too is the trade of poetry, which reproduces human deeds and behaviours. The reason is simple, and is related, at least in Plato's manifest intentions, to the political character of the reflection developed in the *Republic*.

It is not good to imitate and reproduce objects for the reasons that we have already described; nor is it good to imitate and reproduce behaviours, especially reproachful behaviours from a moral point of view.

> It seems, then, that if a man, who through clever training can become anything and imitate anything, should arrive in our city, wanting to give a performance of his poems, we should bow down before him as someone holy, wonderful, and pleasing, but we should tell him that there is no one like him in our city and that it isn't lawful for there to be [...]. But, for our own good, we ourselves should employ a more austere and less pleasure-giving poet and storyteller, one who would imitate the speech of a decent person and who would tell his stories in accordance with the patterns we laid down when we first undertook the education of our soldiers. (*Republic*, III, 398a–b)

Plato is targeting what is useful; that is, the training of the guardians. Yet if this is true, then what usefulness could ever result from the guardians and from the state itself if they use their time to attend a production of *Phaedrus*? Instead of enjoying an edifying performance, they would be witnessing an array of passions and behaviours that are anything but exemplary and which, moreover, an ordinary guardian could decide to emulate.

The matter is clearly delineated: if works of art are particular kinds of objects, as believed by Plato, then our experience with them should be, likewise, an extraordinary experience. It is for this very reason that, rather than dealing with the question of definition, it is necessary to determine the characteristics and the peculiarities of the aesthetic experience. Plato had successfully captured this distinction, just as he had successfully understood art's great potential, especially in regard to ethical procedure and politics. If this were not the case, there would be no explanation for the emphasis he places upon keeping both artists and poets out of his ideal state.

In reality, this choice is motivated by reasons deriving directly from his general philosophy, as much as from his philosophy of art: philosophy can legitimately aspire to assume the task of describing the structures of reality and to guide us towards a reasoned understanding of them. Art, conversely, has the opportunity to determine actions, and actions, of course, have an impact on the world. In the most fortunate case, actions determine the adaptation of the world to our representations – if, for example, we decide to write a book, the actual 'writing' would be the action that would auspiciously cause an impact on reality.

In other words, while a good example can lead to performing a valiant action, a bad example can lead to performing vile or even malignant actions. Therefore, from an ontological point of view, not only does the imitative theory commit to the object that it examines, but also the same commitment is assumed with regard to the experiences that connect us to the objects of our theories. The idea, in other words, is that aesthetic experience maintains a predominantly imitative character.

All things considered, Plato's move is fairly peculiar: though he sanctions the ontological separation between artworks and ordinary objects, Plato reasons as if this distinction did not count in praxis. While he is certain that a representation (poetic or pictorial) of a battle is not a battle, that the representation of a crime is not a crime and that the representation of passion is not passion, he seems to reckon that our experience as enjoyers of the artistic representation of that battle, crime or passion might cause us to demonstrate trivially mimetic behaviour in real life, as if we were unable to recognize the boundaries of fictional space and behaved accordingly.[10]

Though part of reality, fiction is characterized by its own logic. In fact, children, who have yet to understand this logic believe that Santa Claus brings gifts on Christmas eve by way of the chimney, and they are deathly afraid at the sight of the huntsman raising the alleged heart of Snow White.

For this reason, it is both logical and necessary that our experience with fictional objects does not have the same characteristics as our experience with non-fictional objects.

While Aristotle confirms the validity of the theoretical framework laid out by the imitative theory – artworks have an imitative character as the predisposition to imitation is one of the traits that distinguishes human beings from animals

(*Poetics*, 4, 1) – he attests the difference between ordinary experience and aesthetic experience, whereas aesthetic experience must be understood *iuxta propria principia*, that is, across the particular laws that govern it. The adduced proof is exceptionally simple: 'Objects which in themselves we view with pain, we delight to contemplate when reproduced with minute fidelity: such as the forms of the most ignoble animals and of dead bodies' (*Poetics*, 4, 2).

Therefore, a scene that would normally disturb us if we were to encounter it in real life moves us to experience sentiments that are what they are when the scene is an object of pictorial or poetic representation, precisely because our feelings are not involved in the existence of the object that provokes them. This fact entails a decisive difference between experiences in real life and experiences that have to do with objects of fiction: in other words, in the experience of art, we can allow ourselves the luxury of paying attention to details that are usually considered less important. In doing so, our emotions may flow freely without having to worry about the connections that, under normal conditions, we entertain with the world.

In the following pages (infra, 81 ff.), we shall see how Aristotle's seminal ideas have given form to two theoretical orientations that touch upon the question of definition with regard to aesthetic experience: (1) the first concerns the possibility of elaborating a definition that founds itself upon the aesthetic properties of works of art; (2) the second involves the possibility of articulating a definition that is concentrated upon the emotional bond that unites works of art and their audiences.

Thus arises the origin of the divergence between the philosophy of art and aesthetics, amid the realm of the imitative theory, within the distinction between a pursuit of the definition of the ontological status of a particular class of objects and the reflection of our experience with those particular objects.

2 The philosophical question of the twentieth century: What counts as a work of art?

2.1 Types of indiscernibles

The only way we can discover that two different things exist is by finding out that one has a quality not possessed by the other or else that one has a relational characteristic that the other hasn't. If *both* are blue and hard and sweet and so on, and have the same shape and dimensions and are in the same relations to everything in the universe, it is logically impossible to tell them apart. (Black, 1952, 77)

Continuing with Max Black's annotation, if two things display identical properties, these things are two distinct examples of the same thing.

The world is filled with similar things – which, in philosophical language, we call 'indiscernibles' – that, nonetheless, are considered, or treated, as different things. Leibniz was among the first to take up the question from a logical point of view, though Descartes had foreseen that the matter which we shall call 'the question of the different indiscernibles' was of great philosophical, and, notably, epistemological, importance.

While Leibniz was the first philosopher to treat the question formally, Descartes had previously understood, at least potentially, how the question of different indiscernibles enters into the midst of our lives in a fairly inconspicuous manner. Giving shape to what will be a recurrent vexation in Western philosophy, Descartes argued that our life could very well be a long dream – perhaps even one that is unbeknownst to us. We, therefore, may not be able to distinguish a state of waking from sleep; we could be dreaming – precisely as in the case of Neo, the protagonist of the science-fiction world of *The Matrix* – and not realize that our dream shares identical properties with real life; the obvious consequence being that real life, *at least in this case*, is a dream. Certainly, one may choose to think that the problem was entirely created by Descartes, who was, at times, prone to worry over what would be mere futilities for the majority of people.

More recently, Ludwig Wittgenstein asked himself what it was that differentiated two seemingly indistinguishable gestures such as an unconscious movement of the arm (in an attempt, for example, to fight off a fly) and the gesture used to greet someone. Along the same line of reasoning, Peter Strawson (1959, 87–110) asked himself what it is that distinguishes a body from a person. In both cases, it is fundamental to certify that there exist two 'things' that exhibit identical properties and, despite this and in defiance of Leibniz's Law, are separate things. Such questions not only concern, first and foremost, general metaphysics, but also the philosophy of art. As we have already suggested, something odd and philosophically dense with meaning took place throughout the course of the twentieth century: artists suddenly began to produce works of art that were indistinguishable from ordinary objects. In certain cases, these works coincided entirely with ordinary objects – they *were* those ordinary objects.

Paradigmatically, this is the famous case of *Fountain*, the work presented by Marcel Duchamp to the Society of Independent Artists in 1917. Many other works of the same genre would follow: stuffed sharks displayed in art museums (as opposed to being exhibited in museums of natural history, as one would expect) and legal news stories that would become successful novels (perhaps the first being *In Cold Blood* by Truman Capote, followed by *Gomorra* by Roberto Saviano, to name the most famous examples). And what about the cases in which entire parts of nature become works of art? The example of James Turrell may not be among the most familiar, but it conveys the idea quite well. It is 1972 and Turrell is a young and enterprising American artist. For seven months he travels far and wide flying his small plane across western North America, searching for the perfect location. He has an important project in mind: to create the largest work of art in the world.

Along the western boundary of the Painted Desert, to the east of the San Francisco Peaks and to the south of the Grand Canyon, there lie more than 400 volcanoes; on the westernmost edge is one of the oldest craters, boasting over 380,000 years of history, called the Roden Crater. This crater is, undoubtedly, magical. Arizona is a unique place, mysterious and untamed; it is as if an outlandish painter passed through and amused themself by painting everything red. The Roden Crater is famous because since 1972, among the Navajo and Hopi reservations, with the city of Flagstaff behind him, Turrell has been constructing his cathedral of light.

The Roden Crater is in the heart of the desert and reaches a height of 1,630 meters. Around it is pure nothingness that has been coloured red, with one outstanding feature; the mark of past volcanic eruptions, the latest of which dates back approximately 900 years. Turrell began playing with light, and created numerous observatories from which he could behold the cosmos by digging tunnels in the crater. Every single aspect of the *Crater Project* plays on light, space and the concept of rotation. If we were to ask the artist what his intentions are, he would give various answers, but the predominant idea is that his work exclusively represents the conditions and limitations brought about by the perception of light. In short, his work represents light by using light.

Whatever our interpretation of Turrell's initiative may be, we must not overlook the fact that the Roden Crater is the final realization of an entire life's worth of dedication to and research on light. In order to avoid construction projects polluting or altering his project, year after year, Turrell guards a progressively greater territory that surrounds the crater. Few people have had the fortune to descend into the crater. Within it, across an infinite amount of tunnels that unwind across thousands of metres, there stands one of the most beautiful observation posts: the 'skyspaces'. All of the underground passages and posts are oriented according to specific astronomical regulations: in respect to the lunar phases and the ancient light of stars that have died, it is possible to perceive the curvature of the celestial vault by lying down upon an enormous slab of marble. This, too, is twenty-first-century art. This is the theoretical nexus, and it can be expressed by using the title of an article by Michael Kelley: 'Making a Brillo box red, white, and blue is easy. Making it an artwork isn't' (2007, 2).

The prelude to this event, whose philosophical crux was grasped by Arthur Danto,[11] is more or less what we had anticipated it to be. In the second half of the twentieth century, the imitative theory proves incapable of answering the ontological question posed by the avant-garde. Artists are dedicating themselves more frequently to producing common artefacts, oftentimes without performing any type of alterations to their material body, but by simply assembling them and combining them in such a way that they become new objects. It is a short and irreversible stretch from this point to the point of no distinction between simple artefacts and artworks. In a similar context, the need to reconceptualize the realm of works of art becomes evident.

For this very reason, Leibniz's arguments concerning the 'identity of the indiscernibles', applied to the question of the distinction between works and mere things, assume an especially particular centrality in the history of art from the second half of the twentieth century: the pairs of 'different indiscernibles', which crowd our world as much as they do our metaphysics, display a paradox that must be confronted and, possibly, dissolved.

Let us first consider the classic form of the argument, and then proceed to evaluate two paradigmatic instances of its application. The argument, known in literature as Leibniz's Law, states that

> the entities x and y are indiscernible if and only if each predicate that counts as x also counts as y – *eadem sunt, quorum unum potest substitui alteri salva veritate.*

We will now examine two meaningful examples of the application of this law:

1. The case that we shall call 'Brillo box | *Brillo Box*', or rather, the case of the quasi-different indiscernibles.
2. The case that we shall call 'bottle rack | *Bottle Rack*', or rather, the case of the truly indiscernible indiscernibles.

2.2 Brillo box: The case of the quasi-different indiscernibles

Let us consider the first pair, 'Brillo box | *Brillo Box*' (where the traditional font indicates the ordinary object, and the italics the artwork), which, as we will see, can be approached in different ways. Let us suppose, ex hypothesi, that we are dealing with two different objects: the 'Brillo box', designed by James Harvey, containing soap pads and found in American supermarkets, and *Brillo Box*, the well-known work by Andy Warhol that, besides being a box that is very similar to a Brillo box, is *also* a work of art.

Let us examine the two objects more closely. They are two (almost) identical boxes: they both feature the word 'Brillo', written in red and blue and, on either side of the writing there is a stylized red wave. The Gestaltian configuration is the same, though the material with which they are made differs. *Brillo Box* is made of plywood, the difference is difficult to detect with the naked eye. Moreover, *Brillo Box* is larger in scale.

The two Brillo boxes are not truly indiscernible; at least not in the way that Leibniz's Law would require. Nevertheless, Arthur Danto (1981, 54–5) believes that, for all intents and purposes, there is room to discuss this example as a case of identity of the indiscernibles. Let us summarize the argument in Dantian form (1981, vi ff.):

1. supposing that two objects, which we shall call x (*Brillo Box*) and y (Brillo box), are perceptually indistinguishable (they are both Ps),
2. and supposing that only one of the two is a work of art (*Brillo Box*),
3. *then* it must be concluded that the work of art is neither recognizable nor distinguishable by virtue of its only aesthetic-perceptive properties.

It is said that on 21 April 1964, upon spotting *Brillo Box* in the Stable Gallery in New York, where Warhol was exhibiting his collection of *ready-mades*, James Harvey, in the company of his friend, Joan Washburn, exclaimed: 'Oh my God, I designed those!'

Clearly, Harvey had indeed designed the Brillo box, and, in fact, that is the point. The two boxes are very similar – certainly not indiscernible – but we can say that they more or less share the same properties. So, then, why is one a *Brillo Box* and the other a Brillo box? Put simply, why is one an ordinary object (i.e. a simple detergent container), while the other is a work of art?

The Brillo paradox can be dealt with on two different levels: the first concerns the validity of the argument of the indiscernibles, while the second involves the validity of the argument applied to the paradox. The history of art is induced from the theory that our senses alone are not sufficient to resolve the Brillo paradox.

Let us return to the first point; that is, the validity of the argument applied to the Brillo case. Perhaps the most convincing objection to the topic of indiscernibles consists of revealing that if two things share the exact same properties, *then* they are not two different things, but rather one thing. Therefore, in regard to our example, it would not make sense to sustain that two distinct objects exist, but rather that one mere thing and one work of art exist. It would be more sensible to argue that, when looking at Brillo box and *Brillo Box*, we are seeing the same thing – and it would be up to us to decide if they are mere things or works of art.

Let us now consider the specifics of Danto's argument. We must, first, make note of a point: the indiscernibility of the Brillo box | *Brillo Box* case is not so indiscernible, considering that at least *one* property is not identical in both objects. In this particular case, there are two: the material from which the boxes are made and their dimensions. If we take into consideration the observations made by Whitehead and Russell,[12] there are actually four dissimilar properties: the property that x is not identical to x (a property that x obviously cannot share with y if we do not want y to become x[13]), the property of x – which y does not have – of being different from y and the difference in material and dimensions of *Brillo Box*.

Brillo box and *Brillo Box* are not, then, manifestly the same thing, unless we adhere to Leibniz's principle, and this is why it is logically possible to speak of them separately. Moreover, in Danto's argument, the two boxes are not the same thing ex hypothesi. Let us return to the formulation of the argument: let us suppose that two objects, x and y (Brillo box | *Brillo Box*), share all of the same properties, in such a way that both are Ps. Even if the two objects were identical, as required by the principle of identity of indiscernibles, Danto *implicitly* maintains, in the hypothesis of his argument, that they are not, given that Brillo box is an ordinary object while *Brillo Box* is an artwork, as he himself declares. In other words, y (*Brillo Box*) possesses a property f (that it is a work of art) that does not belong to the object x (Brillo box). The two objects, therefore, exhibit different properties (that they are and are not a work of art) that are ex hypothesi. The point is that we *really* have nothing to do with indiscernible objects: the two boxes are not indiscernible on a logical level just as they are not completely indiscernible on a perceptive level.

Supporters of the centrality of the argument of indiscernibles for the philosophy of art could propose that the observation made by Whitehead and Russell can be used in favour of the sustainability of the argument of indiscernibles, and that the emphasis given to the difference of the *third* and *fourth* properties (the material and dimensions of *Brillo Box*) is, all in all, of little importance when trying to explain the enigma concerning the two boxes. In fact, we are faced with a detailed question that is important from a logical point of view, but that is irrelevant to the overall meaning of the argument.[14] Moreover, sustainers of the centrality of the argument could partially reconsider their position, as has been done, by ratifying the example and arguing that the case of the Brillo box is not a good example.

Might the choice of indiscernibles simply come down to inexperience?

We would be able to come to such a conclusion if, in the case of other *ready-mades* that have also been considered works of art, things were different. For the time being, let us make an observation: the accusation of false indiscernibility is not simply apropos to the example the Brillo boxes, but is applicable to all *ready-mades* insofar as it does not concern objects, but rather the premise (2) in the argumentation of Danto's formulation. In all cases, the x's and the y's of the examples are not truly indiscernible because they do not share the same identical properties; in this case, we attribute to object x the property of being an object of art – a property that, clearly, we do not attribute to y. We have not dwelled upon the differences concerning relational properties that exist in almost all cases: *Fountain*, for instance, is oriented in an unusual manner, and the same holds true for *Bicycle Wheel*.

Hence, it would seem that the choice of the term 'indiscernible' is not the most appropriate; it would seem more convenient, rather, to speak of two similar objects: one being a common object, the other being a work of art. If there is a difference, it concerns properties that do not appear classifiable under the category of physical properties. How many properties we are speaking of, obviously, remains to be seen.

In summary, we can affirm that the properties that make an object an artwork are not only found in the object, nor are they only found in the mind of the observer. (I can spend the entire day thinking of the stain on my moleskin as a work of art, but it is very unlikely that the stain will turn into an artwork.) Instead, it is likely that these properties are at the juncture between an object and a mind, an object and an historical-cultural context. We shall return to this point later. For now, it would be worthwhile to reformulate the case of the indiscernibles and to search, among the pairs that come to mind, for two indiscernibles that are *truly* indiscernible; in other words, that do not exhibit the differences in perceptive properties that we have detected in the case of the Brillo box.

Let us consider a famous *ready-made* by Duchamp – *Bottle Rack* – and ask ourselves if a new and better formulation of the paradox is, in fact, possible.

2

Definitions

1 Institutional theories

1.1 The first formulation

Bottle Rack was conceived and made by Marcel Duchamp in 1914. It is easy to deduce from its title that it is an ordinary bottle rack, similar to those found in basements or wine cellars. The original version was lost – it is said that the artist's sister, who evidently was not accustomed to distinguishing artworks from common objects, threw it away while cleaning up her brother's studio – and so, in 1961, Duchamp reproduced it by making four models. We can, therefore, reformulate the example based upon the model of *Brillo Box*. For what reason should the 'bottle rack | *Bottle Rack*' case be significantly different from the 'Brillo box | *Brillo Box*' case? The two objects are, after all, truly indiscernible: save the idea of Whitehead and Russell,[1] we cannot indicate other properties that are able to distinguish the ordinary object from the work of art. It appears as though in this formulation our original question – that is to say, what it was that determined the shift in *status* – actually assumes the meaning that philosophers intended to give to it. The mimetic theory is not equipped to solve the mystery. Let us turn to the numerous institutional theories,[2] the most authoritative of which was formulated in a series of writings by American philosopher George Dickie.[3]

The heart of the first version of the institutional theory is found in these few lines:

> a work of art [. . .] is (1) an artifact (2) a set of the aspects of which has had conferred upon it the status of candidate for appreciation by some person or persons acting on behalf of a social institution (the artworld). (Dickie, 1974, 34)

Dickie's theory gives rise to two very simple intuitions that belong, ultimately, to common sense: works of art are social objects that derive from an act of stipulation, which is, in turn, the fruit of a process that involves certain parts of society and certain specific agents. Artworks, therefore, exhibit two properties: (a) first and foremost, they are artefacts – that is to say, they are material objects intentionally modified by man; (b) in addition, they are somewhat peculiar artefacts insofar as certain properties that they exhibit cause a person, or anyone who operates in place of an institution, to consider these artefacts valid candidates for aesthetic appreciation.

Dickie's idea, at this stage, is rather simple: an artist is someone who is able to create (paint, assemble, write, etc.) artefacts that are good candidates for aesthetic appreciation. His theory embraces common sense: out of all aspiring judges, only a certain percentage actually becomes a judge, just as out of all the candidates for medical school, only some actually become doctors. There are always many disappointed aspirants left behind. Clearly, it is important to understand on what basis some objects are admitted to join the category of works of art, and others are not. Candidates for the occupation of a judge must pass a national standardized test, and medical candidates must finish medical school and, in certain cases, a fellowship. So what about artists? Sure, there are academies, but the question is certainly more complex. In other words, while a judge, throughout their profession, will always perform the deeds of a judge, it is not as predictable that the same will happen for a graduate of one of the academies of fine arts.

The institutional theories appear to be in a more favourable position to resolve the paradox of the different indiscernibles. The art world, and in particular its delegates (that is to say, one or more people acknowledged as having the conventional power to do so), has 'imposed a function' upon a material object – a bottle rack, for instance – transforming it into another object. Magic, one might say. Not at all, according to the institutional theory; it is, rather, a question of praxis and contexts.

1.2 Imposition of function

What does it mean to impose a function? The imposition (or assignment) of functions is a central concept to the social ontology of John Searle (1995, 13–23), and I believe it can be usefully borrowed to explain the position of Dickie. Searle associates this ability with the capacity of all men, and some animals, to impose functions on objects, both natural objects and artefacts. Most important is the ability to associate objects with purposes, or to conceive of objects in order to respond to purposes.

Throughout the course of evolution, imposing functions has proven to be a strategic ability that is fundamental to the survival of our species, precisely because it is highly advantageous to know how to create (or modify) things in order to respond to necessities or to specific objectives.

> As far as our normal experiences of the inanimate parts of the world are concerned, we do not experience things *as* material objects, much less as collections of molecules. Rather, we experience a world of chairs and tables, houses and cars, lecture halls, pictures, streets, gardens, [...] and so forth. (Searle, 1995, 14)

It is important to point out that when we examine an artefact and we consider in terms of the function that it serves (a chair is used to sit down on, or a laptop can be used to write books), we are doing the opposite of what we would do if we were to look at that artefact as an object of design, a similar category to that of works of art. The assignment of functions is particularly evident in the case of artefacts: a computer mouse has the function of making its way through the files and folders of our computer, like a real mouse; a pen is a small tank of transportable ink; an iPod is a reproducer of sounds, but if necessary, it can also become a postmodern archive; we sit down on chairs, and we place objects on tables; we put our belongings away in a closet; we use automobiles to get around. The world is full of objects to which we have assigned functions.

While in one way the case of *Bottle Rack* is similar, in another way it is very different. Duchamp's *Bottle Rack* is an ordinary object that possesses the function that all bottle racks possess (to store bottles, of course). Yet, it has been assigned the additional function of being a work of art – the function that we are interested in. The imposition of the second function has caused the object that was always considered a bottle rack to become a *Bottle Rack*. According to the institutional theory, apparently at a certain point in time t_1 (a particular instant in which 'someone' decreed their fiat) conditions arose whereby out of two indiscernible objects one would be a work of art and the other would remain a useful object. The imposition of function was made possible by a specific circumstance: the fact that there exists a social world, in which common rules, which are accepted by a community, are put into place. It is, therefore, not a matter of magic, but, rather, of procedural mechanisms that establish a shared practice.

Functions can be imposed on artefacts just as they can be on natural objects. We use rivers as navigable ways, mountain ranges to mark the boundaries of a state, cypress trees to embellish cemeteries. In these cases, and in many similar cases, function is a relational property that depends on the structural conformation of the objects as much as it does on the relationship with the subject who perceives it; the users of the artefacts are always the ones who assign functions to objects. In essence, if humans and their cognitive structures did not exist, then chairs would not exist, rivers would not be navigable ways and tree trunks would not function as dikes. But let us return to the distinction between bottle rack and *Bottle Rack*. The underlying idea in the first formulation of Dickie's theory appears to be rather simple: a specific class of individuals, artists, assigns a function ('to be a candidate for aesthetic appreciation') to an ordinary object (a bottle rack, or in a more classic example, a painting). Artists can operate in this manner by virtue of a certain jurisdiction awarded to them by an authority (the art world), which seems to possess all of the characteristics of an institutional structure. The scheme is shown in the Figure 2.1.

I have deliberately described the example in a non-classic direction, referring to Duchamp and to one of his most famous *ready-mades*. If the theory were able to explain how the transformation of the bottle rack took place, it would probably be able to make sense of all the rest – it would be able to find a definition that allows different objects, stylistic descriptions, cultural histories and conceptual situations to be associated by a single definition. The 'art world' appears to exhibit the characteristics of a true social institution,[4] since society has invested it with a specific function: to sanction which artefacts belong to the class of works of art, thereby distinguishing them from all the others. Obviously, in our example, *Bottle Rack* is a work of art, whereas bottle rack is not. This means that Duchamp imposed a function on bottle rack (that of being a candidate for aesthetic

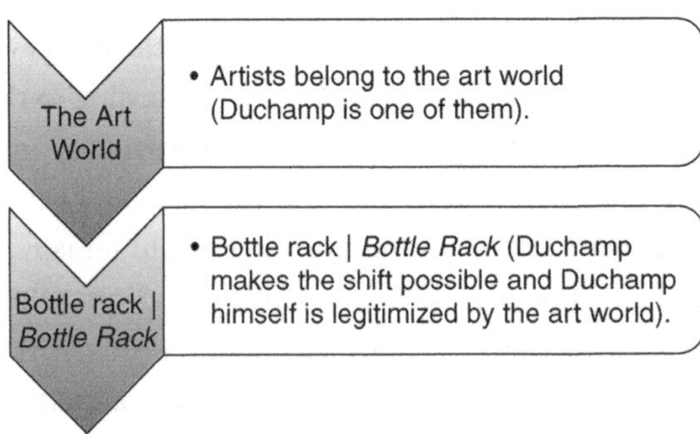

Figure 2.1 The structure of the art world

appreciation) while, in turn, the art world imposed a *status* (*Bottle Rack* is an object of art[5]).

In general, as Searle notes, the creation of a status-function is associated with the conferral of a certain power:

> There would not be much point to imposing the status-function named by the Y term if it did not confer some new power on the X term, and most (not all) creations of institutional facts are precisely conferring powers on the X [...]. In the simplest case, the Y term names a power that the X term does not have solely in virtue of its X structure. (Searle, 1995, 95)

This very state confers a power and certain rights to *Bottle Rack*, which bottle rack does not possess, and which depend strictly on its admittance into the class of works of art. An artwork is a carrier of rights associated with its marketing, its preservation and its conservation; it turns into a cultural and economic asset and its place becomes entirely connected to its value. Some (or many) decide that art is linked to a particular value that calls for its capitalization and preservation, and from here its economic value is derived. Hume would have likely sustained that it is our aesthetic sense that confers value to beautiful things and that promotes their conservation. Hume's intuition would be perfect if it weren't for the fact that artworks that are neither beautiful nor ugly and even very ugly artworks are preserved, conserved and, above all, marketed. As we shall see later, beauty was truly optional for the art of the twentieth century. Nevertheless, these artworks are highly marketable, and include some of the most bizarre objects. We shall revisit this point and deal specifically with the questions concerning the art world.

People and objects, therefore, both acquire power (and value) through the conferral of status. This observation is crucial: the objects that fall under the category of works of art enjoy particular rights that, paradoxically, at times, are not even awarded to human beings. We are accustomed to accrediting to works of art a certain form of exceptionality. As much as it may disturb us that Botticelli's *Primavera* is afforded more rights than an inhabitant of the favelas in Rio – from the point of view of the conservation of World Heritage Sites – this is an accepted and supported fact.

Let us envision a scene. After choosing to display *Fountain* or *Bicycle Wheel* in a given New York gallery, Duchamp seems to symbolically ask the art world for the license that history and tradition have accorded to works such as Raphael's *Resurrection*. At this very moment, the representatives of the art world must develop a series of good reasons to grant the status of 'artwork' to these specific objects, since the traditional reasons were doubted by the artists themselves. If this task, or the majority of it, as Dickie argues, rests upon the shoulders of an institution (the art world), the deciding factor upon which the institutional theory holds itself or falls is linked to the comprehension of the structure and of the dynamics of the art world. What type of institution is the art world that is at the centre of the institutional theory? Is it really the institution that Dickie seems to have in mind? Does it possess the characteristics of the institution? And, finally, does it have the power to do all that the theory promises?

1.3 The art world as a social institution

The art world would not simply implement procedures aimed at confirming the candidacy of a certain object to be become an artwork. The same is true for artists. It has been suggested that it is the artist who advances the candidacy of an object to a work of art. Hence the complementary question: does an institution, or an authority, exist that has the power to decide who is an artist and who is not? Clearly, within this framework, an artist cannot exist without the art world to legitimize them. As a result, Duchamp could not have succeeded in doing what he did if the art world of the early twentieth century had not existed. The question, therefore, lies in trying to understand what the source of legitimization is in the art world. Perhaps we can understand this from the artists themselves.

In general, the institutional theories respond to the objection by highlighting two arguments: first, an artist would not choose an object at random. Rather, one of their skills is to pick out or create an artefact that exhibits specific aesthetic properties. Even if we were to accept this point, the difficulty of pinpointing the aesthetic properties of the *ready-mades* is evident. Is the whiteness of *Fountain*, or the circular shape of *Bicycle Wheel*, in some way suitable for its purpose? It certainly does not seem so, and I believe it would be difficult to argue otherwise. At most, we might claim that *Fountain* exhibits aesthetic properties as any other ordinary object does; it would, therefore, be an arduous task to argue that it is a privileged candidate to become a work of art in virtue of one or more of its aesthetic properties.

The second argument concerns the intellectual profile of the artist. Not everyone can call themselves an artist; as a result, if two indiscernible objects were to exist, only the indiscernible work of the artist would be art, while the other indiscernible, the fruit of the creation of a common person, would remain an ordinary object. So, who are these artists, after all? They are people who are capable of producing new works of art, with knowledge of the history, the practices and the evolution of art. Simply put, artists are people who know both the dynamics and the practices of the art world. It is also true that artists are not the ones who determine a product of human creativity to be an artwork or not: this, rather, is decreed by experts in the field (critics, art dealers, the special press, the big auction houses) as well as, in a small way, the public who visits the exhibits and the museums. Yet again, it is to some extent the experts or, put more simply, those who nurture a certain degree of cultural interest in art. It seems, then, that the institutional theory returns to a crucial, though complex, theoretical point: in order to understand Duchamp, or the work of any other author, it is essential to define the concept of 'art world'. What type of entity are we dealing with? One of the first philosophers to explicitly refer to the art world was Arthur Danto in an article from 1964 entitled just that: *The Artworld*.[6] However, Danto does not establish an exact definition of the *art world* in this article, nor does he elsewhere.[7] Rather, it is George Dickie, his 'unfaithful' prosecutor, who concerns himself with the definition of this concept. In *Art and the Aesthetic* (1974), Dickie traces the fundamental lines of the art world in the following terms:

> The core personnel of the artworld is a loosely organized, but nevertheless related set of persons including artists (understood to refer to painters, writers, composers), producers, museum directors, museum-goers, theater-goers, reporters for newspapers, critics for publications of all sorts, art historians, art theorists, philosophers of art, and others. These are the people who keep the machinery of the artworld working and thereby provide for its continuing existence. In addition, every person who sees himself as a member of the artworld is thereby a member. (Dickie, 1974, 438–9)

If we had to summarize Dickie's idea in one phrase, we would sum it up as the following: the art world resembles an informal institution (that is to say, a social practice or an organization) that functions thanks to ingenuous and followed rules that are not written down.[8]

According to Dickie's theory, an institution confers the status of an artwork. If we consider the matter in more general terms, we might note that, normally, this practice takes place in an endless amount of cases: from marriage, to university degrees, certification exams, the practicing of a profession, the stipulation of a contract and so forth. In each of these examples, a particular institution (the church, the state, a professional association, etc.) has the power to transform an action, or even an object, into something else, by attributing to it a function that is barely reactionary to the physical characteristics of the object or the action, which are considered to be beyond the context expressed by the social act. The instrument used to create these new parts of reality is linguistic and, in literature, we call these statements 'performatives' (Austin, 1962, 6 ff.). We must now clarify if the art world functions in the same way as a state, church, professional association or board of directors of a society; if it is, in fact, an institution that holds the authority to confer a certain form of 'power' on the objects that the artists have proposed as candidates for aesthetic appreciation.

The fact that we have an ingenuous and, for the most part, supported concept of the art world at our disposal legitimizes our supposing that it is, essentially, *something* or, in other words, a certain type of entity. It is, in fact, an entity that 'emerges' (and, therefore, is bound to a dependent relationship) from the elements that form it. The art world exists because museums, artists, artworks, consumers and a market exist. The institution of the 'art world' founds itself upon the union and the integration of all of these elements. In certain cases, this relation seems to be bidirectional: artists like Duchamp exist precisely because an art world exists, and works of art such as *Bottle Rack* exist because museums and collections such as the Robert Rauschenberg Foundation that conserve and exhibit them exist. Moreover, museums and foundations have been approved to do what they do by the art world itself, even though it was determined that the contrary also holds true – The Rauschenberg Foundation exists because works like Duchamp's exist, and must be conserved and passed on.

In general, art theories refer to two different types of institutions: those that Jeffrey Wieand (1981b, 409) classified as 'A-institutions' and 'P-institutions' ('A' stands for action and 'P' for person). An A-institution is one that produces actions whose tokens are 'instantiations' of a particular kind of action (i.e. of a particular *type*). These kinds of institutions distinguish themselves from others because they produce actions that are governed by rules: two people who wish to be joined in marriage can only do so within an institution where certain rules have been pre-emptively accepted and sanctioned. In other words, an A-institution produces a sort of *conventional act*. P-institutions, conversely, are understood as 'quasi-persons', or as agents: they perform actions and can be called upon to account for them. In general, P-institutions act through members who operate by themselves (examples might include state officials, the bishops of a church or the managing director of a society). A state may celebrate marriages through its officials (and can, therefore, perform institutional acts) and some of these acts are particular to itself. (In Italy, marriages can also be celebrated by a P-institution, such as the church, while institutional acts, such as a declaration of war, can only be performed by the government.) In short, the distinction between A-institutions and P-institutions marks a distinction between institutions as acts (or as types of acts) and institutions as agents (Wieand, 1981b, 410).

In his formulation, Dickie makes explicit reference to both A-institutions and P-institutions: the conferral of status to particular artefacts, in order to subject them aesthetic appreciation, appears to be of an A-institution, that is to say a particular type of conventional act. However, when he claims that the conferral of status is operated by a person who acts on behalf of a social institution (the art world or a certain sub-institution within it), he is then thinking, for all intents and purposes, of a P-institution. We are now able to formulate our initial statement: the art world is not a classic social institution and, thus, we must not treat it as such. We now know what it is not. Might we also be able to say – positively – what it is?

1.4 Works of art as tulips: Two worlds face to face

To do so, or at least to attempt to do so, we will use tulips; better yet, we will attempt to discover if the so-called tulipomania – the first economic bubble recorded in the Western world – might teach us something about the topic.

We can embark upon our story by taking into consideration the fundamental historical coordinates of the event whose protagonists, in essence, are certain passions. It all began with the passion for a flower: the tulip. This passion diffused and grew to such a point that it became a mania. Tulip lovers, that is to say, the people who in one way or another dealt with tulips, multiplied to such a degree that from them emerged an actual 'world' – the world of tulips. It was a world that structured itself around specific trends. Soon, one of the most intrusive protagonists of that world would become another passion – the passion for money. Money generally leads to speculation, and this is precisely what generated the first large economic bubble known to the Western world as 'tulipomania'.

What could tulips and works of art possibly have in common? One or two things, maybe three, beginning with an extrinsic and almost colourful element, which is a symbol of how history connects the dots among the things of the world. Once the bubble had exploded, artists accounted for the mania in a disrespectful, often mocking, manner. Among the protagonists who attempted to control the consequences of the economic catastrophe was Doctor Claes Pietersz, one of the most fashionable physicians in Amsterdam. Doctor Pietersz truly loved tulips, and for this reason he never became involved in the mania when it reached foolish levels. He adored the flower to such a point that he changed his own name to Doctor Tulip (Tulp, in Dutch). In addition to changing his name in its honour, Doctor Tulp used this flower as his personal emblem and, in 1622, had a tulip designed as his coat-of-arms. As he gained prestige and authority, Doctor Tulp became personal friends with Rembrandt, who would paint him in one of his most familiar works *The Anatomy Lesson of Dr. Nicolaes Tulp*. He is the illustrious surgeon in the composition, engaged in the dissection of the cadaver of a freshly executed criminal.

As chance would have it, Rembrandt's masterpiece was freely reinterpreted by Russell Connor in *The Pundits and the Whatsit*, the painting that Arthur Danto, the first philosopher to have theorized the concept of the 'art world', used on the cover of *Beyond the Brillo Box* (1992). A fine line now seems to unite the 'art world' and the 'tulip world'. A more substantial connection is the property that tulips share, or have shared, with many works of art: beauty. Until the beginning of the twentieth century, everyone would have agreed that works of art, in different ways, were beautiful. Today, tulips continue to be delightful, while worlds of art, oftentimes, are slightly less so.

The third and final aspect is offered by the respective 'worlds'. The tulips from the 'tulipomania' era share one important point with works of art today: an 'art world' exists today, just as a 'world of tulips' existed in the seventeenth century. As we shall see, this implies that the existence of these worlds is entirely independent from the objects around which they revolve: be they tulips, works of art or financial titles. The world of tulips found itself in a peculiar situation resulting from its connection with the former imponent economic bubble of Western capitalism. Western capitalism saw its first short circuit not at the hand of a war, a dynastic crisis or a conflict between an empire and the papacy, but simply by virtue of a flower. It all transpired thanks to a most fragile and beautiful flower that shook the very structure of the Western economy.

The protagonist of this event is a rare tulip, the *Semper Augustus*, which emerged, partly by chance, partly by the passion of a few tulipomaniacs, into a world that was not its own. All respectable stories include important artefacts, and this one has its own. The tulip fever[9] neither arose nor manifested itself in a sudden or unexpected manner in sober and industrious seventeenth-century Holland. We must travel further back in time to understand how things went. The passion for tulips has a long history that finds its origin in early seventeenth-century Paris. The year 1610 is important for the tulip: flowers become highly fashionable in Paris, and aristocrats begin offering them to their ladies. Initially, it had been customary to give roses, but tulips would soon supplant them by virtue of their elegant beauty. This custom seems to dominate the marriage of Louis XIII in 1615, when it is said that the ladies of the aristocracy were adorned with cut flowers, pinned down to the base of their décolleté, in the groove between their breasts. The most magnificent array of flowers were valued almost as much as diamonds: 'The Dutch horticulturalist Abraham Muntig, writing later in the century, recorded that at the height of the French craze a single tulip of especial beauty – and a cut flower, not a bulb – changed hands for the equivalent of a thousand Dutch guilders' (Dash, 1999, 66). It was a craze, a trend among the nobility, and for this very reason it was destined to convert the Parisian bourgeoisie.

The French were the first to follow this fashion, and a 'mild fever' for tulips began to spread throughout the northern regions of the kingdom. Subsequently, the fashion dispersed all throughout Europe, especially among the inhabitants of the United Provinces. The Semper Augustus was the most sought-after flower, the prototype of its kind. Here is how Dash describes it:

> Of all the varieties acclaimed 'superbly fine', easily the most coveted was a flower called Semper Augustus, the most celebrated, the scarcest, and by common consent the most wonderful tulip grown anywhere in the United Provinces during the seventeenth century – and thus by far the most expensive. Semper Augustus was a Rosen tulip, but to call it simply a red and white flower would be like describing rubies and emeralds as red and green stones. (Dash, 1999, 80)

The main point is that of beauty. The Semper Augustus was beautiful, but this fact was not enough to account for its exceptional fame, nor its irrationally high economic value. There had to be something else, just as there is something else, beyond pure and simple beauty, in Mondrian or in Van Gogh. In actuality, in addition to being very beautiful, the Semper Augustus was very rare; its bulbs could be counted on one hand. We find it first mentioned in a newspaper from 1620, and we know that in 1624 there were 12 examples in total, all of which belonged to a single owner. No one, despite the numerous staggering offers made, was able to convince him to sell them. These were the first traces of tulipomania. At this point, three protagonists are introduced into our story: a passion (the passion the Dutch had for flowers in general, and for tulips in particular), a star (the Semper Augustus) and an unfulfilled wish (to possess *that* flower).

That wish, so difficult to satisfy, prompted the creativity of a host of people: ordinary people, travelling collectors, apothecaries, cultivators and, last but not least, florists. Everyone played a role in the mania and everyone, between the years 1600 and 1634, contributed to expanding the team of botanists and enthusiasts who, in the beginning, would trade tulip bulbs partly as a passion, partly as a game. Cultivators (often crude and imprecise) thereby increased in number and joined those who, by trade, would mediate between supply and demand. Since the Semper Augustus was impossible to obtain – and even if it had been found by raking through every last greenhouse in the kingdom, it still would have been out of reach for the majority of people – a creative and enterprising squad of devoted tulip lovers found a way to multiply the types of tulips on the market. Were they of lesser quality? Perhaps. But they were certainly easier to cultivate and, therefore, more easily marketable. Considering, also, that a tulip did not last an eternity (that is to say, it could not be displayed in the same way as a chair or a suit would be), someone had the idea to print the first illustrated catalogues, which would showcase the selection of tulips, and also promote bargains. Books on tulips, edited by first-class botanists and illustrated by respected artists, multiplied. Like any mania worthy of its name, the tulipomania boasted its own eccentricities.

Tulipomania is the story of a passion. More precisely, it is the story of its transformation into an obsession: the passion for a flower that eventually turns into a mania. It is a bit like when love turns into an addiction – only in our case, the players moved by that passion were not necessarily the first tulipomaniacs. Oftentimes, in fact, the contrary has held true. According to the first documented records, the boom started in 1633 when, in the midst of an economic recession, the Hoorn house, an elegant bourgeois estate, was sold for three tulip bulbs. The bulbs began to be used for economic transactions, replacing money and even gold. It is a privilege that few things have experienced throughout history: animals (that were needed for survival or for work), works of art and capital stock. Tulip bulbs themselves were edible and, quite frankly, fairly similar to onions, which have never been considered stores of value. Moreover, the Hoorn house was not exchanged for flowers but, rather, for two bulbs; in other words, it was exchanged for potential flowers, or for the mere promise of flowers. While a Euro is a Euro, and a bar of gold is a bar of gold, a bulb can become a tulip (considering nothing happens to it during its development), and it can become a tulip of greater or lesser quality. In other words, the unknown outcome, which is related to the fact that we are dealing with a living thing, puts the purchaser at a rather high risk, certainly higher than a more traditional store of value would. At the time, the Hoorn house could have been worth around 500 Florins, which offers the measure of value accorded to those three bulbs.

In 1633, the Semper Augustus was negotiated and exchanged for 5,500 Florins; in 1637, it was handed over for the outrageous price of 10,000 Florins. This king of tulips was worth as much as a fashionable estate that sat on 700 square meters, in Amsterdam, complete with all commodities: gardens, a carriage house, horses, a park, et cetera. In such conditions of widespread madness, who could have resisted the temptation to not only make money from tulips, but also to describe the characteristics of this marvellous world that must have sounded, to most, like an imaginary El Dorado? Indeed, stories about the amazing events of the tulips, and the world of tulips, multiplied. With the stories multiplied the myths, and with the myths the symbolic value of objects emerged. This is how tulips would come to symbolize well-being, beauty, social ascent and money. Of course, there were those who still considered those bulbs simple onions, and found them entirely natural to eat.

Just as a visitor in a museums who, in an attempt to sit down, might well exchange a chair by Kosuth for any ordinary chair, a sailor in the early seventeenth century could have found a tulip bulb in a tavern, where the precious object was bought and sold, and bitten into it as he would an onion.

It would seem that the world is the same wherever one goes. They say that a merchant from Amsterdam once bought a very rare *Rozen* bulb. Heedlessly, he placed it on the store counter. In a moment the bulb was gone. The merchant searched his store high and low, covering every corner, but found nothing. The bulb had disappeared, had been stolen or, simply, had been taken by mistake. As he carefully thought over what had happened, the man remembered that a sailor had entered his store, a foreigner who likely knew very little about the history of tulips. He may have taken the precious object and have done who-knows-what with it. The merchant's hunch was right: after having searched the city thoroughly, the sailor was found at the pier finishing up his meal which consisted of what he deemed to be an onion. The merchant was in a state of despair, the sailor was arrested and the bulb was irretrievably digested. A good lawyer could probably have argued that his client's action involved no criminal intent, seeing as the bulb of a tulip truly resembles a bulb of an onion, and, if we eat onions, then there should be no reason not to eat tulip bulbs – everyone has their own taste, after all. How is one to know, upon arriving in a foreign land and being unaware of the local practices, that in some places in the world, the bulb of a flower is worth infinitely more than that of an onion?

The way in which the story ends is of little importance. It is important, though, to observe how all 'worlds' have, more or less, the same characteristics: they are, or soon become, markets. Not even the world of tulips was an exception to the rule – the transformation from the world of enthusiasts to the world of tulips took place in 1635. That year, the flower market would change forever, due especially to the marketing strategies adopted by florists. Selling a flower was not the same as selling wood, for instance. In the latter case, wood is exchanged, rather than the plant from which that wood was taken. In the case of tulips, the business began with the bulbs, moved on to the flowers and ended with pieces of paper, the promissory notes with which purchasers would buy what would eventually be born within a few months. The bulbs themselves ceased to be the units of exchange, and what were exchanged and paid for were the 'promises' those bulbs held, that they would eventually become flowers. That piece of paper, the promissory note, contained a description of the future flower and the date on which its owner would be able to pick it up.

The system offered certain clear advantages. First, it allowed the tulip market to obtain profits throughout the course of the year: promissory notes could be exchanged at any moment and in any season and, above all, could even be processed in the absence of tulips. The risks, though, were considerable. The buyer could not see the goods – the bulbs were hidden well beneath the ground – and, consequently, there was no guarantee of quality. Florists were forced to trust cultivators who, if needed, could attempt to sell non-existent bulbs. The new system that granted the negotiation of promissory notes was certainly more fluid, but was equally susceptible to a series of risks which, were they to take effect, would be highly burdensome not only for the world of tulips, but also for the Dutch economy at large. Additionally, the new system was sufficiently flexible and could protect and encourage tulipomania. The more the mania grew and spread, the more the system responded, or seemed to respond, to its objective.

This was the historical moment in which an interest in tulips was superseded by an interest in the promise of payment, and the passion for a flower was superseded by the passion for easy money. The trade now involved pieces of paper that stood for property rights. The obvious risk was that in the field of uninhibited transactions, those involved would lose contact with real things, with the objects sold, for the same reason that florists were no longer interested in who bought their flowers or for what reason, or if the buyers had the money to fund their promises of payment. It was, to all effects, the launch of a market of term negotiations applied to the exchange of tulips; that is, to objects whose consistency was significantly more volatile than loads of wood and spices.

A term negotiation is a form of speculation in which the merchant bets the price of a certain merchandise (in this case tulips, but the same could be applied to houses or petroleum), and commits himself to paying a specific amount on an established date. It is a true gamble on the future.

At the pinnacle of the speculative bubble, most florists were entirely concentrated on sales, which were made for personal benefits or on behalf of the rich who used capital to invest. At this point, a new element came into play: the passion for gambling, for risking and for speculative gain. Bargaining would take place where wine and alcohol flowed freely, and would resemble a society game. The scene was far from serious, albeit involving very serious issues.

At the peak of the mania, there were those who bought bulbs for the pleasure of playing a game and winning, or to invest a surplus of money and profit easily, and there were those who took risks and thus fell into debt in trying to gain social prestige. Tulips had become an enormous opportunity, a chance to play a game that, in the estimation of those who played it, generated significant riches.

The collapse was unexpected and devastating. It occurred one evening, the first Tuesday in February of the year 1637, in a tavern in Haarlem, one of the many designated places of trade. During the last months of 1636 and the first months of 1637, exchanges were feverish in volume and price as quotations had reached stratospheric levels. On the day in question, when the situation precipitated, things appeared to be the same as always. As per usual, a recognized member of the association opened the negotiations of the day by verifying the conditions of the market. He put up for sale one pound of bulbs for which the florist was asking a fair price. In a normal situation, those bulbs would have had numerous purchasers. The tulips would have gone to the best offer and the dealings would have proceeded frenetically throughout the day. But conditions had suddenly turned abnormal. Much to everyone's disconcertment, the auction was deserted. This would be the first of a series of similar auctions that would spread panic – everyone wanted to sell, and quickly. After that Tuesday in February, the world of tulips was not what it used to be; in fact, it ceased entirely to exist.

In retrospect, it would not have been difficult to detect the causes of the collapse. During the winter of 1636–7, demand exceeded supply. There were no longer tulips to sell and the market remained accessible to those few people who used their extensive fortunes to negotiate the most expensive bulbs. The absence of economic bulbs meant the impossibility of new subjects, perhaps less wealthy and new to the tulip profession, entering the market. But a market that welcomed fewer new subjects would also see less fresh capital; tulipomania was in a state of paralysis and, consequently, panic.

One additional aggravating factor contributed to dealing the decisive blow: during the final two months of the mania, bulbs of scanty quality were being exchanged at considerably high prices. These bulbs were of value only in the eyes of the speculator; no connoisseur or enthusiast would ever have dealt with them. Even those who would usually intervene in the markets when the bulbs were beginning to fall in price could think of no good reason to buy them. The rest of the story is composed of rather squalid events that are of scarce interest to us. We can, thus, return to our starting point; that is, the comparison between the two 'worlds'.

It may be deduced that the tulip world and the art world are surprisingly similar: the comparison of a few of their characteristics leaves little room for doubt. The world of tulips has its experts and its botanists, while in the world of art we find art historians. Then, there are the authors of the products – specialized gardeners and cultivators on the one hand, and artists on the other. In both worlds, merchants play a central role, as do the travellers who distribute the products throughout Europe. In one world, florists decide which products to wager, while in the other, art dealers choose which artists and works to launch. Both markets endure sudden changes caused by rumours and by the moods of the players that comprise them. Both markets are characterized by speculative forces – the speculative and high-risk game is a central element, and is part of the stake. The bulbs, the tulips and the works of art are all characterized (at least at a certain point in life) by having highly symbolic traits and characteristics. The bargaining among participants of an auction, along with the underlying psychological dynamics, is a primary element of life in both worlds. At a certain point in their respective histories, bulbs and artworks not only acquire an important economic value, but they are also used as trading currencies.

Our comparison shows certain glaring data: the worlds of art and tulips are 'inhabited' by characters that carry out similar functions, despite being given different names (for instance, a botanist is part of the tulip world as an art historian is part of the art world), and the dynamics of the respective operations are nearly identical.

When the tulip world unfurls completely, when all of the energies it is comprised of are composed and coordinated, a certain point becomes central: tulips are no longer only cultivated for personal pleasure or aesthetic enjoyment, but on the basis of pure profit.

It would be worthwhile to ask ourselves what lies at the heart of the tulip world. Surely, it was at first a habit, a trend and, in some cases, a scientific curiosity: the passion for a flower. Yet the strengthening element that allowed a world that not many wanted to be a part of to expand and become a semi-popular reality was the possibility of making money – lots of money – in relatively simple ways.

And the art world? What about its dynamics? Boy, are there stories! They, too, all start with a passion: for art and for its objects, for works of art. Originally, the stories primarily regarded professionals, enthusiasts and patrons. Artists were very good with their hands and using instruments, and knew how to do certain things very well. These abilities made their works objects of admiration and desire. The more creative, extravagant, imaginative and technically skilled they were, the more sought after were their creations. The privileged would then hire or employ them in such a way as to guarantee the perpetuity of the fruit of their work. Artists produced and (by way of them) patrons showcased their economic power. The Italian Renaissance was, perhaps, the age in which these negotiations emerged with most prominence. This can be illustrated through the example of the cupola of Santa Maria del Fiore in Florence, whose plans were conceptualized by the genius of Brunelleschi, and strongly supported by Cosimo de' Medici. The project involved a design for the roof of the crossing of the Duomo di Firenze: it was the largest structure ever to be built. Cosimo sustained the project economically, and it was thanks to him that the monumental and laborious work, that was in construction for over 125 years, saw its completion. To close the cupola seemed an impossible feat, a challenge beyond human limits; for this very fact its construction would have symbolized the glorious affirmation of the city of Florence and, at the time, the affirmation of those who had conceived the project and believed in its realization. The two men were Brunelleschi and Cosimo de' Medici.

Even within this embryonic world of art, where the players are certainly less numerous than in the world of contemporary art, passions play a significant role and, here too, the passions that truly count are always the same ones: money, which is shown first, and power, which is conveyed through the works of art. Just like the first tulip cultivators, artists are moved by a simple, and perhaps rarer, sentiment: the passion for works of art and, for some, the desire to create something truly capable of challenging history.

If up until the nineteenth century the art world is still mainly comprised of passion and a stroke of genius, in the twentieth century its dimensions are decidedly regulated by the market. This means that the passion changes greatly, both in object and in sign, and just as it had occurred with tulips, passion for money becomes the principle factor that regulates all of the interests that revolve around that world; hence, 'artmania'. In the art world, there are at least three designated selling spots: auction houses, galleries and, more recently, fairs. Auction houses, in particular, are the business spots that replace the insalubrious taverns where tulip bargaining used to take place. There is less wine and the sobriety helps avoid regrettable incidents along the way, but, for the most part, the dynamics of the negotiations are entirely recognizable now as they were then. They have a highly entertaining nature and are governed by emotional logic. Like all games, at times they can be risky and crazy and, like all games, they are played by different players following different objectives. A manager might wish to buy a work of art that will guarantee them social prestige, or they might wish to donate it to a museum, with the intent of being invited to join the board of directors. An art dealer might wish to make a purchase upon the request of one of their clients or perhaps to showcase the work in their gallery. Then there are museums that, in certain cases, might wish to expand or strengthen their collections by purchasing works that best represent an artist, while in other cases they might simply intend to hinder the development strategies of a rival museum.

Despite this crossover of objectives, the auctioneer runs the show and does so rather rapidly. It all takes places at an alarming rate and negotiations for each lot last only a few dozen seconds. Decisions are made very hastily, based on emotions, and the psychological dimension plays a significant role in the decision making of each buyer. Known as the 'adjudication effect' in literature, losses have more considerable and challenging psychological consequences than wins do. This all has clearly little to do with works of art, and has nothing at all to do with matters concerning the determination of their definition. Evidently, among the different typologies of worlds, there exists a certain family resemblance.

Let us suppose that, at a certain point in the tulip world, someone begins to cultivate a unique kind of hybrid. These bulb cultivators are committed to producing large quantities of hybrids within a single species in such a way that there will eventually be countless intra-specific hybrids. Some are so different from normal tulips, at least judging by the morphological characteristics, that it becomes truly difficult for a non-expert to distinguish them. At this point, even in the tulip world, the question of recognizing and, therefore, defining the tulip emerges.

Let us now suppose that someone asks the tulip world to shed light on the matter of definition, with the question: 'What is a tulip?' It is plain to see that answering this question is not up to that world. We might, instead, legitimately ask them questions such as: 'In what way can we make profit from a tulip bulb?' or 'How can we create new species of tulips that we can cultivate and market?' and even, 'How can we ensure that tulips will become even more popular?' or, 'How can we in increase business?', 'What were the economic variables that determined tulipomania?' and so forth.

The tulip world arises from a thing called a 'tulip'. It does not create its own object. Instead, it creates the ways in which that object can determine more or less riches or, conversely, it can determine a speculation. The same conclusions hold true for the art world. This is the crucial point from a theoretical perspective:

worlds do not create their own objects, they assume them, they use them and, at times, they modify them.

1.5 The second formulation

The art world, then, does not create its own objects. That is to say, it does not operate through acts that are performatives, while other institutions do. However, since Dickie's theory openly claims the opposite, we shall try to determine where and why he follows a different path. Let us consider, then, if the conventional acts and institutions that act as agents (i.e. the A-institutions and the P-institutions) can effectively form the framework for the art world. In effect, Dickie seems to dismiss the fact that the *art world* is a social institution that operates by following the model of the P-institutions. Better yet, in some ways his model appears to conform to that of an institution with rather frayed and informal mechanisms. In fact, in an effort to clarify, he adds: 'when I call the art world an institution, I am saying that it is an established practice' (Dickie, 1977, 198). His clarification, which essentially resembles a reconsideration, changes the structure of his theory; we might, then, reformulate it in the following manner:

> *x is an object if and only if (1) x is an artefact and (2) is created and/or presented by an agent, who understands all it does, and displays it to an audience that is prepared to understand the meaning of it.*

This second formulation takes into account the theoretical variation caused by the consideration of the art world no longer as an institution but, rather, as a practice.

In this new formulation, then, instead of resembling a traditional institution modelled after a tribunal, a university or even a state, the art world is much more similar to a social practice characterized by formalized and – at times, though not always – shared traits, as opposed to a collection of rules and mechanisms of informal nature.[10] The operation of an institution, in its conception, does not necessarily depend on the codification of all of the norms that are in force within the institution in question. The conclusion, then, is to treat the art world as a practice.

Let us, therefore, try to identify the characteristic traits of Dickie's concept of practice. We have already pointed out the most important property: that it can confer a status – the status of a work of art – to any object, including usable objects. In addition, the conferral of status is related to exercising power.

In other words, it is the art world that possesses the power to determine the transformation of bottle rack to *Bottle Rack*. It goes without saying that this is a transformation with important consequences, both cultural and economic. Who would not want to own *Bottle Rack*, even if not for the sole purpose of reselling it?

This is true. But, as Monroe Beardsley (1976) rightfully notes, if it is always possible to confer a status on behalf of someone (an institution, a group of people or a person in particular), then it is rather difficult to find a case in which this conferral could take place on behalf of a practice. It is clear how one may act on behalf of a P-institution. In an attempt to formalize, we might say the following: a person (or a group of people) *S* acts on behalf of a P-institution *T* only if the action of *S* can be described not only as the action of *S*, but also as the action of *T* (Wieand, 1981b, 412). Wieand's scheme, therefore, assumes the following form: a person *S* (let's say, Duchamp) acts on behalf of a P-institution (the art world) if the action of *S* (to transform bottle rack into *Bottle Rack*) can be described not only as an action of *S* (Duchamp, again), but also as an action of *T* (that is to say, of the entire art world). Hence the first hitch: generally, when we think of institutions that act as agents, we also know the members of the institution. Or if we do not know them, as can be the case with the board of directors of a multinational company, or with a Masonic confraternity, there is always someone, somewhere, who knows them. Customarily, there is a document where all of this information is registered, and it is top secret.

The art world does not work this way: we ought first to ask ourselves who its members are. This does not entail drafting a census; the problem, in this specific case, is that the typologies of the people who belong to the art world are not even clear. There are artists, of course, as well as musicians, writers, sculptors and perhaps, though we cannot say with certainty, architects. What about designers? The answer might be 'it depends'; that is to say, it depends on the intentions that the designer associates with their creation. Let us once again turn to the case of the *Brillo Box*: it was Andy Warhol, an artist, rather than James Harvey, the designer of the commercial product, who exhibited *Brillo Box* and, in doing so, asked that the work be a candidate for aesthetic appreciation. If the same operation had been consciously performed by Harvey, the art world – at least in theory – would have had to respond in the same manner. This is all in theory; in practice, the variables are indeed numerous, and the result is less certain. The problem can be reduced to a matter of fact by observing that, in the end, it comes down to prestige in the respective worlds of affiliation: if one is so fortunate or talented – depending on which way you look at it – to have access to the art world, they will do things that have more value (at least in market terms) compared to the affiliates of the other group. That is how the world works, after all. Clearly, though, if the objects produced by the two groups are indiscernible, it would be difficult to explain the matter to possessors of different typologies of bottle racks. What would we say to the ill-fated owner of the ordinary object? 'Sorry to say it, but the author of your bottle rack is part of the wrong group and, as a result, what you have there is an object that's worth, roughly, 10 Euros'.

Let us now begin our examination of the more relevant objection. Getting back to the question at hand – that is to say, the typologies of the people who comprise the art world – we have established thus far that the authors of artworks are undoubtedly part of it, and in various ways. Our reflection, though, is at risk of becoming circular. Those who produce a work of art are part of the art world, and yet we struggle to identify what characteristics a true artist must have, given that, oftentimes, we are unable to recognize a work of art, not to mention that a large part of contemporary art causes us much discomfort. Moreover, the art world is not only comprised of artists, writers or musicians; there are also critics, historians of art, literature and poetry, art philosophers, curators, art dealers, collectors, as well as actual institutions such as museums and foundations. Curiously enough, we find P-institutions structured in a traditional way (in the cases of museums and foundations) that do not belong to a meta-institution (as would be reasonable to assume), but rather, to a practice (the art world).

The MoMa in New York has formal elements that make it an institution: it has designated members on its review committee and on its board of directors who, throughout the execution of their duties, are subjected to formal and substantial constrains. In addition, there are those who act on their behalf, and are authorized to purchase works, to determine the cultural policies, to search for sponsors, to set budgets and so on. The art world, on the other hand, is characterized by a much looser mechanism: we do not necessarily know who it is comprised of (it is, then, a quasi-institution with vague boundaries that functions – if it in fact functions – by reason of its very vagueness), nor are we able to identify, with clarity, all of the rules that govern it. It is a 'quasi-institution' with vague and sufficiently permeable boundaries, to such a degree that it includes the most diverse of people and the most disparate of institutions, and is able to absorb and promote the most profound cultural changes. Perhaps its way of being is efficacious precisely by virtue of this vagueness that is a vagueness de re, and certainly not de dicto. It belongs, therefore, to the quasi-institution of which we are speaking rather than to the language that we use to speak of it. It would make sense, then, to claim that the *art world* is not itself an institution, even though it can be comprised of institutions in addition to the individuals who belong to it in one way or another. We may, accordingly, imagine a scenario similar to the following: the P-institutions and A-institutions concerning art end up – at least in some instances – expressing coordinate actions, giving rise to practices that are at times shared, and at others revolutionary, just as when *Brillo Box* was accepted into the Stable Gallery in New York. The source of legitimization for museums and foundations is fairly clear: they exist in the same way as universities, schools or even tribunals do and, just like each of these institutions, they receive their legitimacy from the National States. In this case, then, we are dealing with P-institutions that act by producing A-institutions; as a result, the existence of an *art world* is not strictly necessary.[11]

We still ought to place emphasis on one point, which has already been called to attention by the American philosopher Randall Dipert.[12] Dickie not only fails to elaborate a sufficiently articulated philosophical reflection on artefacts, which creates problems for the first point of his definition (we have seen that in Dickie's definition artefacts are candidates for aesthetic appreciation), but he also tries to make sense of the individuation of works of art by postulating the existence of an entity that, in the first version of his theory, should have the same power as that of an institution, despite its not being one, while in the second, and weaker, version it should have the same power as an institution, even though it is declared not to be one.

As we were saying, neither museums nor foundations produce novelties in the field of art; oftentimes these innovations come from art galleries. Traditionally, museums are meant to guard that which has already been consolidated and accredited. The case of *Fountain* is exemplary: Duchamp had been in the United States for two years when his idea for the work flourished. In New York, he came in contact with the Dada movement, and with the avant-garde. The idea for *Fountain* arose when Duchamp, along with artist Joseph Stella and collector Walter Arensberg, purchased a Bedfordshire urinal at J. L. Mott Iron Works, a shop on the corner of Fifth Avenue and One Hundred and Eighteenth Street. After the urinal had been delivered to his studio at 33 West Seventy-Seventh Street, Duchamp limited himself to rotating the object 360 degrees and engraving his signature, or rather his pseudonym, upon it: R. Mutt 1917. At that time, the artist had recently become part of the board of directors for the Society of Independent Artists and decided to propose the work, using a *nomme de plume* (pseudonym), for the exhibit.

After a long and heated discussion that stirred the members of the review committee – the majority of whom had no idea the author was Duchamp – the work was rejected. The Dada artists used the occasion to make a point. Together with a photograph of *Fountain*, the magazine *The Blind Man* published a letter from Alfred Stieglitz that, among other things, underlined a point that became extremely important for the development of new artistic tendencies:

> Whether Mr. Mutt with his own hands made the fountain or not has no importance. He CHOSE it. He took an ordinary article of life, placed it so that its useful significance disappeared under the new title and point of view – created a new thought for that object. (Stieglitz, 1917, 5)

The novelty, then, is not found in the object, but, rather, in the way that we think of it, in the thought that, henceforth, will be associated to the urinal. The importance is brought back entirely to the intentional act of the artist. Duchamp appoints the urinal from the Mott company to assume a new function, to be something different, to be an object that expresses a particular idea of Duchamp's: that is, *Fountain*.

According to Dickie's theory, then, the art world accredits the transformation of fountain to *Fountain*: if we are searching for *Fountain*'s source of legitimization, we cannot stop at Duchamp (who, at the time, was a young artist with no fame), nor can we stop at the gallery that refused the work. It is necessary, rather, to refer to something else: a quasi-institution that, physically, is not situated anywhere, but that emerges from the group of local institutions, from the work of artists and of those who, in one way or another, are involved in art by having knowledge of it and, in the best of cases, experience.

The problem remains and is substantially related to the indeterminateness of the procedures that comprise the framework of the art world.[13] If a game of chess can be played only by those who are familiar with the rules of the game, then, similarly, the game of the art world should be played solely by those who know the regulations. But how is one to take part if the laws are opaque, vague and constantly changing? And, above all, how is one to believe that the game only scratches the surface of its components, and not simply upon the economic superstructures into which they have fallen? It is hard to say. It is accurate to conclude that, according to the institutional theory, this 'something', so vague that it is not clearly definable, has such expansive power that it can determine the occurrence of significant events, which, in effect, happens in other 'quasi-institutions'. However, the fibrillation of financial markets can determine the crises of entire economies, the world of information can influence social and political scenarios worldwide and the tulip world was able to shake the economic structure of an entire nation.

Indeed, it can be easily noted how these types of entities, which we have conveniently defined 'quasi-institutions', and which we can easily liken to fairly particular types of extended communities, are extremely diffused in the contemporary world and in social contexts that, despite being vague in their composition, are especially ample. Certainly, the quasi-institutions determine factual and important changes, but what about the possibility that they can be used as theoretical cores upon which to found the institutional theory?

1.6 Questions of circularity

To conclude our reflection on the institutional theory and its different variants, let us return to John Searle. With the transposition of his arguments to the topic of works of art, we realize, in examining the institutional character of the art world, that there are a series of difficulties. In one sense, works of art must exist for an art world to exist, just as money must exist for financial markets to exist. In another sense, it is also true that without the art world works of art would not exist. The circularity of the argument is evident, and it cannot help but cause discomfort.

If we were to transpose Searle's constitutive rule of social reality, that 'x counts as y in c', to the question of the definition of works of art, we would end up with two distinct formulations. If we follow the first version of the institutional theory:

> *a physical object* (x) *counts as a candidate for aesthetic appreciation* (y) *in an art world* (c).

It is evident from the above statement that *x* and *c* implicate one another and generate circularity. In order to exist, that is, to shift from qualifying as 'candidates for aesthetic appreciation' to qualifying as works of art, works of art need the art world to declare the shift in status. In turn, for the art world to exist, it needs works of art. If, on the other hand, we follow the second formulation of the institutional theory, we must apply certain clearly restrictive conditions:

> *x counts as y if and only if (1) x is an artefact (2) created by an agent, who understands all it does and presents it to an audience that is prepared to understand it.*

A candidate does not always have the necessary requisites, and if they are determined by the field in which they operate, then it is necessary to suppose that the context acts in accordance with certain procedures that, at least as a matter of principle, are detectable and describable. The institutional theories, in their various formulations, do not help us to resolve our original question.

The most general theory, proposed by John Searle for social objects, is unable to account for the specificity of works of art in respect to ordinary objects. While an ordinary piece of metal – a piece of gold, for instance – generally counts as a coin, not all canvases made with minium count as works of art notwithstanding the context in which they dwell.

More narrow formulations, on the other hand, call for an accurate analysis of the parts of the theory that have an institutional character, as well as a procedural one. As we have seen, these parts present habits of circularity, to say the least.

1.7 Regarding x

After having considered *y* and *c*, it would now behove us to focus on the first of the variables: *x*. Searle's version does not help us much, since *x* remains deliberately undetermined. Dickie determines the *x*, in an attempt to avoid running the risk that anything – including the mere idea of a work of art – be considered a work of art. In his version of the theory, *x* must be a physical object, in this case an artefact. In the following pages, then, we will take up the very concept of artefactuality regarding works of art, seeing as the idea that the materiality of a work of art is an essential element of its definition rests upon it.

For our convenience, we shall formulate a statement that is comprised of two parts: (a) works of art are physical objects – according to Richard Wollheim (1968, 4), this part of the theory can be defined as the 'physical object hypothesis'; (b) and are produced by way of intentional actions, in potentially diverse social contexts. The *physical object hypothesis* can constitute a sensible starting point – in view of the fact that it is related to the assumptions of common sense and of the imitative theory – though it is not unassailable. Specifically, this theory must defend itself from two important counterarguments: in the case of certain arts (let us take dance, the theatrical performance of an opera or a narration), the work of art is not reduced to the material object. In fact, the physical object that can be identified in the work of art is not the work of art. The proof lies in the fact that no physical object, that extends into space and time, exists and can be identified, alone, in *Swan Lake* or *The Late Mattia Pascal*. Further proof can be found in the fact that if I ask someone to 'give me *The Betrothed* on the table, to your right', it is doubtful that, in giving me the physical object 'book', my interlocutor will actually give me *The Betrothed*. Better yet, it is highly doubtful that *The Betrothed* is simply the material object.

The same reflections can be applied to the performance of *Madame Butterfly* which I saw in New York on 19 November 2008 at the Metropolitan Museum of

Art. In this case, too, the beautiful opera cannot be easily reduced to a material object – the score? The libretto? On the other hand, I am not entirely sure that the score and the libretto truly give me the same *Madame Butterfly* as the screenplay by Anthony Minghella.

The second objection can be formulated in the following terms: despite the fact that works of art have an irreducibly physical nature, it is nonetheless necessary to accept the fact that the category of physical object is not the most appropriate to account for the specificity of works of art. We shall see how this is a classical argument, formulated by Peter Frederick Strawson who applies it to the ontological difference that separates bodies from people (1959, 87–110), and that will later be transposed to the philosophy of art by Arthur Danto[14] (infra, 132 ff.). Simply put, reductionism does not seem to be particularly advantageous, at least not in this field. To give another example by Wollheim, those who maintain that works of art are, first and foremost, physical objects must take into account the fact that this type of theory supports the idea that a painting from the Palazzo Pitti and a slab of marble from the floor of the Museo Nazionale di Firenze share certain properties (Wollheim, 1968, 10). A formulation of the proposition in these terms – as Wollheim essentially gives us – appears to be, in a certain way, indicative of superficiality: what could seem more distant from a painting found in the Palazzo Pitti if not a piece of the floor (though built with precious marble) of the Museo Nazionale?

As Plato saw it, ordinary objects have the edge over works of art. Upon further examination, we realize that there is nothing strange about claiming that a painting by Giovanni Fattori can share certain properties with a piece of marble. It could, for instance, exhibit the same length, or the same width; it could even share the same depth and both be placed upon flat surfaces. It might even share the same black tone. There are a variety of properties of different natures; if we were to claim that the artwork has all of the properties of the material object, we would be committed to a false affirmation. It would seem, therefore, entirely reasonable to claim that the physical object hypothesis can be considered a good starting point if it is brought back to a more articulated theoretical context.

Nevertheless, the objections raised by Wollheim are relevant as they allow us to focus on two important points, which will be developed in the pages to follow. But first, a clarification must be made concerning the possible reductionist temptations: agreement on the fact that works of art are material objects does not determine a reductionism of the work of art to the material object, as Wollheim seems to believe. A work of art is, rather, a physical object, specifically an artefact, but, as we will have the chance to see, it is not reduced to its physical dimension. That 'something more' that transcends the simple material constitution of artworks is precisely what a good definition should capture. While Wollheim claims that the physical object hypothesis must be false,[15] it seems plausible to argue that it would certainly be false if it were considered separately, while it could be a good starting hypothesis for elaborating an alternative to the institutional theories. Wollheim involuntarily suggests this conclusion when he emphasizes how the question 'are works of art physical objects?' must be further decomposed and reformulated according to two directions: it is necessary to question the physicality of works of art, as much as their objectual nature. In sum: are works of art *physical objects*?

In the breakdown of the statement, two questions of ontological nature are brought into play: the first involves the physical conformation of works of art and their material structure, the second concerns their objectual structure (what type of object is a work of art?).[16] The question of definition puts at stake the possibility of finding a good answer to these two questions and to a third that was left open by the imitative theory: 'What distinguishes an ordinary object from a work of art?' In substance, how is it possible for two different *things* to occupy the same physical space in t_1?

1.8 Artefacts

The institutional theories, especially of George Dickie, have placed an emphasis on the artefactual nature of works of art: they are artefacts proposed as candidates of aesthetic appreciation by their artists. The outcome of their candidacy will be resolved by the institution that holds the power to decide: the art world.

We have already highlighted certain questions regarding the institutional theories, above all the question of reaching a good definition for the concept of artefact. It is now necessary to consider if the point is resolved by the artefactualist theories that find their best articulated exemplification in the position of Randall Dipert. Our question, then, must reformulate itself as twofold into: 'What types of things are artefacts?' and – given that a work of art is (also) an artefact – 'What types of artefacts are works of art?' Dickie's position, like Searle's variant of the theory, presents certain problems that should not be underestimated, above all being the idea that context exercises a function of procedural character that reveals itself as decisive.

Let us suppose that upon discovering a stump of wood on a beach, we notice that it was polished by the sea and now has a particular appearance, and so we take it home: it may turn into something we place in our garden. According to institutional theorists this simple gesture, charged with the intentionality of its author, can confer to the piece of wood the status of artefact and, in addition, its candidacy for aesthetic appreciation (and, in the more fortunate of cases, the status of a work of art).[17]

Another example. Let us suppose that we are picking mushrooms in a forest and, while we are there, we hope to find a decorative plant for our garden. We catch sight of a beautiful fern and decide to take it home and to transplant it to a pot. No sooner said than done, we place it in a well-illuminated space in our living room, fit for the purpose. The reason for which we decide to place the pot in the living room is most likely the same reason that motivates us to buy a painting and use it as if it were an ornament. According to Dickie, the fern that we have transplanted is, for all intents and purposes, an artefact, by the same standards as the log of wood that we displayed in our garden and that we have started to use, perhaps inadvertently, as a chair and, obviously, by the same standards as a painting as well.

In both examples, the important point is that the artefactual character of objects is determined exclusively by the will of those who operate them: in *Art and Aesthetic* (1974), Dickie claims that natural objects can be transformed into artefacts by way of a pure and simple fiat. The stump brought to our garden and used as a something to rest on becomes an artefact that exhibits properties of the same type as those exhibited by a seat and by a work of art. Nevertheless, we must keep in mind that in *The Art Circle*, Dickie formulates the theory by recognizing the limits and defects of his former position:

> In *Art and the Aesthetic* and elsewhere I maintained that the artifacts which are art become so in two distinct ways: by being made (painted, sculpted, composed, and the like) or by having artifactuality conferred on them. I maintained that art such as the *Night Watch* is made, but that some works of art had artifactuality conferred on them. This second notion was an attempt to show how things such as unaltered driftwood hung on walls and the urinal Duchamp used fall within the limits of artifactuality of artists. I now believe it was a mistake to think that artifactuality can be conferred; it just is not the sort of thing that can be conferred: an artifact must be made in some way. (Dickie, 1984, 44)

Now, if by Dickie's own admission, simple conferral of status is not sufficient to determine the transformation of a natural object to an artefact, we are left wondering what else is necessary.

Let us read on:

> I wrote of picking up and hanging on a wall and of conferring artifactuality as if they were one and the same thing; that is, I thought of picking up and hanging on a wall as a way of conferring artifactuality. But while conferring artifactuality

is impossible (as it now seems), picking up and hanging on a wall is quite easy to do. Picking up and hanging and similar actions are ways of *achieving* (not conferring) artifactuality. Of course, it is not just the motion of lifting and affixing or the like which makes something an artifact, it is lifting and affixing or the like plus something else. (Dickie, 1984, 44)

In the end, Dickie is compelled to conclude that artefactuality is not a property that can be attributed to an object by conferral. It is not sufficient to grab a branch and move it in order to transform it into an artefact; rather, it is necessary to perform this action along with *something else*. In order to define what this 'something' is, he formulates a series of distinctions that give life to a fairly articulated casuistry (Dickie, 1984, 44–6):

1. I grab a piece of wood and move it to a different area on the beach, simply to remove it from blocking the way;
2. I pick up a piece of wood and, with my pocketknife, I sharpen its sides. My objective is to construct a sort of lance to catch fish with;
3. or, I pick up a piece of wood and, without altering it in any way, I use it as a utensil to dig a hole in the sand;
4. or, I pick up the piece of wood and – still without altering it – I wave it around to move away a ferocious dog;
5. or, a piece of wood – the same piece of wood – is discovered by a lover of art who brings it home, without altering its physical properties, and puts it on display by hanging it on the wall as if it were a painting;
6. as an alternative, we can suppose that a piece of wood is hung on a wall without any artistic purpose, but simply because that seemed to be the most suitable place to hang it;
7. and, lastly, an internationally reputed artist finds a piece of wood, baptizes it as a work of art and, finally, decides that *that object* is art.

Dickie argues that the piece of wood in examples 2, 3, 4 and 5 is an artefact; while the one featured in examples 1, 6 and 7 is and will remain a simple piece of wood. Furthermore, in examples 3, 4 and 5, the piece of wood becomes an artefact without the alteration of any physical properties, but simply because it is used with a purpose.

To be in the presence of an artefact, then, it would seem that there are two necessary conditions: certain physical properties of the object must be modified with a purpose and the object itself must be used with a purpose. We may, therefore, say:

x is an artefact when the properties of x are altered with a purpose and if x is used with a purpose.

A comparison between examples 5 and 7 proves particularly meaningful. In neither of the two cases are the physical properties of the piece of wood altered, and yet, in one case we have a work of art, and in the other we do not. In one case, the piece of wood is put on display, picked up, brought home and displayed intentionally as if it were a work of art, while in the other case, it is simply identified and baptized as a work of art. How is it possible that such minimal differences, that do not concern the properties of the object, determine the shift from a natural object to a work of art? In both examples, the artist performs an action intentionally – they bring the piece of wood to their home and display it, or they designate it – and, in both cases, they try to achieve a goal, which is the same in both situations: to transform the piece of wood into a work of art. In one case, though, the artist *takes the piece of wood* and *displays* it in his home; in the other, they simply *choose* it. It would seem as though the second condition (according to which a natural object can be considered an artefact provided that it is used with a purpose, while keeping the properties of the object unaltered) must be associated with the idea that an object cannot be used with a purpose unless it is touched, moved or transferred.[18]

Clearly, this is not necessarily so. The Strait of Gibraltar was used to mark the limits of the known world, yet a border is seldom tangible; the moss on the trunk of a tree signifies the north, and it is not necessary to physically touch this signal for it to carry out its task successfully; a row of cypress trees often provokes melancholy because we know that at the end of the pathway, with all probability, we will find a cemetery (and symbols, normally, cannot be held). Dickie's theory appears to be incorrect for one fairly simple reason. A natural object whose physical placement is changed, by an act of intentionality, remains a natural object for all intents and purposes since: (i) the change in placement is extrinsic to the object: that is, it does not change any of the properties that define it; (ii) the intentionality of the subject does not permanently corrode the nature of the object (the block of wood remains a block of wood, just as the fern remains a fern). Now, while a natural object is the way it is without there being a true reason for it, artefacts are the way they are because someone determined their functions in view of a purpose. Furthermore, this purpose is generally recognizable from the physical characteristics of the artefact. Therefore, its usefulness can be found in the fact that it is not necessary to re-explain the intention of the first author.

It will not do much good, then, to drop all distinctions between artefacts and natural objects, nor will it help to sustain that there is no other distinction beyond the one determined by an extrinsic act of the subject. If anything can be an artefact, in the end nothing is, and the result is that the move makes maintaining the distinction rather useless. Let us, therefore, abandon once and for all the path traced by Dickie, and consider a different definition for the notion of artefact.

2 Artefactualist theories

2.1 Natural, artificial, ideal

Our world is full of very different objects. It is not surprising, then, that a true passion for their classification would develop. The habit of recognizing and classifying objects has proven to be a greatly useful operation for the formation of our epistemologies and, accordingly, for the survival of the human species. Whoever claims that it is a simple task to order the different typologies of existing things would be gravely wrong, as Borges's Chinese encyclopaedia serves to remind us. Nevertheless, for our purposes, we need to make a necessary distinction.

The first conceptual macro-differentiation that we must emphasize is based upon a tripartite: the rather simple one between natural objects, artefacts and ideal objects, which establishes an ideal *continuum* directed by the concrete to the abstract. Given its proximity to works of art, we are primarily interested in identifying the categories of artefacts; let us proceed by differentiating them first from natural objects and then from ideal objects.

Natural objects is the most simply identified and circumscribable category, and yet it is accompanied by a series of undertones that can prove problematic. What objects belong to the category of natural objects? The list can potentially be very long: stones, trees, mountains, hills, oceans, rivers, volcanoes, tectonic plates, clouds, even our bodies and the body of Argus the dog.

As we have seen, classification is not always a banal matter. Each body is a natural object: from its birth, until it will encounter death, it is there and is equipped with a certain consistency. In the past, no one would have expressed the least bit of doubt regarding a statement of this type; today the limit between natural and artificial is less defined and the borders are more blurred. When Argus fell ill, we can assume that Ulysses tried to cure his dog as best he could, perhaps by offering him some strange concoction. Veterinarians today do not simply prescribe medications; if necessary, they could easily substitute parts of his body. The same holds true, and is enhanced, for human beings; let us imagine a Gothic version of Hume's mental experiment on the ship of Theseus:

a sort of Frankenstein from the near future. In our version of the experiment, guided by a methodical plan, we will substitute the parts of a human body (internal and external) with the corresponding artificial parts or, even, with parts transplanted from other bodies: heart, liver, lungs, eyes, epidermis, ribs, hair, et cetera. Up to what point can we say that that body is still a natural object? The same goes for memories and the role they play in the formation of personal identity: how many memories can be lost and how many must be preserved for me to remain me? Let us take for instance when someone awakens from a coma and their physical identity is preserved but their memories have been inexorably lost, forever. How many variations can a body or a soul sustain before they become something else? Locke resolves the question in an elegant manner: personal identity revolves around one's memories. If my brain is what it is, it could even be implanted into another body: no one would recognize me, at least not at the beginning yet, nevertheless, I would still be me. But are we certain that my relationship with others – in this case a clearly altered relationship – does not contribute to defining me? And so the story continues.

Ideal Objects. These are objects that in Meinong's classification are identified by the name 'subsistent objects'. *Ideal* objects have a different existence from that of natural objects, but just like natural objects they *do not* depend on human beings.

> They are not tangible. That is to say that the properties of a triangle, of the principle of noncontradiction or of an arithmetic equation do not depend in any way (in terms of their essence) on the work of an architect, a logician or a mathematician. They are discovered, and not invented, just as a continent is. (Ferraris, 2005)

Artefacts. Positioned between the two extremes are artefacts. In general, when we think of an artefact, it is natural for us to refer to a material object of medium scale, an object of a certain physical consistency that is easily held. While it is not so natural for us to think of the ancient Mayan pyramids of Tikal, in Guatemala, as an artefact, we generally do not find it difficult to consider a black Montblanc an artefact, or this very book I am writing. Along the line that we are tracing, which separates natural objects from ideal objects, artefacts occupy a vast frontier territory, which can be extremely blurry at times.

Artefacts are easily manipulated material objects,[19] but what else are they? Let us return to the Frankenstein of our Gothic example. During the normal course of life, many parts of the human body are subject to transformation and are substituted: hair, skin, blood, nails and so on. Even so, we would never say that the human body is an artefact, whereas we could claim so if some of its parts are intentionally substituted. What distinguishes the two intuitions? First, behaviour. In one case (that of the spontaneous changes), there is no intentionality, but nature simply takes its course. In the other case (that of Frankenstein), we can easily hypothesize that, just as in Mary Shelley's story, a mad scientist changes each part of Frankenstein's body and does so in an attempt to fulfil a personal objective or obsession.

Artefacts do not find themselves in nature like clouds or volcanoes do, nor can they declare themselves simple fiats of our will. Rather, they are the result of the work of a subject (unlike ideal objects). We can detect an intentional action, with a precise purpose, at the root of the action of the worker who shaped the clay tile that washed up on the beach, just as there is an intentional action at the root of the action of the mad scientist who substitutes all of the parts of Frankenstein's body. In both cases, the purpose is made clear by the final result – the construction of the tile and Frankenstein's brand-new body. This also happens when a natural object becomes an artefact: a subject, or an agent, observes an object and then modifies it intentionally, on the basis of an exact project or purpose. In order to fulfil this purpose – say, building a house or creating an immortal body – the agent will observe the object and modify certain properties, while leaving others untouched.

Among the manifold properties that an object can exhibit, it is easy to suppose that only some will be directed to make of that object an artefact, for instance, the clay of the tile, but not its weight or its size. Certain properties are the very reasons for which an object was chosen to perform a given function. The whiteness of a piece of paper is particularly suitable for writing, just as the 'function' of a chair responds to ergonomic criteria. Let us take note of a point: oftentimes, the properties that determine the specificity of an artefact have the characteristic of being recognized by different agents (that is to say, by subjects other than those who thought of them in the first place) that identify them as most suitable for the fulfilment of *that specific* purpose.

Having made these preliminary remarks, we are now in a position to follow Randall Dipert who, in his classification, dedicates particular attention to artefacts (1993, 17 ff.). Dipert's classification is fundamentally bipartite and structures itself upon two points – that of completely natural objects (oceans and clouds, mountains and volcanoes and others) and utilizable objects. The first types of objects are objects that, for the most part, are not subjected to intentional modifications dictated by a purpose. The second types of objects are objects that have been realized in view of an objective. Of these, some (i) are not intentionally modified: these are natural instruments (the wooden stump that we use to sit on; the stick we use to lean on when we walk, or to harm an enemy, or to make a coconut fall from a tree). Others (ii) we have instead decided to modify in view of our objectives. Let us take for instance Ulysses, who sharpens and burns the point of a wooden pole in order to blind the Cyclops, or Tom Hanks who uses driftwood to build the raft that will take him away from the island of his shipwreck. Of these objects some (a) are artefacts, while others (b) do not have an artefactual character, and have been modified only to better their usefulness. Among all artefacts some (a.1) have a communicative purpose, others (a.2) have an expressive purpose, while others (a.3) have an artistic purpose. Finally, the majority (a.4) of these objects were built in view of a practical purpose that, typically, is neither expressive nor communicative or artistic.

2.2 Real artefacts: Instruments and tools

For the most part, instruments have an artefactual character: they are used to reach an objective, or else they exhibit specific properties which are modified intentionally by a subject, in view of an end. However, not all things that are directed towards a goal are artefacts: let us consider, for example, a commission whose task it is to redefine the boundaries of two states (perhaps following a war), that defines one of these borders by using a river to separate the territories. Let us also suppose that this river has not been altered in any way. We have subjects who express intentional actions and objectives (to redefine the confines of two sovereign states), an object that acts as an instrument and that is used in view of a purpose (tracing a boundary) and the properties of that instrument were never in any way altered (e.g. neither its basin nor the tracks of its course). The river that separates two opposite banks is, then, a natural object that has become an instrument suitable for defining a different boundary. On the other hand, there are many cases in which human beings purposely modify objects (even natural objects) at their disposal. In cases such as these, instruments – those which Heidegger called 'usable' (1927, 15–16, Eng. trans., 97–109) – must be considered tools and, in general, are distinguished by one or more properties that characterize their function. It is these very properties that make the artefact further recognizable.

2.3 Special artefacts: Works of art

The definition of an artefact that has arisen from Dipert's theory can be used to recapitulate what has been discussed up until this point: 'An artifact is an intentionally modified tool whose modified properties were intended by the agent to be recognized by an agent at a later time as having been intentionally altered for that, or some other, use' (Dipert, 1993, 29–30). The fundamental intuition that seems to characterize the notion of artefact is that of an object that has certain properties that have been intentionally modified in view of a purpose. In this case, the agent has acted knowingly in order that other subjects, in different places and times, might recognize the properties that have been modified, identifying them as properties that characterize the purposes of the artefact. It is, ultimately, the same difference between a chair and a tree stump that a mushroom picker uses to sit on: the chair immediately recalls the possibility of sitting down because this was the explicit intention of whoever built it; the tree trunk, conversely, may or may not be recalled by it. In sum, the artefact 'chair' is not distinguished from the log of wood by the sole fact of being well made and appropriate for human beings to sit on it; rather, unlike the log, it exhibits properties (the function of the chair) that ensure that human beings with different habits, in different times and contexts, consider it a particularly suitable object for that specific purpose.

Things are not always that simple, though. It is not sufficient – or, at least it is not said to be sufficient – to identify certain physical properties of an object in order to be certain of tracing it back to its possible uses, and much less to the explicit intentions of its author. For this reason, as Dipert rightly notes, the recognition of an artefact through the correct identification of its functions is a special human ability, which is directly related to our interpretative capacities (interpreting the intentions of an agent, or the dynamics that govern it within a social context). And so, out of the large sea of artefacts that clutter our world, Dipert isolates two typologies that appear relevant to him and particularly interesting together; these are works of art and linguistic statements. As was the case in antiquity, there is a connection between works of art and statements: both have a communicative function. Since works of art and expressions exhibit, or fail to exhibit, properties that have been modified or introduced by subjects, they always communicate something. For example, the shape of a vase is related, first, to the need to conserve water, and, second, to the will to make known a little discovery – a shape that facilitates the execution of certain operations – to all vase builders or to whomever has had the need to conserve water.

And, yet, if it is true that artefacts have communicative ends, it is equally true that some communicate in a different way. When we hang a sign on our front door that says 'Beware of dog!' we have created an artefact (the sign is clearly not a natural object), that expresses the intention of its author (to warn visitors against possible harm that the dog could do them), and that enables visitors to understand our intention (to advise them that they may find themselves in a dangerous situation). The artefact, therefore, not only communicates something 'about itself', but also with regard to something else, specifically the precise intention of whoever created it. Yet, in many cases – in the majority of cases, according to Dipert – artefacts do not offer information regarding something else; rather, they simply provide information concerning themselves (Dipert, 1993, 103): this is the very element that determines the distinction between ordinary artefacts and communicative artefacts. Dipert's idea, then, is that a given artefact, our chair for instance, communicates something in reference to itself ('I am very functional for your sitting needs'), while a 'communicative' artefact, the sign that warns me of the presence of a dog, for example, informs of something, but in reference to something else, likely to the external world: 'The communicative aspects of the chair (e.g. those that display intentions to get someone to believe it is a good chair, a brown chair, or whatever) cause beliefs about the artifact itself – and these artifactual features of the chair, so conceived, seem incapable of causing beliefs about other objects' (Dipert, 1993, 103). The door sign provides us with superabundant and 'synthetic' information, whereas the chair does not. Dipert's theory is that this argument holds true for the majority of artefacts: with the exception of works of art and expressions. The following is the artefactualist definition proposed by Dipert:

> An artwork is an artifact that has been made with an intention for other agents
> to regard it as an art work (in the sense just described), that is for other agents to
> conceive of its unsubordinated intention (purpose) as being an RIF (expressive/
> representative/symbolic) intention. Its maker in fact intended that when the
> artifact is later perceived or thought about, it will be conceived as an object
> whose purpose was such that its recognition implies its fulfillment. (Dipert,
> 1993, 115)[20]

To summarize: all artworks are artefacts that have the property of communicating something about something different from themselves; in doing so, they stimulate certain faculties, notably those whose task it is to perceive and to interpret (Dipert, 1993, 117).

This theory puts us on the right track by identifying the thread that unites artworks and words, but it does not resolve certain problems. To understand it, let us consider a more complex object, a sort of highly fashionable super-artefact. By using a Smartphone we are able to do a variety of things.

A super phone, like any other artefact, communicates to me many things about itself: for instance, that it is a telephone, but also an iPod, a musical reproducer, featuring a high-definition screen and it also tells me that it is a device equipped to connect to the internet. Despite its very brief life, it can already boast a history that testifies to a true evolution of the species. The history of the Smartphone is interesting from its beginning to its end, and it becomes even more interesting with the development of 3.0 OS software. Perhaps the idea of its developers was, from the start, to decrease the quantity of objects in the pockets of their clients, since occamist parsimony, after all, always pays off. The challenge consisted of making possible an infinite amount of services through a single and highly versatile object: of course it could make phone calls, but it could also check email, keep track of appointments, take notes, avoid getting lost while travelling, make hotel reservations, buy train tickets, complete check-ins to avoid lines at the airport, warn of flight delays, read books, leaf through the newspaper and so on. At this point in history – at the beginning of the year 2008 – a new element has intervened. In Cupertino, it was understood that the iPhone expressed something about its own use, that it expressed something in regard to something different from itself. The super phone, a bit unexpectedly perhaps, shares certain properties with the sign warning of the presence of a dog, as well as with the chair. And the reason is, all in all, quite simple: in less than a year, users had executed a little under 800 million downloads of iPhone applications and, conversely, thousands of developers studying the habits of the users had begun working on specific applications, making them available both by payment and free of charge. It was a short step from thinking that the 3.0 version of the software was to contain an application, SDK, expressly studied in order for the developers to continue doing their job the best way possible, creating and marketing applications that were custom-made for users. But what does all this have to do with the notion of an artefact proposed by Dipert? The iPhone demonstrates well how common artefacts – those such as a chair, for instance – instantiate properties that refer to their usage. Ultimately, they tell us things about those who use them, precisely as is the case of a Louis XVI chair or of Wendell Castle stools, because all artefacts – not only some, as Dipert claims – are 'about' something that does not necessarily refer to themselves. If artworks, just like ordinary artefacts, transmit a series of meanings, then the difference between the two typologies of objects – given that artworks and artefacts are not the same type of thing – will be found in the details, seeing as both the former and the latter seem to carry meanings.

From an ontological point of view, Dipert approves of the first condition posed by Dickie's theory and includes artworks in the category of artefacts. Artworks, like so many other objects, are artefacts; they are, though, fairly particular artefacts – special artefacts. Non-special artefacts, in Dipert's theory, are generally about themselves, while artworks are about other things – we have seen, by proposing a counterexample, how this theory presents certain difficulties. Additionally, artworks, unlike non-special artefacts, do not exhibit any practical purpose; they do not have the objective of intervening in reality in order to modify it. The conclusion is rather bizarre. The fact that art often has a deep effect on reality was already something thought of by Plato who, well aware of his power, had made sure to maintain a reasonable distance between artists and the ideal state. Dipert shows a great deal of ingenuousness with regard to this point. Yet, he does consider a few problems.

Though he admits that art does not leave its mark on reality, it must have some sort of purpose for it to boast such a long history, seeing as mankind would not conserve something for so long if it were useless (Dipert, 1993, 111). Therefore, so far as it does not have practical ends, Dipert claims that art is surely useful in strengthening certain human faculties: as had already been observed by Aristotle (*Poetics*, xi, 1452a–1452ab, xvi, 1454b–1455a), art strengthens the faculties related to recognition. If I wish to use a Picasso to plan a lesson on Cubism, or if I wish to use a hammer to hang that Picasso on the wall, I must be able to pre-emptively recognize each of the two objects. Clearly, the two observations (of the hammer and of the artwork) do not exemplify the same type of activity as faculties and very diverse conceptualizations come into play. In order to explain the matter, Dipert refers to a conceptual traditional horizon. He reasserts how, in addition to the faculties that are capable of interpretation, our senses are involved in our relationship with artworks and, contextually, these senses are particularly sensitive to the aesthetic qualities of objects. It is, ultimately, a recognition aimed at properties such as beauty, harmony, colours, shapes and so forth.

Since the line of reasoning developed by Dipert is founded upon the idea that artworks are artefacts – albeit particular artefacts – from it arises an important distinction between aesthetic objects and artistic objects that is based upon this very point. In fact, any object, including natural objects, can exhibit aesthetic properties: a sunset, a sea storm, the white porcelain mug used to serve hot chocolate at 'Le Monde' on Broadway, a painting, a sonata, a story and so on. However, not all aesthetic objects are artefacts. Accordingly, not all aesthetic objects are works of art: 'I would fussily distinguish between an aesthetic object and an artistic object. The former may simply produce pleasing sensations, while the latter necessarily requires a conceptualization of the object as an artefact – that is, regarding it as an agent's product' (Dipert, 1993, 112). Works of art, then, can without a question exhibit aesthetic qualities, but not all objects that exhibit aesthetic properties are works of art. If this distinction clarifies the reasons for which a sunset is not a work of art, it still does not explain the reasons for which my iPhone is not. It is, ultimately, the product of many agents and, perhaps by chance, it does not fail to exhibit aesthetic properties. Dipert, therefore, identifies two conditions that must jointly apply for an object to be a work of art. The first is that (i) the object must be an artefact; the second is that (ii) this artefact does not exhibit practical purposes.

Compared to the institutional theories, Dipert's definition has the undisputed advantage of delineating more precisely the concept of artefact and, at the same time, of avoiding referring to the art world, which has demonstrated clear limits that we have already mentioned (supra, 48 ff.). Nevertheless, Dipert's artefactualism is not devoid of difficulties: are we really able to distinguish a Brillo box from a *Brillo Box* based on the concept of an artefact? Are we sure that – if we had to choose without the advice of an expert, and we were interested in the artwork rather than the box – we would be able to bring home the artwork and leave the box behind? In addition, to reference less complicated examples, are we sure that a good conceptualization of artefacts is sufficient to distinguish a *Paint by Numbers* by Andy Warhol from the same *Paint by Numbers* made by a child in elementary school? In the end, would Frescoditesta be able to find the answer to his question? I am afraid not. This has already been effectively noted by William E. Kennick, among others, in the previously cited essay *Does Traditional Aesthetics Rest on a Mistake?* (1958, 317–34), as well as by neo-Wittgensteinian theorists. We shall return to this point shortly.

3 The aesthetic definition of art

3.1 Vehicles of aesthetic qualities

This book founds itself upon a specific theory that also comprises one of its central points: it is possible that the philosophy of art and aesthetics might never meet, insofar as their respective objects do not coincide (supra, 7 ff.). We have seen that the realm of aesthetic objects appears more ample than that of artistic objects, and that the philosophy of art in particular seeks to define the ontological status of artworks, while aesthetics (from the etymology of the word) deals with the knowledge that we obtain through our senses; knowledge, therefore, that does not necessarily concern art. So, while the philosophy of art considers works of art and the questions concerning their conceptualization, aesthetics looks after that of reason; that is to say, to the dynamics of the experience that is not connoted in cognitive and logical terms.[21] Art, too, serves as aesthetic experience and is mediated by the senses; nonetheless, as Dipert observes, it appears unquestionably advantageous from a theoretical perspective to understand aesthetic experience as something different from artistic experience. Aesthetic experience is oftentimes configured as a necessary – albeit insufficient – condition for understanding artworks, and it is applied to an undoubtedly larger realm than that of works of art. Furthermore, with the exception of authorized personnel or the insiders, it is more common for an average person to experience a sunset than it is for them to experience a work of art. Aesthetic experiences are widespread, while artistic experiences are less so. It would behove us, then, to remember that it is possible to aesthetically relate to the most diverse range of things: watching a sunset or a cityscape, tasting good wine, listening to the story of travels to a faraway land. The experience that we call aesthetic, and that is a subspecies of the more general concept of experience, depends on the perception of a series of qualities (or properties) that are found in the most diverse and common of objects. These properties are called aesthetic qualities (or properties). Not all aesthetic qualities can be obtained through the senses, but certainly the majority can. Thus arises the privileged bond that tradition has rightfully sanctioned between aesthetics and sensibility.

Aesthetic qualities have a relational nature; that is, they depend on the relationship of the object that exhibits them with the subject that perceives them. While certain qualities belong to objects regardless of the relationship with their subjects, others undoubtedly belong to things, but their interaction with a subject is fundamental for their determination. The blackness of my pen is such only because I am here (or someone with the same physical-biological characteristics is here) to look at it. In order to be what they are, relational properties depend on the response of the subject that perceives them. No matter which decimal system we choose to use in order to confirm that Mont Blanc is 4,810.45 meters tall, it will always remain that tall, even if not one human being were left in the world to determine its height, and even if we were to use an extremely long stack of toothpicks to measure it. On the other hand, if the world were populated not by human beings, but by living beings similar to Godzilla, few would define the Mont Blanc an 'imposing' mountain. While a mountain is what it is, some of its properties depend directly on the relationship that it has with us and with our environment. These are properties that belong to it, but solely by reason of the fact that its relationship with the human environment is part of the history of Mont Blanc. Clearly, we would be mistaken if we were to consider relational properties in the same way as we do subjective qualities. They pertain to our relationship with the world that is determined by the structure of human physicality that is everything but subjective. As we were saying, in principle, an aesthetic reflection may proceed without ever referring to works of art: aesthetic qualities may be equally exhibited by natural objects, just as by the most common artefacts and by certain events.

Within this framework, an aesthetic theory must face two difficult orders: first, it should clarify the reasons for which the analysis of works of art favours the comprehension of the structure as well as the dynamics of our sensible experience. It should also clarify for what reasons the determination of aesthetic properties should help us in matters pertaining to questions of definition. An object's possession of aesthetic properties could be a necessary condition, but it is certainly not enough to be considered a work of art, since the world is full of beautiful things that are, all the while, not works of art. In addition, beauty is an aesthetic quality. The 'aesthetic theories of art' aim in this direction; they claim that an artwork necessarily possesses aesthetic qualities. In other words, aesthetic definitions consider an artwork in the same way that they consider a 'vehicle' of aesthetic qualities and they retain that this characteristic of artworks determined the fact that they make a particular experience possible: an aesthetic experience. This type of approach clearly suggests a specificity of experience related to works of art: it is a particular experience different from the rest, in which we are at ease in dedicating ourselves to perceiving certain specific properties of objects without being distracted by contingent or material necessities. It was not by chance that Immanuel Kant spoke of disinterested contemplation.[22] The aesthetic definition permits us to reconcile quite comfortably the intentions of the artist with the expectations of their audience. There are two conditions that are generally indispensable to this definition: (1) that the artist be guided by the specific intention of producing objects that exhibit aesthetic properties, and (2) that the result of the artist's activity make possible aesthetic experiences.

Therefore:

x is a work of art if and only if (1) it is produced by the intentionality of an agent who intends to confer upon it a certain capacity, that of (2) making possible and favouring an aesthetic experience.

This definition places emphasis on two elements: first, the intentional doings of the artist, who must want the work of art. That is to say, they must lead their action to an explicit end. Specifically, in *Art as Experience* (1934, ch. 8), Dewey anticipates a similar theoretical shift by Nelson Goodman (1978), and revises the classic formulation of the question 'what is art?' by transforming it into one of procedural nature: 'when is art?' In Dewey's theory, in particular, a continuity between general experience and aesthetic experience is traced, while the American philosopher claims that the task of aesthetics consists of re-establishing the continuity between aesthetic experience, which is disinterested and pure, and daily experience. For this to happen, the artwork must be used in the world and never separated from it, since artworks contribute to the comprehension of experience in its totality and also arise from it.[23] The artwork will emerge, then, where the structures of the object relate to the energy, the experience and the emotive dynamics of the subject.

If a supporter of the aesthetic definition were asked to embark on a journey into space-time and, upon arriving in a faraway galaxy very different from our own, he were to stumble upon particular objects that would be considered works of art in his world, based on his theory he would not be able to conclude, beyond the shadow of a doubt, that he had found objects that exemplify works of art in that world. In order to reach this conclusion, in fact, he would have to possess a certain document that attests, with reasonable certainty, that the intention of the authors of these objects was specifically to induce, through the production of them, aesthetic experiences in their audience.

3.2 Intentions

At this point, the reader may foster a legitimate suspicion that the aesthetic definition is a bit too vast, that it does not exclude anything, and that, at the same time, it does not allow for the opposite: to admit among artworks certain objects made to respond to non-artistic objectives and that common sense has considered to be works of art. Let us consider icons, for instance, whose purposes originated from devotional needs and that were later considered, for all intents and purposes, examples of Russian art. Upon closer examination, it becomes clear that this is a fear that we can, at least in part, dispel. The concept of intention upon which the aesthetic definition rests is delineated fairly well. What does it mean to have the intention to produce an object that is capable of causing an aesthetic experience? The artist must have certain beliefs; for example, they must believe that works of art exist, along with a behaviour that guarantees the will to implement them. If I intend to conduct a study on UFOs, I must conceive of the possibility that there exist forms of extraterrestrial life in order to implement the key strategies that are useful for collecting data of their existence. It is also possible that, despite having developed sceptical convictions regarding the existence of other forms of life, I still decide to undertake the endeavour. Even in this case, I would be guided by a belief – 'no form of extraterrestrial life exists' – and I would implement the most useful measures to verify it.

Considering that this is in fact true, it is obvious, then, that an artist who considers artworks as the principle vehicles of aesthetic properties and of aesthetic experience, and then exhibits their work *Fountain*, would prove to be reasoning in a peculiar manner. The principle, perhaps only, experience propitiated by urinals, bottle racks, bicycle wheels, stuffed sharks, unmade beds and such like, is one of estrangement and astonishment.

If the aesthetic definition is not so welcoming after all – there are clear difficulties in accounting for a part of contemporary art in terms of aesthetic experience, for example in terms of aesthetic pleasure[24] – it is out of the question that it might offer any advantages. First of all, it proposes a criterion that, if supported, would allow us to make certain decisions. We could consider all things that were made specifically to provoke an aesthetic experience as works of art, which seems to constitute a good litmus test for judging the quality of artworks. A well-made portrait will not only provoke astonishment in regard to the skill of its author in such a way that my attention is focused on observing the traits of a face that I would otherwise overlook, but it will also lead me in the right direction in terms of recognizing a work of art when I see one.

Beyond this, the aesthetic definition offers a meaningful explanation for why art has enjoyed such a profound and almost unchanged consideration throughout the centuries: humankind loves art because it is the principle vehicle for something that they generally care very much about, as well as the emotions that are related to its fruition. Two important questions remain: the first has to do with the centrality of aesthetic experience in theory, since an artwork may very well have political, moral or even ethical purposes, rather than aesthetic ones.

The second concerns the meaning of the expression 'aesthetic experience' which, until now, we have examined in a knowingly vague manner. Let us try to consider in more detail the nature of the type of experience that we define as 'aesthetic'.

3.3 Testadura and the properties of an artwork

It would be worthwhile to first explain both the structure and the characteristics of aesthetic experience.[25] We can begin by observing that it can be examined under a double profile[26]: the properties of physical objects that determine the dawn of aesthetic experience, or the emotions of the subjects who use the works of art.

Let us consider the first typology which can be defined in the following manner:

> *x is a work of art if it exhibits such aesthetic qualities that it allows subjects to have an aesthetic experience.*

Brillo Box, then, would be a work of art if it were to act causally upon its beholders, provoking in them aesthetic experiences. But, positively, what is an aesthetic experience? Let us imagine that Testadura[27] wishes to describe *Brillo Box* to a friend who has never before seen Warhol's work. Out of the many ways he could choose to speak of it, he decides to describe the work by expanding upon its aesthetic qualities. Testadura begins his description by 'atomizing' the artwork: (a) the colours (Testadura lists them all); (b) the shapes (in this case, too, Testadura carefully describes both the shape of the work and the shapes sketched inside); (c) the measurements (Testadura is precise on this point, too: 6.8 × 6.8 × 5.5); (d) the temporal localization (it has been exhibited in 1964 – Testadura explains – but it still exists today); (e) and, finally, the spatial localization (various copies of *Brillo Box* had been produced, though indiscernible from one another, and each copy was placed in a different location).

Now, it could be that despite such a meticulous explanation, Testadura's interlocutor, Frescoditesta – him again! – is unable to imagine *Brillo Box*, seeing as an account of a work of art is not the same as the aesthetic experience of it. Frescoditesta believes that direct experience is irreplaceable. He therefore decides to build his very own home-made *Brillo Box*: the same shapes (Testadura had described them word for word), the same colours (this was not so difficult either) and, of course, the identical measurements. All of the basic details are accounted for and, so, Frescoditesta gets to work.

Let us suppose that Testadura's account provides such a rich and precise description that it assures that a Brillo box will be assembled in the same exact manner as the *Brillo Box* Testadura saw and, so, Frescoditesta constructs his own *Brillo* by putting together the identical basic details. At this point, a theorist of the aesthetic definition might claim that Frescoditesta is in the position to have a perfect aesthetic experience: all he needs to do is to look at the box and a world (the artwork) will emerge almost magically from Frescoditesta's perception in the exact moment that he collates all of the basic details and all of the aesthetic qualities of the box. By perceiving the artwork, Frescoditesta achieves an aesthetic experience. Problem solved.

Assuming that Frescoditesta has the right intent – he has, in fact, applied the most appropriate strategies for the realization of the artwork – might it be sufficient to consider the aesthetic properties of the work of art in order to have an aesthetic experience? It is quite likely. Assuming that he does have an aesthetic experience with the work, is this a necessary and sufficient condition for Frescoditesta to understand the artwork in order for him to have an artistic experience with the artwork? This is quite unlikely. The unquestionably aesthetically beautiful object will be before his eyes and, unless he is learned in the history of art, Frescoditesta will ask himself why that box should be a work of art. Could Frescoditesta, on the other hand, ever formulate a complete aesthetic judgement based solely upon his sensible perception of the artwork? Clearly not. He might formulate a judgement of taste, by saying if he considers it beautiful or not, but nothing more. And how much might Frescoditesta's perception be related to the prejudice in favour of what is beautiful? That is to say, how much might aesthetic experience depend on the fact that we have a natural predisposition to appreciate beauty, the harmony in shapes, the equilibrium of proportions, the harmony of sounds and the rhythm of writing?[28] In other words, what aesthetic experience is related to the 'kalliphobia' of the historical avant-garde? These matters require reflection; it is possible, after all, that in cases such as these compensatory mechanisms that have little to do with aesthetic experience may come into play. I revel not so much in the formal structure of the artwork but, rather, in the fact that I have been able to fill that cognitive lacuna that separates certain art from common sense; the same satisfaction that we experience when we are able to solve a puzzle or an equation.[29]

The theorist of experience still has a counterargument at their disposal: they could argue that these sorts of difficulties emerge in a scant number of extreme cases – the canonical version of the argument often makes reference to the *ready-mades*. If these are the facts of the matter, we could be dealing with a false problem; that is, we could be dealing with a scant number of 'artworks' that may or may not be artworks. In the end, a good definition should allow us to distinguish works of art from other types of things while, clearly, it could never replace a critical judgement with regard to quality. In classic cases, he might add, the aesthetic definition seems to work rather well. Frescoditesta may have been successful in his endeavour if, in the place of the qualities of *Brillo Box*, he had referred to the aesthetic properties of *The Trace Horse* by Robert Sargent Austin, an etching from 1921 that depicts a cart horse, fully harnessed and ready to work, or even those in *The Holy Family*, painted by Raphael.

We have yet to consider what happens in more traditional cases. Let us take these two works of art: first, the colours (in *The Trace Horse* we have an alternation of black and white, while in *The Holy Family* we see warm colours). Both occupy a space somewhere in the world (*The Trace Horse* can be found in the Fine Arts Museums of San Francisco, while *The Holy Family* is conserved at The Paul Getty Museum in Los Angeles). And they both have an enviable duration of time (*The Trace Horse* is from 1921, while *The Holy Family* dates back to 1483). Even when dealing with these kinds of examples, which are unquestionably the most favourable for theorists of aesthetic experience as the perception of sensible properties causes a sort of aesthetic pleasure that undoubtedly finds no type of impediment in the meanings of the artwork, we may have certain doubts. In cases such as these, is aesthetic experience a necessary and sufficient condition for the definition of works of art? Both *The Holy Family* and *The Trace Horse*, as well as *Brillo Box*, are unquestionably something more compared to their nude physical body which expresses the sensible qualities of the artworks; the only difference is that the meanings found in *The Holy Family* at least appear more accessible to us. Let us suppose that Frescoditesta is an inhabitant of the planet Mars, and that he has arrived on Earth without any knowledge of its history; would his aesthetic experience of *The Holy Family* truly be different from that of *Brillo Box*?

3.4 Disinterest

Aesthetic experience, whatever it may be, seems to be related to a particular feeling of the subject: disinterest. While different modes of life express different degrees of interest towards things, even if measured differently – which, in general, we need in order to live, to live better, to obtain results or to reach goals – aesthetic experience distinguishes itself by being a sort of pure contemplation; one that is indifferent compared to the existence of what is contemplated. No one who is familiar with attending theatrical performances would race to the stage in order to stop the hand of Medea. Adults are generally not entertained by fictional characters just as they are not amused by writing messages to Santa Claus. Instead, they might write a letter that they will insert into a bottle with the hope that it will be found by another human being. Precisely because it does not invest us concretely, this singularly happy condition allows our judgement to move with greater freedom, in order to focus on the details for which we normally nurture a genuine disinterest.

Aristotle had understood the point in his own way: works of art must be judged and enjoyed by making exclusive reference to their internal logic. No moral, ethical or political consideration must compete in the formation of aesthetic judgement. Let us suppose that we attended the premier of the movie *Downfall*, a 2004 film directed by Oliver Hirschbiegel. The plot is constructed around the last 12 days of the life of Adolf Hitler, beginning on his fifty-sixth birthday, 20 April 1945. Devastating madness transpires in a Wagnerian crescendo over 12 days, and the dictator shows signs that he wishes to annihilate the entire German nation, as well as himself. In such a case, a disinterested contemplation amounts to the development of a judgement of the film that prescinds from the moral implications of Hitler's actions. Moral and political reflections have nothing to do with the aesthetic enjoyment of the work, which pertains, rather, to elements such as the cinematographic construction of the story, the performance of the actors, the execution of the direction and so on. It would not make sense, within the framework of the aesthetic definition, to ask ourselves if *Downfall* is an educational spectacle. Considerations of this sort do not involve the enjoyment of the work itself. *Downfall* is about something – the final, frenetic days of the führer and their symbolic, as well as historical, valence – and this something is narrated with specific language. The point, then, is that from the perspective of the aesthetic theory, content is simply an instrument that is functional to the enjoyment of the work.

If we wish to develop a definition that synthesizes the two principle components of the aesthetic experience, we can entrust the formulation of Noël Carroll (1999, 177):

> *x is an artwork if and only if x is intentionally produced with the capacity to afford disinterested and sympathetic attention and contemplation for its own sake.*

The aesthetic theory has the advantage of affixing specific boundaries, since neither natural objects nor common artefacts classify as works of art. Even art's thousand-year-old function in human history becomes a little less mysterious: we have produced art for millennia because it gives us a certain type of pleasure and, as a side effect, certain faculties are strengthened, such as our attention and contemplation.

3.5 Hidden dangers

It appears as though the aesthetic definition as a whole, in its two different declinations, functions rather well. Nevertheless, it is not difficult to detect within it certain insidious problems. Let us analyse them briefly, starting with those concerning the variant of the theory whose objects are aesthetic properties. Two difficulties can be noted with regard to this variant. First, the pervasiveness of the aesthetic qualities: if a theorist of the aesthetic definition defends the necessity of the link that unites perception, aesthetic qualities and works of art, it would be rather simple to object by arguing that it is necessary to identify certain aesthetic qualities that characterize works of art in a univocal fashion, since the world is full of beautiful, ugly, graceful, sublime, dramatic and exhilarating things that are not, and most likely will never be, works of art.

The second difficulty involves an agreement on aesthetic qualities. What are aesthetic qualities? Can we draft a list? The properties that we can discern by way of our senses would certainly count: harmony, proportion, colours, lightness and heaviness, sweetness and bitterness. The qualities that can be discerned by way of intellect would be added as well: unity, grace, harmony, proportion and so forth. Identifying some of these qualities oftentimes seems to be a matter of detail and, yet, this is not the truly problematic point. We must determine, rather, how to handle all of those properties that more and more often we find exemplified in universally recognized works of art, but that do not qualify as aesthetic qualities: silence, ugliness, dissonance, disharmony, disintegration, contrast, fracture, annoyance, irritability – just to name a few. Are these, too, aesthetic properties? And are they vehicles of aesthetic experience?

Not necessarily. *Tibidabo* is a work by Dieter Roth from 1978. If we were to single out its aesthetic properties, the work would undoubtedly give us a run for our money: it consists of the barking of a dog that is protracted without interruption for 24 hours. Together with other works, *Tibidabo* was displayed years ago in a retrospective exhibition at the MACBA in Barcelona. Let us imagine a visitor who attended the projection for the entirety of its duration. What qualities might his aesthetic experience have had? Let us envision the scene. What is the difference between listening to the ordinary barking of a dog that persists for 24 hours and listening to the barking of a dog that persists for 24 hours, but that is a work of art? If a difference does, in fact, exist it is certainly not found in the effects of the barking on its audience. It is safe to say that anyone would become irritated after a certain period of time. In the case of the artwork exhibited at the MACBA, we can choose to end the tension by changing pavilion, while in the case of the ordinary dog we would most likely have to suppress the animal. In the first case, we could also ask ourselves sophisticated questions about how it feels to be irritated, while in the second – probably – we would simply be irritated. The difference, if there is one, is not found in our perception of barking but, rather, in the different ways in which we conceptualize the two events.

The aesthetic theory maintains that where there is no aesthetic experience, there is no art; evidently, in the case of *Tibidabo* there is no aesthetic experience and, therefore, we must conclude that we are not in the presence of a work of art. What about boredom? Might there be a certain proximity with sentiments of disinterest and disinterested contemplation? It is hard to say, though there would seem not to be. It is an indisputable fact that boredom was one of the best-exemplified feelings in the artistic production of the twentieth century. One of the most boring films in the history of cinematography is *Empire* by Andy Warhol. For what seems an infinite number of minutes – 485 to be exact – Warhol's camera remains pointed at the Empire State Building without the slightest movement taking place. It is a black-and-white silent film with a single subject: the *Empire*, shot for an entire day. In this case, too, the only possible (though I do not quite know how aesthetic) experience is most likely that of mortal boredom, from which the spectator can escape only by leaving. According to the terms of the aesthetic definition, not even Warhol's film could be considered a work of art.

Turning to more recent productions, what can we say with regard to the cycle of *Cremaster* by Matthew Barney? The five films not only put to test the patience of any observer, but their structure obligates us to ask an additional question as well: if we were able to survive the showing and we were to admit, without hesitation, that the whirl of colours, shapes and allusions in *Cremaster* transmits an aesthetic experience, can we be sure that this alone allows for the formulation of an artistic judgement? In order to understand the *Cremaster Cycle*, we must come to terms with a quantity of mythological, allegorical and historical references that are necessary to give those five films their due artistic value. In cases such as this, the experience that arises from the perception of the work is a necessary (though not sufficient) condition for the formulation of an artistic judgement.

The question, then, can be summarized in the following terms:

1. We can identify the aesthetic properties of *Empire*, and yet, it is not convincing to maintain that the fruition of this film entails ipso facto the rise of an aesthetic experience;

2. *The Cremaster Cycle,* on the other hand, certainly exhibits, among other things, the aesthetic qualities that give form to an aesthetic experience – exactly as in the case of the aesthetic qualities exhibited by a sunset. Nevertheless, it is doubtful that this experience allows for a good understanding of the work, while it would most likely allow for a good understanding of the dawns and sunsets that frame our days (at least in terms of ingenuous experience).

The second question relates to the modalities of the aesthetic experience: proponents of the aesthetic definition often undertake a type of understanding guided by disinterest. In the end, they say, a successful work of art is capable of stimulating its spectator at an emotive level, playing on the possibility of creating an assonance between the 'implemented' emotions and the emotions experienced by the spectator. Therefore, the depiction of Achille's rage at the sight of his dead friend provokes the spectator to relive the same, or a similar, emotion, without finding himself in an equally complicated situation (*Poetics*, vi). Lucretius was not wrong, in *De Rerum Natura*, when he noted how wonderful it can be to observe a situation that moves our soul to the sublime, provided that we do not find ourselves directly involved in what takes place. The idea, in essence, is simple: events, just as the passions that are related to them, oftentimes devastate our souls and overshadow our minds. A stormy sea has the potential to be beautiful, but we can reach this conclusion provided that we are not on the high seas, paralyzed by the fear of being swept away by it. While this observation clearly applies to the experience of the beholder, the same theory holds true for the author. We must assume that Homer was entirely disinterested when he wrote of Achille's rage, and that he himself was not mad while describing it. Nonetheless, these positions do not account for an optimal argument that is almost as ancient as philosophy itself: we all know that the reason behind much art is not disinterest, but, rather, the opposite desire to manifest a concrete and strong interest in matters of politics and battles for civil and social rights. All of these cases do not come down to disinterested contemplation, but, rather, to obtaining powerful and convinced answers from the beholders of artworks; the desire to change behaviours. It was upon this very intuition that Plato was quick to ban both art and artists from his ideal state.

One last observation concerns the portion of the definition that regards intentionality: works of art are objects produced in response to a specific intention of the artist who is inspired, specifically, by the objective to provoke an aesthetic experience. Yet, are we truly certain that the authors of the Moai statues, the giants carved from tuff that are found across the entire span of the Easter Islands, were driven by this intention? Or that the authors of the first orthodox icons had similar intentions? And what about the artists of *The Dreaming*, the thousand-year-old iconographic stories about the Aboriginal populations of Australia? Not to mention the iconography and the sculptures produced in ancient Egypt, and the art of ancient Greece.

Let us now consider the disinterest which is said to characterize the aesthetic experience. Does it really exist, and is it that distinguishing?

In the Autumn of 2008, in collaboration with a few philosopher and artist friends from the Fondazione Mario Merz and the Accademia Albertina, we planned a festival here in Torino dedicated to the ties between philosophy and contemporary art; a relationship that was manifest from the very title of the event: 'Brillo: Pensiero d'Artista. Festival Internazionale di Filosofia dell'Arte Contemporanea' ('Brillo: Artist's Thought. International Festival of Philosophy of Contemporary Art'). The works in the 'Brillo' festival were to suggest how the encounter between contemporary art and philosophy was dictated by conscious choices – a correspondence of feelings of love, as Ugo Foscolo would say. In order to show these dynamics to the students and to the general public, it was decided that a personal exhibit dedicated to Matthew Barney would be prepared. We organized training seminars for secondary school and university students, as well as for the general public. We met art dealers, journalists and scholars of art and of philosophy. We watched the *Cremaster Cycle* more than once – an experience that, to this day, I consider to be insuperable – together with people from an array of different backgrounds and interests. The students would go on to be evaluated by their teachers, the journalists were to write about the experience, along with the scholars of art and philosophy, while the general public that attended the exhibit, and later the conferences, were most likely interested in learning something more about contemporary art. The New York art dealers who accompanied Barney, and helped him with the exhibition at the Fondazione Merz, were interested in ensuring that the artist's work be looked after in the best possible way (and, of course, they were also very interested in an economic comeback of Barney's works). It would be rather utopic to think that art and artworks belong to the Iperuranio world; rather, art and artworks have much to do with our passions, with our desires and, last but not least, with our interests.

Let us now try asking ourselves: who, among all of the people present at the festival, approached Barney's work out of disinterest?[30] The students? The journalists? The scholars? The art dealers? The general public? It would seem as though this is not a matter of disinterest but, rather, of attention and, therefore, of the attention that we are willing to dedicate to the work, regardless of what it is that inspires us. The concept of a disinterested connection, on the other hand, appears to be the remnants of a rather vague conceptual mythology, which places everything that has to do with art, including works of art, in a parallel and inconsistent reality.

4 Expressive theories

4.1 Vehicles of expression

> O animal grazioso e benigno / che visitando vai per l'aere perso / noi che tingemmo il mondo di sanguigno, / se fosse amico il re de l'universo, / noi pregheremmo lui de la tu pace, / poi c'hai pietà del nostro mal perverso. / Di quel che udire e che parlar vi piace, / noi udiremo e parleremo a voi, / mentre che 'l vento, come fa, ci tace. / [...] Amor, ch'al cor gentil ratto s'apprende / prese costui della bella persona che mi fu tolta; e 'l modo ancor m'offende. / Amor, ch'a nullo amato amar perdona, / mi prese del costui piacer sì forte, che, come vedi, ancor non m'abbandona. / Amor condusse noi ad una morte: Caina attende chi a vita ci spense. [...] Mentre che l'uno spirto questo disse, / l'altro piangea; sì che di pietade io venni men così com'io morisse. / E caddi come corpo morto cade. (Dante, *Inferno*, libro v, v. 88–142)[31]

Francesca strives to translate those sentiments into words, for the benefit of Dante, while her companion remains silent at her side and transforms his feelings into weeping. She does so by choosing the most opportune words that will transmit her innermost feelings, and her words touch Dante's heart so deeply that he is overpowered by them. Together with the poet, we readers experience the same sentiment of pity and affection for those two souls, damned for eternity as a result of such a human sin.

From the time that art and science separated, and distinguished their own fields and objectives, the expression of emotions is one of the traits that has typically been reserved for art, while science has been known to be better equipped to describe the world.[32] One of the main conceptual bipartitions to have characterized modernity starting, at least, from Romanticism is that which separated external reality (the world of phenomena and nature) from internal reality (the world of love, feelings and, more generally, the domain of our minds). While science attends to the former, the latter seems to be reserved for art.

The expressive theory of art[33] has as its premise the idea that art is a sort of privileged field – a laboratory, if we wish to continue the parallelism with the sciences – in which artists research, put to the test and deepen expressions, in an entirely original manner, by trying them out first on themselves and then by depositing them in an artwork, the ideal location for them to reach others and to be transmitted by a universal language. Dante, a profound connoisseur of love and pity, described in a very personal manner two emotions that preserve a universal typicality. What emerged from them are some of the most beautiful pages of Italian literature, and perhaps of all literature: the fifth canto of the *Divine Comedy*.

Within this context, then, works of art are to be considered true vehicles of human emotions. To generalize what we have said thus far we might express the definition of aesthetics in the following terms:

> *x is a work of art if and only if it is the result of the intentional action of a subject (the artist), who (1) experiences an emotion to which they give (2) an expression (3) that is personal, in a work of art (4) by using a universal language that is able (5) to transmit the emotion to a broad public.*

The fifth canto of the *Divine Comedy* is the product of the intentional elaboration of Dante who, having directly experienced the emotions of love and pity – or, better yet, being in love himself, and likely seized by love in the very midst of his narration of the two unfortunate lovers – finds a way to clarify the nature of his sentiments by using his own words and expressions so effectively that they reach the broad public in their purest form. It should be noted that it is not necessary that condition number 5 be present in all of the formulations of the theory, as it is possible to claim that the clarification the artist uses in reference to emotions does not involve being communicated to others. After all, the lovable Miss Beston (the secretary at Marlborough, the gallery that managed the work of Francis Bacon) not only looked after the artist in the most motherly fashion, but she was also committed to stopping the painter from destroying his own paintings. Perhaps Bacon did not only paint for himself, but he most certainly made an effort to separate himself from his works; he therefore did not necessarily paint for others.

4.2 The denied space of fiction

We have already emphasized how each definition expresses necessary and sufficient conditions, and the theory that unites art and the expression of emotions is no exception. Therefore, the theory that states that art expresses emotions should be understood as a necessary condition (a conclusion that appears to be false) from a threefold point of view. It is false from the point of view of the author, just as it is equally false from the point of view of the artwork and, finally, it is correspondingly false from the point of view of the spectator. According to the expressive theory, an artist (just as a writer or a composer) intervenes in their own emotions in order to transmit them in a unique way through their work of art. The underlying idea, then, is that these emotions are found first in the artist, after which they are transferred to the work of art; in other words, an artist must, in some way, experience the emotions expressed in their works. If this were true, then the history of art, literature and music would be a sort of inventory of human passions, vices and virtues together: Manzoni would have been familiar with vice and sanctity, Dante would have personally experienced all of the sins, as well as the virtues, of the world and so on and so forth. Clearly, this is not so: there is no reason for which it is necessary to believe that an author (or even an actor, for that matter) must experience first-hand the emotions that they describe. That is to say, it is not necessary to assume the existence of a causal relationship between expression and expressed emotion. It is not imperative that we be mad in order to describe the rage of Achilles. In fact, generally, authentic rage must be experienced rather than described.

> Consonant with this is the idea that an expression is causally linked with what is expressed. The expression on a face, for example, may be the effect of the fear or anger or sorrow a person feels, the facial configurations at once arising from and showing forth that emotion; or James-Lange-like, the emotion may arise from perception of the bodily expression. In neither version will this stand up very long. A pleased expression may be due to politeness and endured with discomfort; and fear may give rise to an expression of abject approval that drains rather than bolsters confidence. An actor's facial expression need neither result from not result in his feeling the corresponding emotions. (Goodman, 1969, 47)

An actor does not have to be all of the characters that they play; rather, it is necessary that they know how to represent different characters, and this can happen precisely because there is no identification between an actor and the characters. If the author of Medea were to feel the same emotions of a mother who kills her own children, there is no reason why they should not end up performing the same tragic acts. Fortunately, though, stories in literature, music and art are not brimming with the deeds of the authors who experienced the stories that they told. There are certain techniques, familiar to all good authors, that allow rage to be represented in an appropriately rage-like manner, which ensures that the spectators will adopt the description of a rage-like mood as intended by the author. In short, the space of fiction is not the same as reality, and it is governed by its own specific rules. In addition, it should be noted that many works of art once were, as they are still today, the product not of inspiration – that is to say, of the well-known emotions experienced by artists – but of commission, which shows how the emotions that an artist does not experience, and perhaps has never experienced, can be represented very well – perhaps even better.

As we were saying, from the point of view of the work of art, as well as of the spectator, this theory is false. In fact, it would a good idea to emphasize how there are many examples of artworks whose principle objective has nothing to do with the artist's will to express emotions. As a consequence, not even the reaction of the spectator is thought to be at an emotional level, yet it could be considered a cognitive response that causes them to reflect upon the emotions implemented by the work of art.

Abstract art and conceptual art are rarely characterized by having a strong emotional impact. Obviously, a supporter of the expressive theory would find themself forced to exclude from the category of works of art those works that are not tied to emotions. In order to do this, they would need a supplementary argument, since their theory, at this point, is about to take a regulative turn. Or they might argue that, though they may not be aware of it, an artist already finds themself in an emotional state when they work, just as a spectator is in an emotional state when they observe a work of art.

In a way, the idea that our experience is always emotionally connoted is a basis for discussion, just as it is equally disputable to say that a beholder of Malevič's *Black Cross on White Background* can be overcome by emotion as they observe the work. It is unclear, then, why the emotional connotation that marked Mario Merz while he worked on the *Fibonacci Sequence* should be more important, to the comprehension of the work, than the emotional connotation of Pythagoras at the exact moment in which he discovered his theorem.

One more point may be observed in reference to condition 5 (the public). We have emphasized that there is no reason to assume that a direct causation exists between an author and their artwork by means of expression. The same conclusion must be derived with regard to the public. The theories that traditionally stress the influence of emotions on the public (such as, for instance, Aristotle's theory of catharsis) seem to imply that the public's response is proportionate and reinforced. Ugolino's cruelty is depicted on stage and, in some way, that emotion is transferred to the public that distances itself from it and, in doing so, frees itself of it. But this theory, too, is rather weak: the public's response is not always proportionate to the emotions that are expressed in a work. Surely, the public does not feel the same jealousy that torments Othello: they may feel compassion for Desdemona, anger towards Iago and pity for Othello. While the spectators will not be overcome with the same despair experienced by Juliet, they may very well be distraught while hearing the story of a shattered love. Ultimately, that which is expressed can be different from the emotion that arises upon reflection, and, in the majority of cases, it is.

Nevertheless, it may be noted that even if the relationship between an expressed emotion and expression is not regulated by a relationship of causation, it is still necessary to postulate a certain type of relationship, since it is fairly unlikely that a frowning face could make us think of a happy person (Goodman, 1969, 47).

That said, it would clearly be different to state that works of art 'can' express emotions but, as we have seen, this is not the objective of a proponent of the expressive theory of art. Sacred art can certainly express emotions; at times, it may have even been the opportunity for an artist to express their specific feelings. Nonetheless, its principle objective was to recall the public to their devotional duties.

A rather important observation remains to be made. Let us consider collectively all of the conditions that we have listed, and let us admit that they help us distinguish what is art from what is not art. Are we truly certain that the definition cannot be applied equally well to things that we would never be willing to consider works of art and, therefore, that it is not too broad? I have always loved to travel and jot down fragments of the places I visit, along with stories that I happen to hear, in a notebook that is now well worn. Oftentimes, I keep track not only of my memories, but also of the emotional hues of my trips. All of the ingredients are present, but would we be willing to consider that notebook a work of art? It is quite unlikely and, certainly, not a blind bargain.

As we shall see (infra, ch. 4), the idea that works of art are vehicles of emotions, among other things, puts us on the right path, though it is a path that must be travelled differently from that suggested by the expressive theory. We can, however, begin to make an assessment. The definitions that we have examined thus far, along with strong basic intuitions, have demonstrated some fairly important weak points. After much theorizing, the legitimate suspicion may arise that it is not possible to find a solution for the questions related to the definition of a work of art. This was, in fact, the very conclusion supported by neo-Wittgensteinian theorists.

3

On the Impossibility of Definition

1 Neo-Wittgensteinian theories

1.1 Family resemblance

Wittgensteinian thought[1] is inspired by the idea that as much as we may strive to diligently classify and subdivide works of art, even those recognized as such by the art world, it is extremely difficult to identify something that they have in common and that goes beyond a certain resemblance,[2] a vague feel of family, that allows us to determine that something is really a work of art. This difficulty is so deeply rooted that after two thousand years of philosophical history we have yet to resolve it. As a result, the more than legitimate suspicion may arise that it is a poorly postulated and unsolvable philosophical problem.

Let us turn to William Kennick (1958, 317–34) for the formulation of the argument. Let us imagine that we are in a spacious warehouse that contains many objects, of all different types, and that some of these are works of art while others are not. The warehouse is packed with paintings, sheet music, books of all genres, work tools, plants, flowers, wood, model houses and model churches, vases, newspapers, stamps, stones, musical instruments and much more.

Now, let us assume that we instruct an employee to bring out *only* the works of art, leaving all the rest inside of the warehouse. Let us also assume that this individual does not have at their disposal a 'definition' that could allow them to distinguish what a work of art is from what it is not: they are bereft of an instruction manual. Let us also assume that they have never thought about the issue; they have never asked themself what rules or definitions they should follow in order to be able to recognize a work of art if they happened to encounter one. According to Kennick, it is reasonable to assume that the protagonist of the story would be capable of carrying out the task at hand.

Let us now imagine that this same individual is asked to bring out all of the 'significant forms'[3] that they find in the warehouse, as well as all of the 'objects of expression' or – we might say – all of the communicative artefacts. It is safe to say that the individual would feel uneasy: in some cases, they might be able to recognize an art object if they saw one, but to recognize a significant form or an object of expression is certainly a more complicated feat. Kennick concludes that, in order to make the necessary decisions, it is best to put aside the question of definition and to be guided by habit or, perhaps, by good taste.

Kennick's strategy, then, is clear: we must renounce solving the question of definition. He offers two reasons in support of this strategy. The first has to do with the age of the problem: if for over two thousand years philosophy has been asking itself the same question, perhaps it is time to give up as we put ourselves at risk of squaring the circle. The second reason behind the strategy concerns opportuneness: we may, in fact, not be in the appropriate historic conditions to establish a definition. If it is true that not everything can be made an object of definition, then it is also true that not all moments in history are suitable for establishing a definition. Let us find out why.

1.2 What type of concept is the concept of 'art'?

> The problem with which we must begin is not 'What is art?', but 'What sort of concept is "art"?' Indeed, the root problem of philosophy itself is to explain the reaction between the employment of certain kinds of concepts and the conditions under which they can be correctly applied. If I may paraphrase Wittgenstein, we must not ask, What is the nature of any philosophical x?, or even, according to the semanticist, What does 'x' mean? [...]. (Weitz, 1956, 30)

This is the most important point for Morris Weitz (1956, 25–38)[4] who, in explicit Wittgensteinian style, points out how the philosophy of art attempts to define that which cannot be defined, 'to state the necessary and sufficient properties of that which has no necessary and sufficient properties, to conceive the concept of art as closed when its very use reveals and demands its openness' (Weitz, 1956, 30).

Weitz emphasizes two points in his argument. First, he claims that opponents of the philosophy of art may be right when they argue in favour of the impossibility of identifying the properties that characterize works of art as works of art. Especially throughout the course of the twentieth century, works of art have assumed such unique stylistic determinations that it may well be impossible to find the scarlet thread that unites such different exemplifications because that thread simply does not exist. Weitz's critique is severe and deserves to be considered closely:

> I want to show that the inadequacies of the theories are not primarily occasioned by any legitimate difficulty such e.g., as the vast complexity of art, which might be corrected by further probing and research. Their basic inadequacies reside instead in a fundamental misconception of art. [...] Art, as the logic of the concept shows, has no set of necessary and sufficient properties, hence a theory of it is logically impossible and not merely factually difficult. (Weitz, 1956, 27–8)

In order to conduct a study on conceptual reconnaissance, the concept that I intend to examine must not be subjected to further modifications. In other words, I must use a closed concept – a concept that is certain not to present itself in the future in new and different exemplifications. It is plain to see how an ordinary definition permanently runs the risk of becoming rapidly unusable as each new form of art could require its modification.

Preliminarily, we must ask ourselves if philosophers are in a position to consider the question of definition. One simple fact seems to yield a negative response: a significant amount of art is produced today, just as in the times of Weitz. It would seem that the concept is not closed, but, rather, very open. In fact, it is founded upon practices that must be permanently expansive, though not necessarily revolutionary. (Chinese art, for instance, is more apt to be expressed through minor variations rather than radically changing its paradigms.)

> 'Art,' itself, is an open concept. New conditions (cases) have constantly arisen and will undoubtedly constantly arise; new art forms, new movements will emerge, which will demand decisions on the part of those interested, usually professional critics, as to whether the concept should be extended or not. [...] What I am arguing, then, is that the very expansive, adventurous character of art, its ever-present changes and novel creations, makes it logically impossible to ensure any set of defining properties. We can, of course, choose to close the concept. But to do this with 'art' or 'tragedy' or 'portraiture,' etc., is ludicrous since it forecloses on the very conditions of creativity in the arts. (Weitz, 1956, 32)

What should the philosophy of art attend to, then, if it has failed to define the objects that are included in this particular field? Weitz's solution is very simple: the question must be formulated differently: '[...] rather, What is the use or employment of 'x'? What does 'x' do in the language? This, I take it, is the initial question, the begin-all if not the end-all of any philosophical problem and solution' (Weitz, 1956, 30).

A step further must be taken towards the formation of a good critique of art; one that will identify the characteristics of artworks that are often underestimated for different reasons.

Indeed, for a long time Weitz's objection had seemed convincing, especially because during the 1950s, similar Wittgensteinian arguments were used and applied to different research areas of philosophy.

Nevertheless, it is important to emphasize one difference: neo-Wittgensteinian theorists were never sceptical of the possibility of recognizing a work of art. Rather, they criticized the possibility of this objective being reached through the question of definition. How, then, are we to resolve the problem presented by Kennick's mental experiment? This is not a trivial problem considering that, if it were to emerge as an insurmountable difficulty, many of our practices would be seriously limited. It is to this degree that the concept of family resemblance plays a fundamental role.

How must a museum director, an art dealer or, simply, an art enthusiast conduct themselves if they wish to purchase a work or to write an *expertise* or to give advice to a friend? Should we amicably suggest that they abandon their undertakings seeing as they are potentially dedicating themselves to impossible activities?

As a matter of fact, Kennick claims that it is absolutely possible to make a decision, just as it is possible to make a value judgement with regard to the qualities of a work of art; in fact, we do so every day in very similar and more banal cases. Just think about how many different types of pens we have used, or simply seen. From primitive wood styluses, to the ultraclassic biros, from ballpoint pens, to liquid ink pens; from elegant fountain pens all the way to the ultramodern digital pens, and there is reason to believe that mankind will produce many more that will respond to the needs of the users. The point is clear: do we need a definition of 'pen' in order to recognize one when we see one? It is highly unlikely. Perhaps it is not so important to use a definition to do the majority of the things that are important to us. If, while handling a certain object, we discover certain properties that are similar to those that we normally associate with pens – for instance, that we can write with it – then we would have reason to use the object at hand as if it were a pen. The situation is simple; if we belonged to a population whose custom it is to write its laws, stories and science in the sand, then even a wooden stick would be an excellent pen.

The same reasoning holds true when it comes to works of art. If it is true that no one work of art is identical to another, then it is also true that works of art share certain traits. Therefore, if we had to propose a rule that would prevent us from hanging a canvas made of lead in our living room instead of a masterpiece by an abstract expressionist, we might suggest a few simple precautions. First, we should draft a list of undisputed masterpieces, after which we should take each work and make note of the properties that they have in common or that are similar, as exhibited by the members of a single family.

While philosophers may never be in the position to establish a definition, by following this simple operation, they will be able to formulate (by accident or by choice) sophisticated value judgements regarding works of art. In short, this means that they obtain access to the field of art criticism. The destiny of the philosophy of art, then, is to transform itself into critique.

Before moving on to counterarguments that have been directed towards neo-Wittgensteinian positions, we must comment on one point. Neo-Wittgensteinian theorists do not formulate a definition in coherence with their premises; rather, they formulate a theory founded upon three equally fundamental points:

1. Philosophy of art has persisted in treating the concept of 'art' as a closed concept, while, clearly, it is an open concept.
2. If we accept point 1, it follows that, in order to recognize that which is art from that which is not art, we must not use a definition, whose formulation is impossible from a logical point of view. We must use the method of 'recognition by analogy', which, in literature, is known as the method of 'family resemblance'.
3. Though it involves an awareness of the limits of the philosophy of art, this theoretical shift sanctions the ultimate transition to art criticism. (Weitz, 1956, 36–8)

In response to the observations made by Wittgensteinian theorists, Maurice Mandelbaum (1965) formulated a good argument that allows for the overcoming of what seems to be an important impasse: in certain areas of reality, relational properties cannot be disregarded. These properties have two fundamental characteristics: they exist exclusively within the relationship between subject and object, and they do not primarily involve our senses.

The list of the properties 'that the eye cannot decry' (Danto, 1964, 580), but that are indispensable for the understanding of works of art, is a very long list. As we shall see, this is a decisive topic in view of the formulation of representational theories.

Yet, before tackling this final set of theories, it would behove us to make additional reflections regarding the neo-Wittgensteinian position. First, certain considerations must be made from a critical point of view. Is the neo-Wittgensteinian theorists' metacritique of the philosophy of art so potent as to liquidate questions which they have been trying to answer for centuries, in just three simple steps?

1.3 Not all that glitters is gold

We have noted how the strength of neo-Wittgensteinian criticism lies essentially in the fact that it focuses on a seemingly banal, but potentially revolutionary point: philosophers have always considered the concept of art as closed, as this is the only way for them to formulate a definition that is not transient. Nevertheless, in doing so, they are obliged to decide on a stance when faced with a contradiction: they either choose to 'close' the concept, causing a detachment as opposed to artistic practice that is unlikely to surrender and pay heed to philosophers, or, sooner or later, they will be forced to conclude that their theoretical project is destined to fail.

Let us attempt to formalize the argument by following Noël Carroll's model (1999, 212):

1. Art can be expansive.
2. Therefore, art must be open to the permanent possibility of radical change, expansion and novelty.
3. If something is art, then it must be open to the possibility of radical changes, it must be able to expand and it must be able to renew itself.
4. If something is open to the possibility of radical change, expansion and novelty then it cannot be defined.
5. Suppose that art can be defined.
6. Therefore, art is not open to the permanent possibility of radical change, expansion and renewal.
7. Therefore, art is not art.

The argument is paradoxical, making the strategy proposed by the neo-Wittgensteinians linear: seeing as paradoxes are generally avoided in philosophy, we have no choice but to abandon the lines of reasoning that have generated them.

Nevertheless, an important detail is hidden deep within the argumentation, one that is worth paying attention to as it could invalidate the line of reasoning. Gottlob Frege instructs that in certain cases different names can have the same reference. In his judgement, this warning should protect us from the temptation to multiply entities unnecessarily: the morning star and the evening star are not two different things but, simply, two different names that indicate the same thing (the planet Venus). We must, however, also be vigilant about the opposite risk of not realizing that one single name can be used to refer to two different things.

This is precisely what occurs with the neo-Wittgensteinian argument: Carroll observes that they use the word 'art' to refer to two different things. In one sense, when they speak of 'art' they refer to artefacts, or to works of art, while in the other sense they imply the artistic practice. Ultimately, then, the neo-Wittgensteinian theory supports the argument according to which a closed concept is not compatible with the concept of art as artistic practice, which is known to be an open concept. If these are the facts of the matter, one might rightly ask, then what is the problem?

The reference to artistic practice, in particular, is evident in the third statement, which claims that if something is art then this something must be open to the possibility of change and of continuous renewal. Obviously, only artistic practice can have these characteristics, as opposed to artworks that were never truly completed, but this, once again, would be a factually false assertion. The fifth statement, on the other hand, where it is assumed that a definition must be possible, is a manifest reference to works of art. After all, the philosophy of art has always predominantly concerned itself with artworks rather than artistic practice.

Hidden within the argument, then, is not a paradox but, rather, an ambiguous use of the term 'art': artistic practice is characterized by continuous transformations, by profound changes and, in some historical periods, by actual revolutions. Works of art, on the other hand, are simply what they are, beyond all possible historic transformations.

Unless we should make a categorical error, there is no reason for which we should not assume that a closed concept, a work of art, does not coexist with an open concept, artistic practice. Art philosophers, on the other hand, do not aim to normalize practice but, rather, to find necessary and sufficient conditions to establish an essentialist definition. In fact, a research program whose aim would be to define science and to take up the idea of an innovative, imaginative and even revolutionary scientific practice would not be cause for trouble.

Let us assume, then, that the concept of artistic practice can be kept open without difficulty; in fact, in accordance with what we have claimed thus far, it must be left open in such a way that it will be able to express the unique nature of creation. As a result, a new objection arises: wouldn't this mean that any object can be a work of art, which would lead to the concrete possibility that nothing is a work of art?

Therefore, if it is true that the critique of the alleged closing of the proposed argument by philosophers of art presents a fallacy, then it would seem that the second argument made by the neo-Wittgensteinians – family resemblance – offers a good pretext to distinguish that which is art from that which is not art without the need to rely upon a definition. The formula is quite simple: it would be sufficient to draft a sort of catalogue that guides our understanding and that includes a group of undisputed masterpieces. The catalogue would feature works that no one would ever venture to challenge. This catalogue would be used as a basic guide and would be expanded by using analogies. Let us suppose that it includes: *The Odyssey*, *In Cold Blood*, the *Mona Lisa*, and *Don Giovanni*. Following the guidelines of the methodology of family resemblance, we could make the following additions:

The Betrothed: *The Odyssey* and *The Betrothed* share at least one property. They both tell the adventurous stories of their protagonists.
Gomorra: In both *In Cold Blood* and *Gomorra*, police reports and legal acts are essential to the development of the plot of these two non-fiction works.
Woman with a Hat by Henri Matisse: The *Mona Lisa* and *Woman with a Hat* are both portraits.
Beethoven's *Ninth*: The *Ninth* and *Don Giovanni* both lead to the sublime.

And the list could go on. In the end, the method of family resemblance does not require us to pay attention to certain qualities rather than others, nor does it refer to a minimum, numeric threshold of properties that must be shared. It simply requires a generic family resemblance that translates into a generic sharing of properties. It is due to this very generality that the theory exposes us to the most significant risk; that of grouping everything together.

To be clear, I might ask: why not include in our catalogue the colourful rug I bought in a market in Guatemala? After all, it exhibits more or less the same colours as *Woman with a Hat*. And what holds us back from including the nursery rhyme that was sung to us when we were to fall asleep as children? After all, it too is composed of notes, just as *Don Giovanni*. And while we're at it, we might as well include the coin that we received as change after paying for our coffee; it is a material object just like *The Betrothed* and the *Mona Lisa*.

The moral of the story, then, is this: the family resemblance method is too loose for it to be useful. Nonetheless, a proponent of the neo-Wittgensteinian position has one card left to play: they could point out how philosophers of art are not better off considering that, whereas they did not include rugs and nursery rhymes in their inventories, they chose to include urinals, boxes of detergent, snowballs, unmade beds, embalmed animals and other oddities.

In reality, this is not the case. While many philosophers would not deny that these, too, are works of art – especially supporters of the institutional theories and, as we shall see, of the representational theories – there still exists a subtle difference that factually separates them from neo-Wittgensteinian theorists.

Many philosophers argue that the urinal, and, therefore, possibly any material object, *can be*, in certain conditions, a work of art, though this doesn't mean that it automatically is one. Neo-Wittgensteinians, conversely, are obliged to take the stance that any object that resembles a work of art (that is to say, that shares certain properties with an object that is universally considered a work of art) must be a work of art. The theory is far too ecumenical.

The neo-Wittgensteinian stance has two solutions at its disposal. The first is to accept the theory implied by its position, that is to say, that any given object, in any given historical moment, is a work of art. This idea, which is particularly challenging from an ontological point of view, affirms that there is no difference between a number and an artwork.

If, on the other hand, the neo-Wittgensteinian theorist wishes to avoid this conclusion, they still have the possibility of reducing, at least partially, the range of possibilities used by the family resemblance method by suggesting which properties we should favour as we conduct our research on resemblances. It goes without saying that in order to perform this operation they must suggest necessary and sufficient conditions and, therefore, must carry out the very job that they intended to avoid; that of the philosopher of art.

2 Historical narratives . . .

The neo-Wittgensteinian theory showcases numerous weak points. Therefore, in order to support an argument that is not glaringly absurd, it returns to the philosophical inquiry that is typical of the philosophy of art: the analysis of the concept of art and of its definition. Which brings us back to our starting point.

The failure of the Wittgensteinian approach, which is the same failure of those who claim that the resetting of philosophy is a good option for responding to eminently philosophical questions, does not yet demonstrate that the idea of turning to an alternative to the method of definitions is, in itself, wrong.

This is the very orientation of the theorists who claim that after many attempts to reach a definition, only half of which were realized, it may be necessary to deal with praxis, since many of the central questions in the philosophy of art have relevant practical relapses for the experts in the field. Afterwards, if possible, we might give the floor back to philosophy. A good alternative might be to ask ourselves how would an art critic, a museum director or an art collector determine whether or not they are dealing with art.

Let us consider a concrete and noteworthy case: how was Clement Greenberg able to discern the genius of Jackson Pollock before anyone else? How was he able to understand that the painting that emerged from those gestures was not simply the ostentation of a hothead?

Theorists of historical narratives[5] offer a simple answer: Greenberg succeeded due to the strength of the historical and theoretical aspects of his narrative – in short, it was thanks to the incisiveness of his critical effort.

To understand what this really means, we might consider a theory formulated in the philosophy of history. Just as for neo-Wittgensteinian theories, the philosophy of history has been the source of inspiration for the philosophy of art on several occasions. We are talking about what occurred with regard to the theory of narrative sentences, formulated by Arthur Danto in *Analytical Philosophy of History* (1965).

2.1 … Or narrative sentences

What is a 'narrative sentence'? For the time being we might express ourselves in the following manner: a narrative sentence is an explanatory model concerning our understanding of historical facts and of the theoretical model that the philosophy of history may use to direct expectations regarding them.

Theorists of the spiritual sciences[6] were the first to establish a separation between them and the natural sciences, as they pointed out how the difference in object – the former deals with objects in nature, the more solid and better-quantifiable realm of reality, while the latter have as their object the actions of mankind and their moral and practical life – must correspond to a difference in method (Dilthey, 1959, Eng. trans., 11 ff.). In other words, while the natural sciences can count on the regularity of their laws, which easily allows for the empirical verification and the resulting falsification of inadequate, or no longer adequate, theoretical models, the phenomena which are dealt with by the spiritual sciences are neither equally stable nor equally regular. For this reason, scientists must formulate different explicative models.

Let us consider the historiography that, in the spiritual sciences, is considered the science par excellence. What should an historian do to carry out their research in the best way possible? Let us assume that they are interested in reconstructing the events that lead to the discovery of America. They will inevitably have to consider the primary and secondary sources. In order to extract the necessary information from the primary sources, they will carefully study the archives, examine the current events of the time and will investigate the documents that are still accessible. They will then turn to the secondary sources: they will read other historical works, take into consideration archaeological finds, literary works and works of art.

Let us now assume that our historian is the most competent and able expert to have ever existed. Let us further suppose that they are an ideal chronicler (Danto, 1965, 149 ff.); the perfect chronicler who knows all that happens, the moment it happens, and keeps track of every single occurrence by jotting them down in a notebook. This notebook resembles an extensive tablet, like Funes's memory; it contains traces of all that has been, and it does so without the minute possibility of error. Now, with the presence of this super-chronicler, one might conclude that there is no longer any need for historians: it is enough to read the chronicler's notebook in order to have the answers to all of the questions that plague us, including our curiosity about the discovery of America. By reading the notebook, we will know everything, and we will know it without the fear of being contradicted.

We have left out an important point: our beloved ideal chronicler, ex hypothesi, has a complete cognition of the present, and only the present; in other words, they are not able to look beyond the moments of the occurrences they record. They cannot even cast a glance at the future, and have little memory of the past seeing as they simply record it in their notebook.

Danto argues that the best chronicler in the world – better yet, the best chronicler possible – will never be a good historian precisely because of their inability to look towards the future, or to write their chronicle 'from the future' (Danto, 1965, 149 ff.). The reason behind this is very simple: the story of the discovery of America cannot simply record the events that form the ideal chronicler's present. It must also take note of the facts that followed those events, some of which will determine, in a sort of fantastic retroactive action, the meaning of what occurred on 12 October 1492. Numerous events followed that extraordinary discovery, and those who wrote the story of those happenings had to take them into consideration, since an historic judgement that neglects future events would not be a good judgement. The present can be fully understood only in light of its consequences which, in part, allow for its redescription. Present and future, then, form a new mereological object that can only be considered in its entirety, otherwise historical understanding would completely miss the target.

The statements that we use to describe this strange object are particular sentences called 'narrative sentences'. The general characteristic of these propositions is found in the fact that 'they refer to at least two time-separated events though they only *describe* (are only *about*) the earliest event to which they refer' (Danto, 1965, 143). Ultimately, in order to formulate a true description of the part of history that we identify as the 'discovery of America', historians must use statements that keep together three temporal dimensions: the year 1492, the years that preceded it and certain select events from the enormous mountain of happenings that followed that year.

2.2 The history of art as narrative

Why have we taken this brief excursion into the field of the philosophy of history? For one simple reason: those who aim to stay away from the strategy of definition favour the strategy of 'explanation' and consider it one of the most practicable variations. Explanation is nothing but a type of narration.[7]

It is said that when experts must decide if an object is a work of art or not, they construct a narrative that is able to harbour it and explain it. If an appropriate narrative is available, an expert will adopt it, enhance it and, perhaps, even continue it. If they are talented enough, they might even think of a brand new one. As in every story, the narrative of the history of art has a beginning and, perhaps, will even have an end. Some theorists[8] believe that with the second half of the twentieth century began a new narrative and, therefore, whether or not we are aware of it, we are moving towards a different horizon, whose story has yet to be told. In other words, the idea is that the narrative begun by the wonderful story of Vasari,[9] continued by many others after him, has come to an end since the artistic practices of the twentieth century would have been far too heterodoxical compared to the Vasarian theoretical cornerstone, according to which drawing is the foundation of all arts – especially those which, according to Vasari, are the three arts par excellence: architecture, sculpture and painting.

Without necessarily sharing the same view as those who identify with a new narrative, it is still true that an interpretative technique that can explain the art of the twentieth century is comprised of the idea that, in this period in history, art consisted primarily of an intense reflection of its own status. It was not about representing things, or moods, let alone imitating something. Rather, it was about reflecting upon art as such, in order to understand what it is and how it works, by testing its extreme limits of expression.

In painting, artists such as Georges Braque, Pablo Picasso, Jackson Pollock, Yves Klein and Jasper Johns aimed to give particular prominence to the concept of two-dimensionalism, and stressed the fact that paintings are nothing but two-dimensional objects, not three-dimensional worlds as painters had led us to believe for centuries. This part of the narrative, therefore, was comprised of an eminently cultural project developed by artists who were committed to reflecting upon the epistemological status of their art.

Within this narrative, even an apparently paradoxical work such as *Brillo Box* by Andy Warhol is explained insofar as it belongs to the realm of meanings where the ontological question on art is posed. Warhol, then, does not ask himself 'what is art?', but, rather, 'what distinguishes an ordinary object from a work of art?' and, above all, 'why are ordinary objects not works of art, considering that certain ordinary objects are in fact works of art?'

A good narrative sentence, then, can find an explanation even for the most bizarre of artworks. Only the description must be linked to the right historical precursor – in the case of *Brillo Box*, the predecessors are Cubism and, earlier still, neo-Impressionism – in order to demonstrate how that single, large narrative actually continues into the work of art that is last in line, in order of time and of transgression.

Noël Carroll uses conversation as an effective metaphor in order to convey the idea:

> The narrative approach attempts to handle the developmental aspect of art – including its local developments – by treating it as a conversation. As in a conversation, so in artistic practice there is an expectation of artists that they be concerned to make original contributions to the tradition in which they work. (Carroll, 1999, 255)

Generally, in a conversation, we expect each interlocutor to contribute by bringing forth their originality, by adding something of their own, by dedicating themself to the questions posed by the past while, at the same time, posing new ones. The field of narrative sentences within the history of art is assumed to do just this. Each artist makes their personal contribution which is connected to tradition and, in turn, is justified. Just as in everyday life, those involved in the conversation also decide which artworks are relevant (because they involve the protagonists of the conversation) and which objects qualify as artworks.

Let us consider a fairly well-known case. Andy Warhol shot the film *Sleep* in 1963. In the movie, the artist depicts the sole actor, and his then-companion, John Giorno, as he sleeps. The film is 5 hours and 20 minutes long, and it is a sort of dry run for what Warhol would realize the following year, with *Empire*. What fun! The fact that these two films were shot by the inventor of Pop art deserves further reflection. What might the meaning be behind a movie camera that is pointed at a man who sleeps for hours without interruption, or at a Manhattan skyscraper while virtually nothing happenings? One of the elements that characterize the beginning of Warhol's film production is his attention to movement, which is understood, paradoxically, in its absence. In both movies, movement is largely absent; its presence is noted by virtue of its very absence.

While *Sleep* does not tell a story, *Empire*, even more radically, exhibits not only the total absence of a storyline, but also of any form of movement: it is utter fixity. Now, it is not difficult to imagine the reaction of the very first spectators: not only did they have to overcome their boredom, but also, more properly, they had to find a certain meaning for such eccentric films. They had to invent a new narrative, or at least a new development for the portion of the narrative that claimed that movies are images in motion.

It was at this point that the narrative expanded, allowing for Warhol's works to be included in the history of film. Two stories could have been told upon the release of Warhol's works: the first trivializes the films, reducing them to the necessity of the technical instrument. To shoot the film, Warhol used a Bolex camera in 1963, and an Auricon in 1964. Neither of the two were easy to handle and, therefore, one could have concluded that the artist made a virtue of necessity. He neglected movement, shots filmed at 24 frames per second were projected at 16 frames per second (the speed of old silent films), and the use of black and white completed the effect.

We could choose a different path, instead, and develop a more sophisticated narrative. We might imagine that, as will be the case on multiple occasions, Warhol wished to compel the spectator to reflect upon the artistic (in this case, cinematographic) medium. It is within this very idea that the conversational theory interjects by suggesting a different move. Traditionally, cinema has told stories. If a story is particularly engaging and sophisticated, the spectator's attention is diverted from the medium and committed to the object of the narrative. What if we were to try to tell a story without a storyline? When narration is missing, movement is also missing, and one's attention focuses on the medium and, inevitably, on movement's faithful companion: time.

Those who are accustomed to travelling know that when movement is missing, time slows down; it expands and becomes the absolute protagonist of our interior lives, and we feel it in a special way. Saint Augustine (*Confessions*, XV, 14.17) was certainly right: if someone were to ask me to explain what time is, I would most likely realize that I am unable to define it. If, however, I am catapulted into a clear absence of movement, then I will be face to face with time. Perhaps I will still be unable to conceptualize it, but I will not be able to not feel it.

This is a good way to close the gap of meaning that seemed to separate Andy Warhol's first cinematographic works and traditional and consolidated filmography. The conversational theory did not answer the question posed by the definition of a film, but it still explained why, for all intents and purposes, Warhol's two films must be considered films. Its objectives are perhaps minimal when compared to those of theorists of definition, but nonetheless they are unavoidable. And, yet, this position also has its share of snares.

One of the questions posed with urgency by contemporary art has to do with the opaqueness of 'background' ideas that should allow for slow and steady conversation to take place. In this sense, not only is the meaning of single works problematic, but also quite often the very cultural context – the art world – is perceived as being rather opaque.

Perhaps a visitor in a contemporary art museum appreciates the originality of a work, but is unable to grasp its relevance; that is to say, they are unable to understand the reasons for which that work was assigned a prominent position within the story of the history of art. The solution proposed by narrative theorists is that, as in any good conversation, the lacuna may be repaired by simply reviving communication wherever it was interrupted or where it presents problems. In fact, it is normal for those who are not professionally involved with art to have a hard time following the evolution of practices which, in certain historical periods, are very rapid and complex. Furthermore, narrative theorists claim that the idea that art was open to better understanding before the twentieth-century avant-garde is simply the result of a prejudice caused by a larger use of expressive, representational and mimetic instruments.

I reckon that we can agree that not all understandings are equal. We may be under the impression that we perfectly understand the art of Giotto because we understand the subject matter; we are familiar with biblical stories and we see them depicted fairly explicitly. Yet, in the end, it is clear that a comprehensive understanding of the art of Giotto is very different.

The second point highlights a more complex question and, in my judgement, is quite problematic. It has to do with the legitimacy of the creation of inventories of reference works. We have already stated that the narrative theorist chooses to trust consolidated practice: tradition will dictate which works of art belong to the class of artworks, beyond a reasonable doubt.

Let us suppose that we accept the premise of the argument and that we avoid emphasizing that whoever began the narrative (Vasari, for instance) must have established it by using an initial conceptualization that is useful for separating good works from bad. This is precisely how the canon that we still use today was created.

Let us imagine that the beginning of the narrative presents no philosophical problems, which would be dealt with by general philosophy and metaphysics, similar to what occurred with the neo-Wittgensteinian positions. Let us take into account one possibility: Let us suppose that the director of an international museum of contemporary art is requested to do two things. First, they are requested to include in the museum's collection the artworks by a young Tarzan, who has lead a life of solitude in the jungle. The artist does not speak (at least not the way we speak), and he is not familiar with any of the stories that mark our civilization, not even our languages. Anthropologists, however, were able to ascertain that Tarzan uses a strange way to engrave leaves in order to communicate with someone, though it is not clear with whom.

The second request has to do with drawings (which might as well have belonged to an artist from the school of Picasso) that were sketched by a central-African tribe. Anthropologists have discovered that those drawings comprise a highly sophisticated alphabet, through which those populations share their thousand-year-old history. It is a story made of symbols that to our sensibility, which is accustomed to abstract art, may recall pictorial, and not figurative, works.

These two examples emphasize how, in certain cases, it is neither simple nor opportune to expand the narrative to such a point that it includes products that are clearly foreign. This is perfectly evident in artistic traditions that emerged and developed independently. Let us take, for example, oriental art and its heterogeneity, compared to our tradition. Since merging different traditions into a single story seems to be a stretch, what other possibility is left for narrative theorists? Will they be confined to stories produced by the cultural perspective to which they belong?

Whatever the answer may be, I believe that the fundamental point remains unaltered. The strategy chosen by narrative theorists is a problematic one. When we put forth a typically philosophical question, such as the question on art, it is not possible to keep philosophy out of the picture (after all, no one would think to disregard cosmology when establishing a convincing response to the question of the origin of our solar system).

Nevertheless, the narrative theorist's strategy draws attention to a point that has already been stressed by the institutional theories (supra, 43 ff.), and one which we will reflect upon in the following chapter: works of art are social objects, and so whichever theories intend to define them must not neglect to take this element into account.

3 The documental theory

The normalist theory, formulated by Maurizio Ferraris, is a quasi-definition since, while it responds to the question of ontology, it maintains that the explanation cannot be formulated in theories of necessary and sufficient conditions.[10] This theory boasts a strong relationship with common sense, with which it has much in common, and it seeks to be regulative in the name of a Hegelian motto: not everything is a work of art because 'if anything can be, then in the end nothing is' (Ferraris, 2007, 8).

A building block for a more general social philosophy is the theory of 'Documentality'.[11] The normalist theory considers works of art as a particular class of documents, equipped with a very particular function and role that Ferraris effectively calls 'inscribed artifacts' (Ferraris, 2009, Eng. trans., 49–54). An artwork is, first and foremost, a material object (in this case an artefact) that is characterized by a specific inscription. According to Ferraris's formulation, everything can be summarized through the formula (Ferraris, 2009, Eng. trans., 263 ff.):

Object = Inscribed Act.

3.1 Art, life's recreation

Let us proceed in an orderly fashion. While delineating his general theory of the social world, Ferraris captures both the similarities and the differences between artworks and the most traditional of documents. Unlike true documents, in other words objects that hold a regulative power and that bind us to specific obligations (such as contracts) or that simply attest a status that holds a social value (college diplomas, marriage certificates and so on), the sole utility of artworks is to better the quality of our *otium* (leisure time). If a college diploma changes the social status of whomever obtains it, then a work of art will ensure that they acquire prestige and, in certain cases, wealth. Documents are, therefore, indispensable to our daily activities, while artworks, high art and low art alike, are useful exclusively for our recreation:

> For all the advantages that may flow from an aesthetic education and for the entire turnover generated by the market in art works, films, rock concerts and literary bestsellers, the fact remains that the basic reference point is that of recreation, which is altogether different from the world of intentional treaties, driver's licenses, checks, supermarket receipts and parking tickets. Art works [...] are inscriptions of acts that have no practical purpose and, at the same time, they are material objects that have no instrumental value. (Ferraris, 2009, Eng. trans., 272)

In short, while documents are power reserves, works of art are designated for entertainment. This idea overrules the Platonic position that, as we might recall, attributes to art the possibility of etching upon human actions. It would appear that Plato was well aware of the fact that works of art can influence and determine behaviours more than well-structured arguments can; artworks, therefore, possess power.[12]

In Plato's time, mass media did not exist; yet, stories were told, just in a more antiquated manner. Singers and poets would tell stories that would influence behaviours, especially those of the younger population. Stories and actions are not connected by a causal relationship – that is to say, the former do not necessarily determine the latter. Rather, the intervening relationship is almost certainly mimetic, as the psychologists who speak of the 'Werther effect'[13] are well aware when referring to the relationship between the narration of a resounding event and the social imitation that follows. It is of little importance if the narrative is based on true events or if it is fictitious. All in all, very little changes.

Good stories – stories that are well written, with a good narrative structure – can undoubtedly lead to action, especially imitative action, much more so than the Pythagorean theorem can. Art, then, does not necessarily determine actions, but in some cases, through imitative or empathic effects on its audience, it can still happen. So, as we continue with the dichotomy between artworks and documents, it may be a good idea to soften it up a bit: documents are necessarily included in the sphere of the *negotium* (business) – so far as no one would find it disreputable to see a homeowner's college degree hanging up in their living room, as if it were a painting – while artworks mainly, though not exclusively, have to do with our free time.

Within this context, the normalist theory argues that the ontology of artworks can be better captured within the field of the general theory of documentality, through the examination of the notion of a 'document'. It is logical and consequential, then, to ask ourselves what characteristics must be present in the particular documents belonging to the class of artworks. A good answer would allow us to recognize a work of art when we see one and, most likely, would help Frescoditesta resolve his puzzle.

3.2 Not everything can be a work of art: An ontology

How are we to go about this? First, we must adhere to a series of simple rules, the first of which consists of not believing that anything can be a work of art under certain conditions. Ferraris has a different take on the example favoured by exceptionalist theorists: what works like *Fountain* tell us is not so much that 'anything can be an art work' but, rather, that works of art must necessarily be 'things' (Ferraris, 2009, Eng. trans., 272 ff.). Ultimately, artefactuality is the most relevant characteristic that allows us to create an ontology of artworks. What Duchamp did, therefore, takes up a long tradition: that of the directors of the old *galéries* who exhibited in their collections not only objects of the fine arts, but also those from everyday life. A very similar case can be found in today's generalist museums (the Metropolitan Museum of Art, for instance) that more or less explicitly adopt a vast definition of art, taking into account not only the fine arts, but also all that can be produced by a culture. It is not rare for works of art to be considered objects that were made to serve a purpose. It is not by chance, then, that the Met is overflowing with utensils, furniture and jewels, since it broadly takes into account artefacts that also happen to be documents.

The exceptionalist theory, however, does have an argument at its disposal: it could object that the difference that separates Duchamp's ready-made from the utensils displayed at the Met is the same difference between one of Andy Warhol's *Paint by Numbers* and a 'paint by numbers' that I might paint in my free time. Duchamp and Warhol charge their respective objects with meanings that are very different from their original non-artistic objects, and the artists' intentions makes them different from their counterparts, which are utensils or documental finds. Such an answer also explains the ontological complexity of reality seeing as, within the exceptionalist context, a wheel can be a mere utensil, a document that attests to the evolution of the techniques of field work and, finally, a work of art. *Ready-mades* are certainly extreme examples; they are works that are found at the limits of their class. The majority of artworks respond to much simpler criteria, as that of 'size' (Ferraris, 2007, 77). As we were saying, not everything can be a work of art. In fact, in relation to space, artworks are generally neither very large nor very little. Relative to time, they cannot have an infinite duration; not even a very long one, for that matter. To this end, the normalist theory openly finds inspiration in the unity of time, place and action that is at the heart of the Aristotelian idea of tragedy. The precept from which Aristotle draws inspiration is rather simple: in order to write a good tragedy, he advises not forcing the spectator to make logical strides, not to bore them by confining them to their seat for hours and, finally, to tell stories that have a good plot; that is to say, a beginning, a middle and an end. These are all sensible rules, and, yet, human patience has apparently been refined if an astounding number of people have become hooked on *The Bold and the Beautiful*, knowing very well that they could die before finding out how it ends. Aristotle was undoubtedly wise, but his wisdom did not prevent certain people from creating works that were 'out of range'.

Ferraris formulates his ontology of artworks based on six points (2009, Eng. trans., 271–82):

1. *Art is the class of artworks*. Practices that, over the centuries, have had poietic goals produce all artworks. In other words, they essentially produce things that have a physical dimension, a temporal duration, a spatial placement and that are perceived by our senses. It is a class that includes numerous examples and, yet, is not infinite seeing as though not everything can be a work of art.

2. *Artworks are, above all, physical objects*. A work of art that merely exists in the mind of its author is not yet a work of art. This means that it is a physical object and that it relates with us primarily through our senses. One might think that this is the case for the majority of objects in the world. In reality, as the normalist theory rightly notes, the centrality of the *aisthesis* has too often been undervalued by the philosophies of art of the twentieth century, which are primarily interested in accounting for the work of the avant-garde who favour the conceptual, rather than sensible, aspects of artworks.

3. *Works of art are social objects.* In order to exist, they need our senses as well as other human beings along with their social and historical worlds. Art has a long history from which a discipline eventually emerged. This history would never have existed or been told if there had only been one person, or people without a common culture, in the world.

4. *Works of art only incidentally provoke understanding.* If someone were to decide to treat a novel as if it were a guidebook, or to go to London in search

of Sherlock Holmes's house – as has happened before – they would surely be in for a disappointment. We may very well find something true written in a novel, and a painting may very well provide us with the necessary material to partially reconstruct women's fashion of the seventeenth century, but the point is that, unlike chronicle, history or the sciences, an artwork does not necessarily have to follow the truth.

5. *Artworks necessarily provoke sentiments.* In his fifth theory, Ferraris further explains the document analogy and detects it within the emotional dimension related to artworks. Just as fines or college diplomas, works of art produce emotions or minute sentiments. Unlike a fine that generally involves us directly and that produces circumstantial sentiments, works of art generally cause us to experience more general, at times universal, emotions.

6. *Artworks are things that pretend to be people.* This theory is deliberately provocative and recalls a passage by William James in *The Meaning of Truth* (1909, 189–90). James was of the idea that even if we had an automaton at our disposal that resembled a human being in every way, it could never replace a person (a girlfriend, for instance) in the flesh since it does not foster sentiments and, accordingly, we cannot expect to be replaced. If, however, we happen to fall in love with an automaton or an object – such as the ill-fated protagonist of Marco Ferreri's film, *I Love You*, who falls in love with a female-shaped key chain that recites those three words at the sound of his whistle – the consequences are unpromising. It is best, then, to avoid automatons and key chains. And, yet, from a certain perspective, automatons and key chains resemble one another insofar as they can instigate our emotions, just as a person could, only artworks and key chains will never reciprocate.[14]

3.3 A quasi-definition: Artworks as documents

It is now further evident that the key chain that whispers 'I love you' calls our attention precisely because it is part of the story of a work of fiction. This does not hold true for the myriad of kitsch objects that clutter our lives: oftentimes the only sentiment that they provoke is bother. Therefore, following the normalist theory, we may identify a first difference: artworks provoke a typology of sentiments similar to those provoked by people. They make us feel enthusiasm, emotions and sentiments; sometimes they entertain us and other times they sadden us. They achieve all of this without having recourse to anything and, most importantly, without serving any particular purpose, unlike other social objects that are documents (Ferraris, 2009, Eng. trans., 277 ff.).

In Ferraris's classification, then, artworks are a type of social object. As social objects they distinguish themselves from natural objects (for instance, mountains), and from ideal objects (such as numbers or theorems), because of a peculiar trait of all social objects: they are historical objects characterized by relational properties. The relational and historical character of artworks, then, is a necessary, albeit insufficient, element for the constitution of their identity. Obviously, once the ontological topic has been addressed, it becomes important to identify the properties that distinguish works of art from artefacts that are not artworks.

Let us now consider the definition of a social object[15] and of documents, social objects par excellence:

Object = Inscribed Act

This, in full, means that the social object is the result of a social act – that is to say, an act between (at least) two people – that is characterized by being inscribed upon a certain physical surface. Let us return to artworks and ask ourselves what it is that makes the neon lights in my house lamps, while those used by Dan Flavin in *Icons*, artworks of our time?

> Inscription, which confirms the continuity between art works. On these grounds, I believe that the best way of explaining that peculiar kind of object that is an art work is *Work = Inscribed Act*, and this formula should be understood as a necessary but not sufficient condition: for there to be a work, an inscribed act is needed but it is obvious that there are many inscribed acts that are not works. (2009, 277)

We ought to pay attention to a point that shall become especially significant when we deal with representational theories, and that marks an important difference with respect to these positions (infra, 132 ff.). The normalist theory does not speak of objects that vehicle or, better yet, incorporate, inscriptions. Rather, it refers to acts that are inscribed; the act is inscribed and is the bearer of inscriptions. Within the realm of the visual arts, this holds true for works of art that fall within the most traditional of canons as well as for the avant-garde.

> The specific reason why I think that the rule *Work = Inscribed Act* is preferable to the formula "X counts as Y in C" is that it applies to all forms of art, where

Searle's version is applicable only to ready-mades. Francis Ford Coppola did not just take a load of celluloid and baptize it *Apocalypse Now*: if he had done so, perhaps a better title would have been *Laocoön*; but he didn't: what he did was compose the script, meet backers to whom he explained his project, asked for permissions, signed contracts with the actors and distribution houses, and so on; and what he filmed, registering on celluloid, depended directly on those acts and the inscriptions that followed from them. The same goes for old art works [...]. (Ferraris, 2009, Eng. trans., 278)

The theory that an artwork is the inscription of an act and not of a concept allows the normative theory to distance itself from the idea that an artwork is the expression of certain conceptual content or, we might say, of a certain representation of the world.

4 Frescoditesta's can opener and the cluster theories

The group of 'quasi-definitions', that is to say, the theories that seek to provide a list of jointly sufficient, albeit unnecessary, properties for the identification of a work of art, while also accepting the perplexities expressed by the neo-Wittgensteinian theorists, deserves to be completed by mentioning cluster theories.[16]

By means of a logical 'cluster' structure, these theories provide lists of properties that aim not at providing us with definitions in the traditional sense but, rather, at offering certain criteria of orientation that allow those who wish to formulate judgements and to make choices to do so. As Adajian (2007) explains, when considered individually, none of the properties found on the lists produced by the cluster theories comprises a necessary condition for the object that exhibits it to be a work of art. When considered jointly, however, the properties on the list are enough for the object in possession of them to be considered a work of art.

There are numerous lists, and they can overlap considerately. As an example, let us consider the list proposed by Berys Gaut (2000, 28–9): (1) possession of positive aesthetic properties as, for instance, beauty, grace and elegance. These are, essentially, properties that have to do particularly with our senses and with their ability to provoke aesthetic pleasure in us. The list also includes (2) the idea that artworks are able to express emotions, (3) that they are intellectually stimulating – let us keep in mind that one of the essential components of a work of art are the relational properties such as interpretation. (4) Furthermore, given the unavoidable material component of artworks, formal properties – in other words, the aspectual character of works – are presumably fundamental. Beyond aspectual and material qualities, the communicative component should not be undervalued, (5) artworks must have the capacity to communicate complex meanings to their perceivers, (6) to bring forth the personal point of view of the artist, (7) to be the product of a creative imagination, (8) they must be artefacts or performances that attest to the high degree of technical ability of their authors and (9) fall within a certain artistic genre or form. Finally, (10) we must not overlook the intention of the author, which must be explicitly artistic.

Let us assume, then, that Frescoditesta is still busy in his uncle's warehouse, and that he is observing an object that entirely resembles a can opener. How will he behave after he remembers reading of the cluster theories? For starters, after he asks himself if the can opener that he sees laying on the workbench could be a work of art or not, it will be clear to him that if that object exhibits some of the properties listed by the theory, *then* it is a work of art. In fact, in this typology of theories the object (the can opener) relapses to the concept (work of art) even if only some, or few, of the properties identified by the theory are exhibited by the can opener. It is not necessary, then, for the can opener to have been built as a result of the explicit intention to produce an artwork that is beautiful, or that moves us. It is sufficient that its sinuous shapes, for example, lead Frescoditesta to reflect upon the differences that separate 'masculine' from 'feminine', or that they signify the special technical skill of its designer, or that someone designed that can opener not with the intention to open cans, but, rather, with the intention to create a work of art. That said, it is still necessary that the can opener exhibit at least *some* of the properties identified by the theory, though it is not important *which*.

There are three fundamental types of objections that the cluster theories allow room for: the first is the very group of properties that comprises the list. Oftentimes, the lists are long and complicated, and it is not very clear what criteria they were created with (Davies, 2006). Good observational skills? Common Sense? Sound practical judgement? An understanding of the history of art? Or, perhaps, of the history of philosophy, together with historical-artistic knowledge? The second objection questions who should have the authority to formulate these lists: we must assume, in fact, that they are not readily available, made somewhere in nature. Some properties – the ninth on Gaut's list, for example – can be identified only after having taken into consideration another definition, which would project the theory in a logical cycle that is difficult to manage. The third, and final, objection is that while the clusters of properties identified by the different cluster theories are relatively interchangeable (the lists made by Gaut and Dutton, for instance, are truly similar), they still do not coincide. For example, Gaut includes aesthetic properties in his list that are excluded by Dutton, who explains how aesthetic properties derive from the union of properties that comprise the list (which are not included in his version) and the subject's experience of the artwork. Two fundamental questions remain unanswered, and appear to be inescapable: whose job is it to write up these lists of properties, and what criteria must be used to identify them, given the need to avoid circular results?

4

Works of Art as Social and Historical Objects

The road that we have mapped out thus far shows how after the dismissal of the mimetic theory, philosophers implemented very different reflections in order to define the concept of art, the majority of which concentrated on a fundamentally metaphysical choice – the adoption of a descriptivist perspective – and a monist approach. With the exception of the institutional theories, it is the aesthetic qualities, the artefactual aspect, aesthetic experience and even the intention of the author that provide criteria from which the distinctive features of a work of art are to be detected.

We may, therefore, divide the theories into three large families: the first seeks to define art by focusing on the intrinsic properties of artworks. It essentially focuses on the concept of artefact by structuring a true phenomenology intent on identifying, even if in negative terms, the characteristics that make it a work of art by distinguishing it from an ordinary object, or an object with semantic value.

The second family is the product of a broader vision and is characterized by its more careful reflection on the role of the subject, on the specificities of the subject's experience during the fruition of artworks and on the social dynamics involved in the verification of the concept of art. The theories that discuss the very possibility of a definition have also been of particular worth: in addition to emphasizing the intrinsic difficulties of the most controversial positions, they have also stressed a third factor – the role and importance of conceptual history. The final chapter of this book will be dedicated to the theories that are constructed with this threefold polarity in mind: the physical object, the subject and their social reality and, finally, the history of the particular narrative that is the history of art – in short, the positions implemented by the *philosophy of art* in its proper sense.

We have already mentioned that artworks belong neither to the class of natural objects, nor to that of ideal objects. A mountain or a number can be a work of art – just as Mario Mertz's *Fibonacci Sequence* and Turrell's *Roden*

Crater are – but certainly not just any number or mountain. Similarly, common artefacts are not works of art: *Object*,[1] by Meret Oppenheim, is a work of art, but surely the same cannot be said for ordinary cups and saucers. Therefore, there must be something that distinguishes *Object* from an ordinary object. The crux lies in identifying that 'something'.

The theories that we shall now examine sustain a fundamental point: no matter what direction we choose to travel in order to face the question of definition, monism is not the right path.

It is a well-known fact that works of art are objects (from here on out the term will assume its broadest meaning) that are closely related to two potentially different typologies of objects: the author and the users. We must not overlook the latter, for it is here that the intentional and decisional action of the artists and the experience of the consumers converge. Works of art are what they are because a subject intentionally decides to realize them through specific modalities while taking into consideration, among other things, the responses of the subjects within a type of experience that does not necessarily coincide with ordinary experience.

And, yet, this is not enough: to some extent, the identity of an artwork resembles that of a person. That is, their identities are somehow defined by aggregation: the former is defined by the collection of stories of its perception, while the latter is defined both by the collection of actions performed by that individual and by their consequences. People and artworks, then, are defined by a collection of their intrinsic properties, such as the actions that they produce, the narrative of the effects of their actions and by their history which, in the case of art, as opposed to people, is thousands of years old. These are properties that, most of the time, the eye cannot decry (supra, 81 ff.).

Through inspired ideas and weak points, the theories that we have examined up until this point have made possible the following consideration: in order to formulate a good definition, it is necessary to bundle together three highly different spheres: the metaphysical-ontological sphere, the social sphere and, finally, the historical sphere (since art, just like philosophy, is like an old woman whose life story comprises her identity seeing as, at least in these domains, what we do today is directly related to that which has been done before us).

Therefore, if it is certain that no present-day philosopher tries to understand if the Earth is really comprised of air, water and fire, then it is also true that certain questions that philosophers continue to analyze are related to the original question. As we shall see, the same goes for art: few contemporary artists are interested in the questions posed by beauty or mimesis, yet they create many of these questions by simply discussing antiquity or the Renaissance with artists. In this way, history persists.

This is the opposite side of the coin that argues that there must exist certain characteristic traits that allow us to liken objects created two thousand years ago to objects created in our own century, within a single concept and without the similarities among the two being evident. The heart of the matter lies in the intuition that compels us to believe that works of art are always the same type of thing, despite innumerable stylistic variations. It is precisely the solidity of this intuition which we shall now verify.

1 Historical contextualism

My claim is that when the most unlikely things are offered [...] and when Picasso offers his *Demoiselles d'Avignon*, Beethoven his *Eroica* Symphony, Sappho her odes and the ancient Egyptians their hieratic murals, there is something common in what is going on in these cases which allows us to recognize all the upshots as art from our current perspective, despite the fact that a lot is going on which differentiates them, and despite the fact that the *concepts* of art prevailing at those various times are by no means the same, and in some cases – the earlier ones – may even be absent. (Levinson, 1993, 411)

Jerrold Levinson's insight is akin to what was typically associated with common sense, at least until the eve of the twentieth century, and I believe that it deserves to be conserved despite the multiple upheavals brought about by the avant-garde movements. At the same time, it is around this very intuition that contextualism builds its own definition.

The idea introduced by the theory of historical narrative and resumed entirely by contextualism – along with similar theories that deal with this perspective[2] – is that there are no properties of an object, no particular effect on a spectator, no specific trait of a particular experience that is able to determine the concept of art in a distinguishing and univocal manner since this 'also' depends on an historical relationship – that is, the relationship between the artist and his historical past, his practice and consolidated tradition (Levinson, 1993, 419).

As we were saying, the contextualist definition resumes this idea and places it side by side with a second important point: the valorization of the intentionality of the author. Levinson's position is most likely the most mature; compared to Carroll's theory, which is explicitly against the possibility of establishing a definition of the concept of art, it considers itself to be a definition that exhibits three characteristics: (1) it appeals to the intentionality of the author; (2) it exploits the contribution of history; (3) it 'is not' a variant of the institutional theories.

Let us begin with the definition proposed by Levinson in an essay from 1989 entitled *Refining Art Historically*, which he would develop and optimize in 1993 in his article *Extending Art Historically*:

> An artwork is a thing (item, object, entity) that has been seriously intended for regard-as-a-work-of-art, i.e., regarded (treatment, etc.) in any way preexisting art-works are or were correctly regarded, so that an experience of some value be thereby obtained. (Levinson, 1989, 29)

The motives behind Levinson's theory are clear and are conveyed in his rejection of the institutional theories. The reasons for this decision are eminently theoretical: in his view, the game that is being played involves, on the one hand, those who believe that art is simply the product of a series of social stipulations and that it is, therefore, absurd to try to define something that is the mere expression of the choices made by certain wielders of power (those who comprise the art world). On the other hand, it involves those who believe that even if any object can be a work of art, this does not mean that it, in fact, is.

At the heart of the matter lies Levinson's conviction that the semantic or lexical games of prestige serve little purpose. If, instead of asking 'what is art?', we ask 'when is art?', the situation is no different; at most, we explicitly renounce a definition. What is important for Levinson is that the different formulation is not relevant given that it is not supported by a truly profitable theoretical strategy.

Levinson's critique of Wollheim's position, who considers his theory to be among the numerous subspecies of the institutional theories (1980, 157–66),[3] is especially incisive and can be summarized in four points (Levinson, 1989, 8):

1. The institutional theory violates the intuition that there be a certain connection between being an artwork and being a good artwork.
2. The institutional theory violates the idea that art making be an important activity, apart from the artistic value – provided this exists – of what is made.
3. It considers *ready-mades*, and similar works, central to the economy of its definition, while they would otherwise be treated as extreme cases.
4. Finally, the institutional theory fails to answer a question that Levinson considers to be fundamental: shouldn't experts who candidate an artwork

for aesthetic appreciation do so based on good reasons – that is, based on reasons that are understandable?

Therefore, Levinson's work, which distinguishes the contextual theories from the group of institutional theories, aims especially to emphasize the fact that works of art cannot be the product of a mere action of auto-referential stipulation by certain members of the art world. If we are dealing with stipulations, then the reasons for this stipulation must be clear and supported and, most of all, must not arise out of thin air considering that art boasts an especially long tradition and history. As we might recall, the institutional theories had trouble accounting for the artworks that were not the product of a deliberate and conscious decision of their author. Levinson's answer, based on an important historical sensibility, is much more elegant: by painting the tall trunks of the sequoia trees, Tarzan can 'have the intention' to provoke a certain form of aesthetic pleasure in those who observe them. However, it will be up to us, belonging to a culture that has institutionalized art as much as it has history, to connect that intention to the traditionally understood artistic production. Nonetheless, Tarzan's is an extreme case: in the majority of situations – including the most eccentric – the problem of relating intentions to the history of art is not an issue since artists (just as poets, writers, composers, etc.) always work within an historical tradition.

Given that the intrinsic properties of artworks help neither to define the concept of art nor to separate that which is art from that which is not, just as when dealing with the concept of aesthetic experience (which can be instigated by 'objects' that have nothing artistic about them, as can be the case with drugs), Levinson directs his attention to the properties that are not seized through the senses, such as the special artistic intention of the author – an intention that we can relate to the known and consolidated expressions of the concept of artisticity.

There ultimately exist two ways of proposing that an artefact be considered a work of art: the first is for the artist to implement an explicit intention that is related to the history of art – that is, to the products that belong to the history of art by general consensus. The second is for the author to implement an explicit intentionality that, in a certain period of history, has been recognized as 'artistic'. This position is clearly compatible with the Tarzan-artist scenario.

In an even more mature formulation, then, Levinson can argue that

> Contextualism is the thesis that a work of art is an artifact of a particular sort, an object or structure that is the product of human invention at a particular time and place, by a particular individual or individuals, and that that fact has

consequences for how one properly experiences, understands, and evaluates works of art. For contextualism, artworks are essentially historically embedded objects, ones that have neither art status, not determinate identity, not clear aesthetic properties, nor definite aesthetic meanings, outside or apart from the generative contexts in which they arise and in which they are proferred.[4]

Therefore, anything can be a work of art, provided that it emerges from or is connected to the narrative that is the 'history of art'.

The value of the definition is clear: Levinson's work highlights what is an apparent banality that has been too often underestimated by contemporary philosophy of art. Unlike science, art is intrinsically related to its history and, accordingly, any definition that prescinds from this point cannot help but be gravely insufficient. Yet Levinson's contextualism presents the rather serious risk of being perhaps too vast of a definition. This is the very theme of the objections made by Richard Wollheim (1980, 157–66), Crispin Sartwell (1990) and Noël Carroll (1999, 241–8).

1.1 The weaknesses of contextualism

The criticisms of the contextualist definition are significant from different perspectives. The observations made by Wollheim, to whom Levinson makes sure to reply (1989, 27–30), mark a certain distance when compared to the institutional theory and its attempt to base the definition of the concept of art on the explanation of mechanisms that have a nearly exclusive social nature.

For this reason, contextualism does not postulate the existence of a phantom institution, to whom it entrusts a central role such as that carried out by the art world in the context of the institutional theory. Furthermore, the definition is formulated in such a way that it includes the extreme cases such as the *ready-mades* and conceptual art in general, without founding itself primarily upon the *borderline* arts.

On the other hand, arguments such as that made by Crispin Sartwell (1990, 157–8) which, as we shall see, fail to hit the mark, allow us to better define the differences between a descriptionist position, à la Levinson, and an explicitly regulative position. Sartwell's criticism is rather accurate: the theory is too vast and does not allow a classic question in the field to be resolved: the relationship between an artwork and its copy.

Let us suppose, says Sartwell, that I am an established and talented painter. One day, I decide to paint a composition that is in every way similar to Rembrandt's self-portrait housed in the Metropolitan Museum of Art. My product is, ultimately, a high-quality copy. In the wake of my enthusiasm, and in order to avoid being classified as a forger, I decide to make every effort to ensure that my painting will receive the same consideration as the original Rembrandt. And so, I skilfully replace it with Rembrandt's masterpiece without being caught.

The question posed by Sartwell is this: based on Levinson's contextualism, how can we deny the copy of Rembrandt's masterpiece the status of a work of art? Indeed, we cannot. And yet, it seems to me that the more interesting question is: 'why should we?' It is clear that the copy is a work of art; the question, perhaps, is if it is a good work of art or, even, a masterpiece. This is an important point as theories – especially those of regulative nature – often tend to confuse the questions that concern identity with those related to quality.[5] Philosophy concerns itself with the former, while the latter belong, or should belong, to art criticism.

Sartwell shows us that this confusion is at the heart of his objections in the second counterargument to Levinson. We may not be convinced by the example of the copy of Rembrandt's portrait. Yet, let us take the example of a sophisticated IMB computer, equipped with mobile appendages that have the same function of our arms and our hands. The computer has been programmed to produce objects and, among the many it produces, it creates one that is very similar to Rembrandt's self-portrait.

Yet again, the theory is of little help: upon what basis can we justify our choice to 'not' consider the computer's product a work of art? Once again, the answer is none.

Sartwell treats the two examples as if they were more or less equivalent when, in reality, they are not. In yet another example, it is supposed that a chimpanzee – an artistically talented chimpanzee – is capable of painting Rembrandt's portrait. Neither the chimpanzee's painting nor that of the IMB have anything to do with Rembrandt's painting or with its reproduction. This is because the Rembrandt and its copy are products that were created intentionally with an explicit artistic aim, whereas the other two works are accidental artworks – that is to say, they merely resemble the actual artworks. The difference is substantial and contextualism emphasizes the theoretical point very well. The excessive hospitality of the contextualist definition is another question all together.

Carroll rightly stresses how it is a good idea to explain the idea of the intentional bond that connects an author to their artwork, though it founds itself upon an excessively undefined concept of intentionality and is, for the most part, summarized in the intention to produce 'something artistic'. If, then, an inveterate Japanese traveller, who photographs everything that he encounters, were to think that each click of his camera produces a work of art, since his intention is to duplicate – in the mimetic sense – the monuments in Paris, the parks in New York or the ruins in Rome, it would be difficult to prove him wrong based on the arguments that Levinson gives us.

This is the first point for which a solution is not easy to find. The second, equally important, point is a question that is found in many of the philosophies of art that we have already dealt with, and it concerns method. Challenging each and every argument and putting them to the test by using all of the imaginable counterexamples is not necessarily the best strategy. This is an observation that has already been made by Arthur Danto who, for this very reason, does not entitle his masterpiece *Analytical Philosophy of Art*, as would have been expected following the trilogy of *Analytical Philosophy of History*, *Analytical Philosophy of Knowledge* and *Analytical Philosophy of Action*.[6] Electing a definition of art that prescinds from the formulation of a broader scope of presumptions on the human universe as a whole is an elementary operation.

2 The question reproposed: Homeless objects

The Brillo Box seems at first to enter the artworld with the same tonic incongruity the COMMEDIA DELL'ARTE figures bring to Ariadne's island in Strauss's opera. It appears to make a revolutionary and ludicrous demand, not to overturn the society of artworks so much as to be enfranchised in it, claiming equality of place with sublime objects. For a dizzy moment we suppose the artworld must be debased by allowing the claim [...]. But then we recognize that we have confused the artwork – 'Brillo Box' – with its vulgar counterpart in commercial reality. The work vindicates its claim to be art by propounding a brash metaphor: the brillo-box-as-work-of-art. And in the end this transfiguration of a commonplace object transforms nothing in the artworld. It only brings to consciousness the structures of art which, to be sure, required a certain historical development before that metaphor was possible. [...] But I am speaking as a philosopher [...]. As a work of art, the Brillo Box does more than insist that it is a brillo box under surprising metaphoric attributes. It does what works of art have always done – externalizing a way of viewing the world, expressing the interior of a cultural period, offering itself as a mirror to catch the conscience of our kings. (Danto, 1981, 208)

Resolving the difficulties we encounter when defining an artwork is certainly not a simple task, and this has been proven by the long road we have travelled thus far.

Let us briefly recapitulate. After having determined the realm of the philosophy of art, and distinguishing it from aesthetics, we examined a series of theories that all had the question of definition at their core. It has become clear that, beyond the strong and weak points of single theories, the best strategy is to not insolate philosophical research pertaining to art and art's objects from other fields of philosophical research. We should use this as a starting point and continue a while along a negative route (so to speak) by asking ourselves to which 'ontological houses' our homeless objects[7] cannot at all costs belong. Before we are able to find an appropriate accommodation for them, it may be useful to continue our exploration of the neighbouring area, as the artefactualist theories have begun to do, keeping in mind both the arguments of Mandelbaum and of Danto, (supra, 81 ff.), that have emphasized the importance of the properties that elude the eye (and, in general, our perception),[8] and the classic argument proposed by Strawson (1959, 87–117) who puts us on the right path for resolving the enigma of an artwork by discussing what constitutes the difference between a person and his material body. From a metaphysical perspective, the point remains the same: to find a way to understand the distinctive features of objects that fail to be captured by a reductionist perspective. Let us return to the imitative theory and, once again, face questions of ontology because, as we shall see, these are the very questions we must use to tackle the question of definition.

As we have seen, the imitative theory poses the ontological question, but it does not resolve it. The institutional theories, on the other hand, simply outline the ontological question only to transport it, in a rather simplistic way, into a social environment. The artefactualist theories, which reduce an artwork to its material aspects, miss the target as they struggle to relate to the properties that are indispensable to the definition of an artwork, but that do not have a physical determination. Prompted by Mandelbaum's observation (supra, 103 ff.), let us once again pose the ontological question and ask ourselves what was missing from Dipert's ontology that prevented it from hitting the mark.

2.1 Representationalisms

In one of Joseph Kosuth's most significant works *One and Three Chairs*, the artist puts three chairs on display: an actual chair, a photograph of a chair and, finally, a copy of the dictionary definition of the word 'chair'. As is often the case in conceptual art, this artwork represents itself – in fact, it represents all of the chairs in the world – and, at the same time, it implements a philosophical theory through images that, rather than trying to portray a chair, indirectly show us the types of depictions of chairs that exist and what it is they have in common. As a result, when we refer to chairs, we have three different options to choose from: we can build a chair, take a photograph of a chair or establish a definition that captures the meaning of a chair. All three options refer to the same archetypal object – that is to say, the idea of a chair – and so the spectator is invited not only to observe the aesthetic qualities of a chair, but also to ask themself questions regarding what connects, say, the photograph of a chair (therefore, the image of a chair) and a chair depicted through a discursive description. What relationship exists between these typologies of objects, which are so different on a phenomenal level, and, yet, appear to be similar from a certain perspective?

Kosuth's work does not simply invite the spectator to reflect upon the dynamics of our systems of representing reality. It goes one step further – a highly refined step from a conceptual point of view – as the work is dedicated to implementing this conceptual reflection by reflecting upon its own identity. It is, in fact, within this very work that the artist structures his response to the question that we have posed thus far: 'what is a work of art?'

It is certainly possible to produce art without asking ourselves what art is or what artworks are. Kosuth's is a second-level operation, a bit like when Descartes emphasizes our nature as thinking humans by asking us to reflect upon the modalities of our thinking activities. We can exercise our abilities to think and to analyse, and we do so without giving any thought to the fact that we are thinking and without considering the modalities of our thinking. Similarly, we can make art, because we like to or, perhaps, because we were taught to, without looking for a definition of art and without understanding the theoretical meaning of what we are doing.

The need to address the question of definition heightened significantly when, upon auto-interpretation, art unintentionally realized that its aim was not to imitate reality. Kosuth's work is, ultimately, an epistemological investigation carried out with the use of an artist's instruments. As much as this strategy may appear estranging (at least at first), it is entirely legitimate. Art, in other words, can take itself as subject matter, just as for centuries it did daily life, mythological tales or devotion and its expressions of faith. It is clear, however, that when it decides to take this path, art manifests a natural proximity to philosophy. It is not surprising, then, that philosophy would favour the comparison with conceptual art, provided that a good definition must be able to explain the most diverse typologies of art, regardless of the evolution of styles.

Regardless of variations in style and taste, the art of Kosuth, Duchamp, Warhol or Jasper Johns does with images what the philosophies of Gorgia and Plato sought to do, the only exception being that the instruments of art and philosophy are, obviously, different. Philosophers and conceptual artists essentially raise a single philosophical issue.

It is for this simple reason that conceptual art serves as a privileged observatory for philosophers who wish to take up the question of definition: it would be a bit like claiming that epistemology is the privileged seat from which to question nature and the dynamics of thinking – which does not change the fact that we could reflect upon the modalities of our knowledge even in a park, while taking a walk.

The typology of the theories that we are preparing to examine, which we shall call 'representational', do not exclude a priori a reflection on contemporary art, with the understanding that it is there, more than anywhere else, that it assumes a philosophical and conceptual dimension as it completely reflects upon its epistemological status.

2.1.1 *A generous ontology*

Alexius von Meinong brought to light the curious paradox that the breadth of the realm of objects is superior to that of existing things.[9] In order to explain this fact it might be useful to acknowledge the existence of objects that do not include existence among their attributes, but that, nevertheless, must possess a certain form of being since much can be said about them.

Franz Brentano, on the other hand, rightly pointed out how all of our mental states have characteristics of objectivity, whereas Meinong realized that it is necessary to classify among objects not only objects of knowledge, but also, for instance, those of the imagination, or even hypothetical objects. Therefore, dealing with what is, was or will be is not sufficient, considering that there are things – Grisu the tiny dragon, for example – that do not exist. That is to say, that they do not exist here and now in the world that we know and they have never existed. We would not be able to find traces of Grisu's relatives regardless of how many museums of natural history we visit and, given the notions that we possess, Grisu will always and only be an imaginary character.

And, yet, there are many stories about Grisu, which leads Meinong to the conclusion that an object may very well have a 'Sosein' (essence), even without having a 'Sein' (existence). In other words, an object (Grisu) can be one way or another (it may have wings and want to be a firefighter) and not even exist (that is to say, even if Grisu is never assigned the predicate of existence).

The reason for which Grisu or the current king of France put our ontologies in such an uncomfortable situation is because we harbour a certain difficulty in acknowledging that although we cannot prove the existence of certain objects, it is still possible to prove many of their attributes. Meinong believed that this discomfort is attributed to a prejudice that is as old as the world itself: that human beings are in favour of that which exists, the 'prejudice in favour of the real'.[10] In other words, we are more likely to believe that a child is intelligent (i.e. an object to which we can easily predicate the category of existence) rather than an imaginary dragon.

Nevertheless, one might say that works of art do not exist the same way as Grisu does. While certain works of art depict fictional objects, like dragons and fairies, an artwork is an object that has a specific physical consistency and that, therefore, exists in space and time. For what reason are we inclined to call on Meinong's ontology?

Getting back to our problem – that is, identifying the most appropriate ontology to resolve the question of the definition of artworks – it may be a good idea to clarify what type of 'house' Meinong imagined for objects that have subsistence without having existence. First, we must ask ourselves why it would be worthwhile to seek a house for these objects. The reason is a metaphysical one: as we shall see, the existence of a work of art is quite similar to that of Grisu insofar as it does not exist in space and time. The material object exists, just as its properties exist (its colours, its shape, its size and so on), but the artwork does not exist.

Let us get back to Grisu. Although he does not exist, it is still true that, as we were saying, we can think of him and even discuss the most minute details regarding him. Like many of us, the little dragon has an impossible dream: that of becoming a firefighter. He has a father, Fumé, who is a noble descendent of the Draconis lineage, and who relentlessly attempts to bring his son to his senses by asking him to abandon his dream. He also has a beautiful red firefighter helmet. Grisu lives in a specific place: the Valley of the Dragons in Scotland, a tourist destination where Fumé is the main attraction. The little dragon is so stubborn that rather than dreaming of erupting volcanoes and destructive fires, he yearns for the red fire-engines that he has never been given the chance to experience, in spite of endless recommendations from his benefactor, Sir Cedric McDragon and his wife, Lady Rowena McDragon. Despite being continuously disappointed, Grisu is always energetic and has many jobs: he is a secret agent, a stoker, a director, a servant, a jockey and a nuclear and naval engineer. Together with Fumé, Grisu discovers many important things, such as his coming from a faraway planet.

The dragon-firefighter has a highly intense life and, yet, common sense claims that he does not exist. Grisu's story indirectly demonstrates at least three things: first, that we can easily speak of objects that do not exist, like dragons or golden mountains. Second, it shows us that human beings are able to understand each other very well when they speak of dragons or golden mountains. Most importantly, though, it demonstrates that – according to Meinong's theory – these objects 'are something' regardless of the fact that they (not our representations of them) are found in space and time.

We can formulate statements about Grisu that are true or false: if we claimed that Grisu's house is in Sicily or that his wings are yellow, we would be formulating erroneous and, therefore, false affirmations. If, on the other hand, we were to claim that Grisu's dream is to one day become a firefighter, no one could claim that we are wrong.

Here is the metaphysical question: we can predicate a series of properties of an object, even if that object does not have a physical consistency. In other words, an object can be this way or that way (it can be green, have wings and wear a firefighter's helmet) without having a being – that is to say, without existing (Meinong, 1904, 127). For example, it is a fact that the golden mountain does not exist. It is a fact just like any other fact, save that it is a fact that concerns an object that does not feature existence among its properties.

Can we treat flying dragons the same way we might one of the paintings from William Blake's *Great Red Dragon* series, for instance? Flying dragons have no spatial-temporal location, while Blake's series does. One painting is housed in New York's Brooklyn Museum, two in the National Gallery of Art in Washington and the fourth at the Rosenbach Museum and Library in Philadelphia. A reason exists and it is found in the fact that Blake's paintings exist as works of art thanks to relational properties – properties that depend on the subject, a bit like the 'group of dice' concept Meinong speaks of.

Let us return to objects that do not have a classic spatial-temporal existence. As we have suggested, it seems quite contradictory to predicate something about objects that do not exist – this is the conceptual tangle dubbed 'Plato's beard' by William Quine – and, in order to bypass the paradox, a double strategy has been devised:

1. claim that non-existent objects have a mental existence;
2. distinguish between essence and existence – a strategy adopted by Russell in *The Principles of Mathematics* (Russell, 1903, 441).

Nevertheless, Meinong rejects both solutions. Regarding 1, he is of the idea that the thought of the round square can exist but, for all intents and purposes, it does not exist either in thought nor for thought. Furthermore, he refuses the idea according to which all non-existent objects must have a certain form of pseudo-existence (a mental existence, for instance), on the basis of the observation that there are many non-existent objects that have never been thought of by anyone and that will, most likely, remain unthought-of.

The notion that cellular phones did not exist at the end of the nineteenth century did not become a fact when someone first thought of a cellular phone. The cellular phone was a non-existent object even when no one thought of it, when scenes like this took place: '. . . George, I'll tell you where you can reach me, I'll be at: 362–9296 for a while. Then I'll be at 648–0024 for about fifteen minutes. Then I'll be at 752–0420, and then I'll be home at 621–4598. Right, George. Bye-Bye . . .' These are the lines spoken by Dick, the neurotic master of availability, in Woody Allen's film from 1972, *Play It Again, Sam.* Certainly Dick would have felt less anxiety and would have lived a simpler life had he had a single number; a cell phone number. Be it as it may, in Meinong's view, the cellular phone was already an object when Dick was going through so much trouble to be available, only, the cell phone that would have been useful to him did not have the properties of an existing object.

Let us now consider 2. Russell's position regarding this point is well known:

> *Being* is that which belongs to every conceivable term, to every possible object of thought – in short to everything that can possibly occur in any proposition, true or false, and to all such propositions themselves. [. . .] '*A* is not' must always be either false or meaningless. For if *A* were nothing, it could not be said not to be; '*A* is not' implies that there is a term *A* whose being is denied, and hence that *A* is. [. . .] Numbers, the Homeric gods, relations, chimeras and four-dimensional spaces all have being, for if they were not entities of a kind, we could make no propositions about them. Thus being is a general attribute of everything, and to mention anything is to show that it is. (Russell, 1903, 449)

Put simply, Russell claims that a bit of being is not denied to anything or to anyone. In reference to existence, however, the discussion is markedly different. In Meinongian terms, the being of which Russell speaks becomes *Quasisein*: just as in Russell, this strange being pertains to everything. Moreover, it differentiates itself from other forms of being by not having opposites: if it did, in fact, have them, then objects would have to possess a superior *Quasisein*, which would set us back to an infinite regress – an option that is not impossible, but that certainly seems extremely unlikely. The decisive factor that pushes Russell to reject the theory of the *Quasisein* is the impossibility of acknowledging that there are a variety of beings to whom it is not possible to oppose a non-being. The motives behind Meinong's stance are understandable: if the term 'being' has a meaning, then the statement '*x is*' must contribute to broadening our understanding, and this can only occur if it is thinkable that '*x is not*'.

Meinong's theory, then, can be formulated in the following manner: a pure object has no relation to a being or a non-being; both cases are external and extrinsic to it. If we were to answer the question 'what is an object?' by following Meinong's theoretical instructions, we could say that what an object is (its authentic essence) consists of a number of instances of *Sosein*. The object 'dog', for example, is determined by such attributes as 'being an animal', 'having four legs', 'being a mammal' and so on. This kind of attribute is possessed by the dog-object regardless of its existence: the dog's being a mammal or Grisu's being a dragon are such notwithstanding the existence of dogs or dragons.

As we were saying, Meinong claims a spot for the non-existent object within his ontology, and he does so based on the following arguments: (a) we can identify certain facts that concern non-existent objects; (b) these facts have a mind-independent existence; (c) these facts pertain to non-existent objects.

Let us attempt to formulate some examples by taking into consideration a few of Meinong's most well-known arguments. First, (i) literature features positions that claim that negative facts cannot be compared to positive ones (this is the 'weakness of negative facts' argument). For example, the fact that dragons do not exist is somehow considered less of a fact than that which states that people speak or that dogs are mammals. Yet, what remains unexplained is how we can agree with relative ease that dragons and phoenixes do not belong to this world if we presume that the agreement is not founded on the apprehension of something that is – that is to say, of the non-existence of dragons and phoenixes.

Then there is (ii) the argument that attempts to relate the negative – which, as we have stated, is, for the most part, bothersome – to the positive (the 'irrelevance of the negative' argument): the fact that water is odourless and tasteless (and, therefore, devoid of a smell or taste) is related to the lack of the property x, which is the property that confers smell and taste upon water.

Meinong could very well object that nothing guarantees that things must be as they are required by proponents of positive facts. In fact, it would be quite difficult to entirely remove the negative, and understandably so. Even if we were to have before us all of the concrete objects that comprise the universe, along with the primary properties that compose them, we still would not completely know the universe unless we also knew that the universe that we are examining is comprised solely of those objects and those properties. Thus, we cannot not involve a negative fact – specifically that which states that no other facts, objects or primary properties exist in the universe that we are studying.

It is also possible (iii) to acknowledge the existence of negative facts and, at the same time, to deny that certain facts concern non-existent objects (this is the theory of non-existent objects without facts). The statement 'Grisu does not exist' does not concern Grisu but, rather, all of the other positively existing objects in the universe, none of which we can predicate the same properties which we attribute to Grisu; none of which, then, can be Grisu. This is a position that has been defended in literature by Moore and supported by Russell, who state that we must not have any worries regarding the existence or non-existence of the objects that we deal with.

In the case of an object of which we have immediate perception, for instance, it would be worthwhile to ask about its colour or about its size, but not whether it exists or not. Therefore, by asking, 'does Grisu exist?', we are simply asking if something exists with the property of being green, of wearing a firefighter's hat, of spewing flames and of having a father whose name is Fumé. Nevertheless, the meaning of Meinong's argument[11] is not brought into focus by the objections of Moore and Russell. In fact, it is not a matter of determining if some of the objects that exist can be different than they are, but, rather, of demonstrating that certain other objects (specifically objects that do not have a spatial-temporal existence, but whose nature is nonetheless determined) should be included in our ontological catalogue.

Despite all attempts to abandon references to negative facts, it is necessary to acknowledge that, in some way, non-existent objects are objects that have definite properties (though, of course, the creators of Grisu, Nino and Tony Pagot could always decide to add or eliminate certain properties at their pleasure) and are absolutely identifiable, just is as the hole (a non-existent object) of a doughnut.

The ontology that Meinong has in mind is, therefore, more complex than the one that Dipert uses to outline his artefactualist position, for instance. That which exists not only is in a trivial sense; according to a less trivial meaning of the term, 'there are' also things that do not exist, either because they do not have an existence in our physical world or because perhaps they do have a physical existence in the world, but that type of existence does not fulfil the form of their being. In order to find a home for these types of objects, Meinong introduces a new category: objects of higher order.

2.1.2 Objects of higher order

Meinong's idea – put very briefly – is that a negative entity must be 'something', insofar as certain properties can be predicated of it.

Similar considerations hold true for physical facts since, in the Meinongian view, it is not possible to represent without representing something, just as it is not possible to judge without judging something. Accordingly, neither representations nor judgements can lack content; hence the distinction between the content and the object of a representation, as well as a judgement (Meinong, 1899, 386).

The idea itself is fairly simple: we are capable of numerous representations – many of them are of things that exist and many are of things that do not exist. Some have an extensional content (the representations of things that have an existence in space and time) and others an intentional content (the representation of Grisu, of Mickey Mouse or of Paolo and Francesca). I can represent my former apartment on Manhattan Ave., in New York (that exists even though I am far away), just as I can represent the difference between two colours (that does not exist anywhere, and does not exist in the same way as the apartment on Manhattan Ave.). The representations that concern the apartment in Manhattan can be true or false (or, even, partially true and partially false), because that apartment truly does exist in the world – and specifically in Manhattan – whereas the representations of the difference between two colours, Grisu or works of art are neither true nor false precisely because they are representations of things that do not have an existence beyond our representations of them.

While in all of these cases the representation exists, this does not mean that what is represented necessarily exists: in other words, neither Grisu nor the golden mountain exist, but my representations of both do exist, and these are intentional representations. Therefore, both objects of dragons and objects of 'groups' of dice, as well as artworks, have to do with our representations. In the case of dragons and artworks, the representations are intentional, while in the other, the representations are extensional. In the case of artworks, the representation is embodied, or transported, by a material object; in the cases of the group of dice and dragons, the representation is nowhere to be found beyond the minds of those who established the concept of 'group' or 'dragon', and it is eventually found in their language.

Aside from an artefact's embodiment of a representation (to which we shall return shortly), there is another element that distinguishes dragons from works of art. Normally, dragons remain what they are, and works of art do not. Depending on how we interpret the representation incorporated in the artefact, the object can (or cannot) become a work of art. In other words, it can or cannot be that which we define, in Meinongian terms, an object of higher order.

Icons are widely known to be the figurative expression of Christian doctrine that we read in the Gospels. It is for this reason that in the Slavic languages they are not painted, but written. Iconography required significant technical and spiritual preparation insofar as the pictorial practice was to allow the painter to come into contact with divinity. Precisely because of their theological content, icons were not signed and were considered the direct work of God that expressed his perfection by way of human hands. For a long time, in fact, they were not considered works of art as they were, rather, devotional and sacred symbols steeped in theology and philosophy (Florenskij, 1922).[12] And yet, considered under a different, less devotional and mystic, light, they are works of art; objects that represent something of the sacred world that they present to the worshipper. Representations have an intentional character in the case of icons, too. Whereas the representation of Grisu concerns nothing but Grisu, icons represent something else, and this something else can be descried or not. More importantly, it can be descried only by those who use theoretical and cognitive instruments to do so: a devoted Russian who has not the faintest notion of art or its history will only consider the icon from a devotional perspective.

Let us briefly return to Meinong. It would be absurd to claim that a representation exists, but that its content does not: both Grisu and the difference between the colours red and green exist within my representation and only within my representation. In other words, we would be unable to find them if we were to search for them in the external world. It is from this very realization (that arises rather naturally from Meinong's discourse) that the distinction between the object, the representation and the content of the representation emerges. The representation is the common act that does not change (if I were to represent a round square just as if I were to represent Grisu), while the content of the representation varies from time to time and the represented object can be absent, non-existent, not real, not physical and so forth (Meinong, 1899, 388).

Falling within this framework are objects of higher order, whose salience, in metaphysics, is brought about by 'dependence':

The intrinsic dependence [. . .] can also be described in this way: we are dealing, there, with objects which are built on other objects as their necessary presuppositions. Looking from this angle, we are justified in calling objects which are intrinsically dependent on those objects which are their presuppositions, in the sense just indicated, objects of higher order. In order to complete the requisite terminological conventions we must add that objects on which such objects of higher order seem to be resting are called inferiora. But an object which is built on another object is called the superior of the latter object. (Meinong, 1899, 387)

Within the Meinongian framework, objects of higher order 'emerge' from relational representations (or relations) and from complexions[13] that regulate the relationship between *inferiora* and *superiora*.

Let us consider four dice on a gaming table. The group of four dice is something (we gather them together naturally), and it is different from each dice considered separately (the group is formed through connections of relations and complexions). What we have, then, is a new inhabitant of the populous Meinongian world. Once again, we are dealing with a real object and not with a state of mind: its apprehension requires an activity of the mind that is not part of the object. Moreover, the whole (i.e. the group of dice) has properties that do not belong to the single units of the group but, rather, to the group as such. It consists of four dice, and the parts that comprise it can relate to each other in different ways, and the relationship between the parts is of relative cohesiveness (I can draw them together or pull them away from each other, but if I slip three into my pocket, the group no longer exists).

Compared to non-existent objects, and to their relationship with reality, the group of dice has a relatively simpler life: first, because the dice are positioned somewhere (specifically on a table), but also because this table exists, in the trivial sense of the world (that is to say that it is a physical object present in space). If we decided to locate Grisu or the golden mountain, we would be in a rut. And yet, the group of dice does not exist the same way each dice does; it has a different form of existence, which is related to that of each individual component of the group and does not result from the simple sum of the properties of each of the dice.

Therefore, the new object that we define 'group of dice' emerges from the relationship with and the composition of single objects (the four dice), possesses its own qualities and is an object of higher order. It is a *superiora* and, by definition, every *superiora* requires one or more *inferiora* upon which to base itself. And, yet, the *inferiora* are not related to the *superiora* by the same symmetrical dependence (they can very well exist without the *superiora*), and should a *superiora* be based upon an *inferiora*, as we were saying, it would still be possible to know an *inferiora* without having to refer to the *superiora* to which it is related (Meinong, 1899, 386–7).

There are, therefore, two important theoretical points to keep in mind: first, that the whole is not reduced to the sum of the parts of which it is comprised and, furthermore, that the new object has its own, autonomous, form of existence.

The theory that we are about to examine is that works of art belong to this very class. A good way to explain their ontological structure, then, is to integrate the representational theory (which sustains that works of art are vehicles of representation) with Meinong's ontology.

2.2 Giacomo di cristallo, or on embodied representations

When Alexius von Meinong philosophized about objects of higher order, he did not have works of art in mind specifically. Nonetheless, one of his pupils, the philosopher Stephan Witasek, applied the Meinongian idea to art and, particularly, to musical objects (Witasek, 1904). We will soon have the chance to consider how the theoretical intersection of the Meinongian idea of objects of higher order and the representative theories resides in the attempt to oppose itself both to reductionist attitudes (which link the ontology of art to the artefactual aspects of the material object) and to the sensibility of the perceiver. The presumption, therefore, is that there is a common thread that, from a metaphysical perspective, associates a group of dice, a painting by Dalì and any ordinary person. This thread is comprised of properties that do not have a properly material and physical character, but that are a determining factor for the three dice to constitute a 'group', for a picture by Dalì to be an artwork and not simply a coloured canvas and for a man to be a person and not a mere material body. Put simply, to define the class of artworks by insisting primarily upon their physical structure would be like wishing to get to know someone by focusing exclusively on his or her body. In the latter case, we would get to know the body, but little about the person, while in the former case we would get to know the aesthetic properties of the object 'work of art', but little of the work itself.

The important point, then, is this: while it is fairly easy to understand the reasons that lead us to argue that we do not know a person if we can boast only of a familiarity with his or her body (as thorough as it may be), it is not equally as easy to determine that which we need in order to be certain of our understanding of a work of art. We can say that we truly know someone – let's say, a friend – when we know their ideas on important matters, when we are able to predict their reactions or, even, when we know exactly what they would think in a certain situation. In other words, the better we know someone, the more things we know about their interior world, the more we spot things about them that the eye cannot decry through an understanding of, for instance, their thoughts, beliefs or even their convictions.

It is astounding to think how little the physical structure of our thoughts, comprised of brain cells, has to do with their semantic content. This very astonishment must have moved Descartes when he theorized the separation between *res cogitans* (a thinking substance) and *res extensa* (a corporeal substance). From that very moment, philosophy began to hypothesize that human beings were composed of two distinct substances: one which is material and consistent, and the other which is intangible and, as such, more valuable. The former being the receptacle of the latter, while the latter is incorporated in the former and, therefore, invisible, but is the very core of thinking and conscious human beings (Descartes, 1641, Eng. trans., 1993, 20).

No two things are more diverse than a material body and a thought (in all of its declinations: a judgement, a belief, a desire, etc.). Thoughts inhabit bodies, and we can keep track of their presence. We see them, for instance, emerge from behaviours, words or complex actions. Basic actions, conversely, are, in some way, naked and are expressed without giving shape to particular meanings, or without being induced by an intentional action. In any case, thoughts are never seen alone, sitting on a chair, or relaxing in an armchair.

In *Favole al telefono*, Gianni Rodari tells the story of Giacomo, better known as *Giacomo di cristallo* (Giacomo made of glass), a child just like any other – only with an invisible body:

> You could see through his arms and legs just as if they were air or water. He was made of flesh and bone but he looked as if he were made of glass. If by chance he happened to fall he didn't break into pieces. At most there would be a transparent bump on his forehead. You could see his heart beating, and his thoughts flickering like colored fish in their tank. (Rodari, 1962, Eng. trans., www.energybulletin.net/stories/2010–08–20/giacomo-crystal)

When Giacomo, a lively child, happens to tell a lie, everyone takes notice instantly as a ball of fire pierces through his head. The ball of fire is a sort of mark, which seems trivial, but for those who know Giacomo it assumes a perspicuous meaning: it is a lie. In other words, it is a thought that is intentionally meant to deceive, and it 'inhabits' Giacomo's head just as blood and bile inhabit his body. Yet, unlike bile, which simply runs through an organism and accomplishes specific biological functions while being itself, the ball of fire refers to something else by revealing Giacomo's lies.

Rodari offers a concrete and physical body to Giacomo's thoughts in order for the reader to be able to imagine them and to distinguish their nature. Stories like Giacomo di cristallo's must have inspired the work of the neuroscientists who researched thoughts by utilizing techniques of functional magnetic resonance normally used to assess the functionality of the organs of our body. In this way, scientists do not 'see' the sentential content of thoughts, but they 'see' (or they should see) something that represents them – a sort of coloured map by areas of the brain in which each colour has its own key and respective meaning.

The important point of the story for our purpose is that thoughts and representations are in some way transported from our body or, better yet, incarnated in a body from which, at times, they emerge in verbal, formal or signal form, allowing them to be taken part in and shared. And so, whether thoughts are symbolized by the ball of fire that pierces Giacomo's head, or extrapolated (in a less distinct manner) from the mapping of a brain, or they transpire from actions, in each case they are in need of something that will lend a body to the sentential content which they themselves are.

2.3 Semantic vehicles

Let us take a step back and reconsider the matter from the idea that a work of art is an inscription and that this inscription is the representation of a subject. In short, and according to the formulation that I shall use in the following pages, a work of art is a 'semantic vehicle' that houses, or embodies, a representation.

Arthur Danto (Danto, 1968, 1981)[14] introduces the idea of the semantic vehicle by borrowing it from epistemology and positively applying it to the ontological discussion of works of art. Danto argues that works of art share the same ontological region that is occupied by natural language.

Danto clearly harks back to Strawson and borrows the underlying idea: an artwork is a material object that embodies 'something', beyond the original material structure, that renders the object a different kind of object. It is, in other words, a new complex of commodities. A person is something more than the sum of the parts of their body, just as an artwork is different from a simple artefact. This is so primarily because there exist properties that the eye alone cannot see, but which the mind has access to: goodness, generosity, courage, personality, character, altruism, selfishness and so forth. These are qualities that we can infer from the behaviours of those who perform acts that are good, generous, courageous, altruistic, selfish and narcissistic, but that could not be deduced simply from the features of a person.

In the previous pages, we have seen how other theories have also contributed to developing the idea of an artwork as a 'vehicle' of something, be it emotional content or aesthetic qualities. But Danto's idea is, in some way, more general: like words, works of art are positioned within the space that separates human beings and the world, and they are, ultimately, among the vehicles to which human beings entrust their representations. In this respect, they embody the meanings, or representations, of the world.

The line of reasoning that we shall follow within this framework will be comprised of two stages: first, we shall explain what a semantic vehicle is, after which we shall attempt to identify the peculiarities of the semantic vehicles that are works of art. Let us begin with the first point and ask ourselves, 'what is a semantic vehicle?' The term, ultimately, says it all: it is something that has the property of transporting meanings by embodying them.

A large part of twentieth-century philosophical reflection consists of showing how the world is full of these particular objects. They are scattered just about everywhere: a river can become a border between two states, a ream of paper can become a novel, a piece of paper can become a banknote and Joseph Ratzinger a pope. In all of the aforementioned cases, the theoretical crux is metaphysical in nature: some things cannot be explained by simply making reference to the physical structure of the object insofar as they contain 'something more', and this something appears to be what characterizes their essence.

In order to develop our first important epistemological distinction, we must first distinguish the semantic vehicles that have to do with truth (linguistic statements that can be true or false, for instance) from those that do not entertain any relationship with the truth (as, for example, works of art). This, however, does not mean that we cannot get muddled, for instance, if we visited St. Petersburg using *Crime and Punishment* as our tour guide. Even when a correspondence between a work of fiction and the world seems to exist, the author is not obliged to respect it. As rightly noted by Roman Ingarden with regard to the habits of the average reader:

> He frequently searches in the literary work for objectivities and situations that are similar to those he knows from his own life, and he considers the work to be 'true' if he in fact finds such objectivities in the work. By the same token, the naïve tendency of the reader to judge the work from the point of view of 'truth' and 'untruth' leads to the reading of reproduction and even Representation functions into the object stratum. This sort of thing, however, is occasioned by inappropriate readings and has very little to do with the real structure of the given work itself. (Ingarden, 1965, Eng. trans., 246)

Danto adopts an ample acceptation of the idea of 'semantic vehicle' by situating it within an epistemological perspective preluded by representational materialism.

From this perspective human beings, too, are semantic vehicles as they are bodies upon which representations are inscribed:

> The important insight of representationalist materialism is that we are built on the principles of texts, of words made flesh, and that a complex trade-off must be made between what a sentence means in the text of one's life and what it means as such. And the former is a function, one might say, of how the texts of our lives have been written. (Danto, 1989, 248)

Let us, once again, consider Giacomo who, from this point of view, proves to be a rather interesting case. As we were saying, Giacomo is a child who is marked by the misfortune of having a transparent mind: when he tells a lie, for example, his brain is penetrated by rays that resemble balls of fire, by bad thoughts that have the same aspect as the scorching boulders thrown by ancient catapults, or by gentle and playful thoughts that resemble the feathers of a bird. But that's not all; what bothers Giacomo the most is the fact that his friends can see when he is devising an idea. In other words, they see him develop his representations 'about something', usually about the state of things in the world – his friends, the following day's quiz, the soccer game or even his unpleasant teacher. Everything that Giacomo represents finds a place in his mind: meanings are housed in a brain, in a mind and in a body. Those meanings, to some extent, are related to Giacomo and to his life, but, in a way, they are also independent of him. Giacomo, then, is a semantic vehicle, too.

2.3.1 Inscribed beliefs: People who are semantic vehicles

In a particular sort of way, then, Giacomo – any Giacomo in the flesh, for that matter – is our first semantic vehicle: he has the ability to represent the world and his representations are inscribed somewhere in his brain. Furthermore, he possesses the wonderful ability to reflect upon this skill. This is a second-level ability that, as observed by Descartes, belongs to few species – perhaps only to human beings.

An initial distinction that Danto simply alludes to, without completely carrying out (1999a, 93), is ontological in nature: natural objects per se are not semantic vehicles, though they can become them in certain cases and at the hands of mankind. Humans, on the other hand, are always semantic vehicles.

In order to seize the epistemological meaning of the matter, we must turn briefly to the reflections that concern the philosophy of the mind, as the concept of semantic vehicle has to do with the idea that human beings formulate thoughts and beliefs fit to represent external reality. Philosophers have often considered the examination of beliefs to be a useful testing ground for understanding the operations of the human mind. Due to this conviction, they have taken particular care to resolving what it appears to be, for all intents and purposes: on the one hand, beliefs are equipped with sentential content – that is to say, they can be true or false. Giacomo, for example, can have the belief that 'Napoleon abdicated on 14 April 1814', and his belief is true since, according to historians, this is the actual date of Napoleon's abdication.

If, on the other hand, we consider the matter from the perspective of the functioning of the mind, it would seem as though belief is a process, given that there had to have been a moment (presumably during a history lesson) in which someone explained to Giacomo that Napoleon abdicated on that very day. In that specific moment, a belief that did not used to exist (Giacomo knew nothing of Napoleon until that history lesson) took form within the mind of the boy.

Beliefs, then, present themselves as processes, or as objects that are characterized by a temporal duration. All would be well up until this point if it were not for a contradiction that makes the development of the argument difficult to continue in this direction. The problem lies in the fact that the propositional content ('that p') 'Napoleon abdicated on 14 April 1814' cannot be true in a time t and false in a time t_1. Put simply, the temporal properties which we attribute to beliefs are incompatible with the propositional content of the beliefs themselves, since that which is true or false and that is expressed in the form 'that p' cannot, at the same time, be that which begins to exist, endures and, finally, has an end. It is true at this moment, just as it was true on 14 April 1814, and it will be true forever that Napoleon abdicated on that infamous day. It therefore goes without saying that the statement affirms something that is not subject to the passing of time.

There are, in large part, two theoretical strategies[15] that are implemented to obviate this problem: the first emphasizes the fact that it is not the propositional content of the belief (the 'that p') that begins to exist, but, rather, the mental state (the belief that p). This requires that when we say 'A believes that p is true', we do not mean to say that p is true, but that it is true that A possesses that particular belief, which has nothing to do with the truth or falsity of 'that p' (a belief that I have now may very well, one day, reveal itself as false). This stance seems to claim that a similar thing – the mental state 'that p' – can have a propositional content and a temporal duration.

The second strategy, on the other hand, emphasizes how philosophers of the mind are not very interested in the sentential content of statements; what they concern themselves with, rather, are the dispositional states related to things like beliefs – and these states are obviously neither true nor false. According to this position, then, Giacomo has the belief 'that p' (which is a propositional content) if, and only if, in him exists the 'state' of belief that p (a state that, as previously mentioned, possesses temporal properties).

Now, it is known that the dispositions are neither true nor false (unlike their propositional content), and that they have a beginning and, predictably, will have an end. By adopting this strategy it seems that we can avoid a paradox: that of the same object – belief – to which we associate temporal properties and sentential properties.

The reflections that Danto develops concerning semantic vehicles, which belong to the positions that, as a whole, are labelled 'representational materialism', emerge from this framework to respond to the need to structure a theory of the mind that exceeds the Cartesian distinction of the substances and, therefore, explains the shift from the physical to the mental in the simplest of terms. According to Collins's observations (1979, 229), at least three authors were working in the same period of time to build a metaphysical structure (albeit through different declensions and languages) for the position that is referred to in literature as 'representational materialism': they were Arthur Danto, Jerry Fodor and Gilbert Harman.[16]

As we were saying, declensions bring forth different takes. Danto affirms that beliefs are sentential states of people, Harman treats them as memorized inscriptions, while Fodor speaks of internal representations that are created in the language of thought. Nevertheless, the underlying idea is the same: they all agree that the mind is the centre of beliefs and, therefore, of 'things' that share the same structure and the same properties of a statement, and that are associated with the well-defined state of belief. In other words, Giacomo believes that 'Napoleon abdicated on 14 April 1814' because he finds himself in a state that makes that belief possible.

> I have no evidence that there are sentential states, only persuasive arguments in their favour. But in the end my theory is an empirical one. Why should we not suppose that someday sentences might serve to individuate neural states, so that we might read a man's beliefs off the surfaces of his brain? We could find out *what* he believes in this manner. (Danto, 1968, 96)

Perhaps Danto had read of Giacomo di cristallo when he wrote these lines in *Analytical Philosophy of Knowledge*. Be that as it may, his idea is quite similar to that of Gianni Rodari, though the latter is imaginary. Most importantly, the idea lays out a classic metaphysical question: that of the mind-body relationship, which

Danto resolves from an utterly materialist point of view (it is no coincidence that a collection of his essays from the second half of the twentieth century is entitled *The Body / Body Problem* [1999]). From the perspective of representational materialism, the problem does not consist of the difficulty of explaining the relationship between two different and separate substances (mind and body) but, rather, of explaining how it is possible that from a material substance there should emerge complex dispositions, such as beliefs.

Danto's theory is structured in two phases: first, it demonstrates how a separation of mind and body does not exist; it demonstrates how the mind is inscribed – physically inscribed – within the body through traces that are presumably arranged in a very similar manner to the grammatical structure of languages; traces inscribed within our bodies.

Danto develops this point by making a comparison of two paradigmatically opposite epistemological models: that of Nietzsche and of Descartes. Danto's judgement, which refers to the considerations developed in Gilbert Ryle's *The Concept of Mind*, is that the introduction of the separation of the substances entailed a multitude of problems from a metaphysical point of view by unfolding problems that were practically insurmountable. It was not necessary to separate mind and body, due to the exceptional idea that multiplying the categories that we use to explain the world is not only redundant, but also counterproductive.

The reasons for representational materialism's criticism of Cartesian internalism rest fundamentally upon two arguments. The first is related to the excessive number of concessions to scepticism which, in Descartes, prove to be particularly insidious.

As we might recall, Descartes (1641, Eng. trans., 20 ff.) claims that knowing is a 'second-degree activity'. Thinking, in its most noble acceptation, is above all a self-conscious thinking. Therefore, we 'think of the fact that we are thinking'. What does this mean? It's quite simple, really. While the majority of our activities are unreflective, or are accompanied by a minimal amount of self-consciousness (before crossing a street, for instance, we simply pay attention in order not to be run over by a car), in epistemology, we often focus our attention on understanding the modalities of our thinking activity, as well as on our ways of knowledge. This thinking that involves our thoughts is, at least for Descartes, the authentic starting point for any good epistemology that, to be called scientific, must prescind from the contribution of the senses. The following passage is highly renowned:

> Surely whatever I had admitted until now as most true I received either from the senses or through the senses. However, I have noticed that the senses

are sometimes deceptive; and it is a mark of prudence never to place our
complete trust in those who have deceived us even once. (Descartes, 1641,
Eng. trans., 14)

The beginning of the *First Meditation* is rather decisive. It introduces doubt and
is substantiated in three phases: the senses, dreams and God.

Descartes recalls how he once exchanged the truth for falsity and, in order
to prevent this misfortune from reoccurring, and taking into account that our
senses could deceive us not only occasionally, but even systematically, he decides
to suspend all types of certainty, including the most common. In reality, sooner
or later, we all experience the deception of our senses. I once took a trip across
Death Valley in the scorching, suffocating heat of the Mojave desert. Upon being
alleviated by the air conditioning, at every turn, I would seem to catch sight of
a lake, despite being well aware that not even a trace of a lake could be found
there.

My eyes were certainly deceiving me. Yet, it is also true that *normally* I do
not see lakes wherever I look (and if I did, it would be a source of worry).
This is the point precisely: Descartes assumes that our senses can deceive us
continually, though it is clear – simply because millennia of human evolution
demonstrates it to us – that, for the most part, they seem to work rather well.
Of course, we could always conjecture that we are constantly deceived by our
senses because, perhaps, life is a dream. This hypothesis, however, is quite risky
and likely ineffective: our species has proven to be, all in all, well organized and,
from the point of view of evolution, victorious. For what reason, then, should
we believe that our sensibility is systematically unreliable? Reason would prove
the contrary.

After identifying the reasons for the distrust towards our senses, Descartes
takes up the topic of dreams – that is to say, the possibility of confusing reality
with a dream. In this case, too, he offers an extreme case that occurs very
rarely:

> How often does my evening slumber persuade me of such ordinary things as
> these: that I am here, clothed in my dressing gown, seated next to the fireplace –
> when in fact I am lying undressed in bed! (Descartes, 1641, Eng. trans., 14)

In reference to dreams, too, the heart of the matter is distrust. As he observes
in his *Sixth Meditation*, his eyes are not the only things to have deceived him
about the shape of towers in the distance (1641, Eng. trans., 50); at times, in his
dreams, he believes to be somewhere different and, perhaps, to be in a different
position.

If a consolation exists, it is the fact that these types of dreams are not common: they are the dreams in which we have perception of ourselves and, perhaps, even of the fact that we are dreaming. Let us try to apply our doubt to a dream: 'I believe I am sitting near the fire, but I am dreaming; therefore, perhaps I am not sitting near the fire.' As André Gombay wisely notes (2007, 17), the example is a bizarre one:

> Something sounds askew here, even at first hearing. One oddity is the second clause. There do exist 'lucid' dreams – dreams that one is aware of having and where, if one spoke, one might say 'I am now dreaming that . . .' [. . .] So be it; but lucid dreams are an anomaly, and surely we cannot require our Cartesian doubter to be having just that kind.

Our senses certainly do not deceive systematically, and the same must be concluded for dreams, with the sole exception of the particular cases of lucid dreams which Descartes has in mind.

It is plain to see how a rather insidious hyperbolic tendency is hidden within the argument. First off, because, as we mentioned, our senses generally work well: transforming occasional delusions into systematic delusions would be biting off more than we can chew. Our senses, on the other hand, do not resemble human beings, whom, after deceiving once, we are right in suspecting will eventually deceive again. They are, rather, similar to sophisticated mechanisms that, at times, can relapse.

This means that reaching a systematic poor functioning of perception (visual, for example) from a few of its periodic stumbles is an all-together unjustified conclusion that would need better arguments and that, as a whole, is truly of little benefit for our lives.

The majority of activities which we are usually involved in occur without 'us' (the part of our conscience that is delegated to reflect upon what we are thinking and doing) worrying or spending energy to check on them; without having to rely upon a sort of auto-check of our representations, as Descartes would have wanted.

It is with reference to this very point that Friedrich Nietzsche makes one of his most famous criticisms of Descartes: neither humans nor animals can be steadfastly distracted by second-level activities. The cognitive resources used by human beings are oriented towards survival. If we were regularly involved in secondary occupations – argues Nietzsche – then a large part of our faculties would be deterred from their principle objectives. It would, therefore, be reasonable to hypothesize that this does not occur and that 'thinking about thinking' is, at most, a habit of philosophers.

In considering the third phase, God, we must keep in mind the two main criticisms that have been made with regard to the topic. The first is that made by the 'doubt-dramatizers' who express a variation of the position formulated, paradigmatically, by David Hume in *An Enquiry Concerning Human Understanding*: 'The Cartesian doubt, therefore, were it ever possible to be attained by any human creature (as it plainly is not) would be entirely incurable' (Hume, 1748, 97). Next we have the positions expressed by the 'doubt-sceptics' who say that, far from being indubitable, Cartesian doubt and the deceiving God argument is but a pseudo-problem. If we are not even certain of the existence of God, then for what reason should we imagine him as a being a deceiver?

Be it as it may, Descartes remains solid in his defence of the legitimacy of this doubt, arguing that if God did not exist, then it would be all the worse for atheists who believe they are immune to the subject by reason of their atheism: 'the less powerful they [atheists] take the author of my origin to be, the more probable it will be that I am so imperfect that I am always deceived' (Descartes, 1641, Eng. trans., 16).

Therefore, the argument of God's intentional deceit, which is examined and discarded by Ugo Grozio in *De Jure Belli ac Pacis*, is covered extensively by Descartes who, though being a believer in God, doubts God in an almost excessive manner:

> Be that as it may, there is fixed in my mind a certain opinion of long standing, namely that there exists a God who is able to do anything and by whom I, such as I am, have been created. How do I know that he did not, bring it about that there is no earth at all, no heavens, no extended thing, no shape, no size, no place, and yet bringing it about that all these things appear to me to exist precisely as they do now? [...] But perhaps God has not willed that I be deceived in this way, for he is said to be supremely good. Nonetheless, if it were repugnant to his goodness to have created me such that I be deceived all the time, it would also seem foreign to that same goodness to permit me to be deceived even occasionally. But we cannot make this last assertion. (1641, Eng. trans., 61)

André Gombay compares Descartes to Othello, who also has doubts without having a reason (2007, 21): just as Othello was furiously jealous, despite not having grounds to doubt his wife, so too did Descartes, with equal and unmotivated intensity, doubt God. The reasons for Descartes's doubt are based on human imperfection: if God truly wanted the best for us, then we would be able neither to deceive ourselves nor to do wrong. We can reach this conclusion provided we clearly understand the reasons for divine choices and actions (which, for a believer, is an act of much pride).

In this respect, the point made by Descartes is similar to that which we discussed regarding the criticism of sensibility: sometimes we make mistakes. If God were truly good, he would not have allowed for this to happen – not even once. Perhaps, then, he is not that good, and we are, in fact, able to deceive ourselves since, one might say, the fact of being human implies making mistakes from the very beginning. It goes without saying that the universe is inundated with imperfections and errors that exist without their cause necessarily being God, and without this having to bring about systematic doubt. Taken in small doses, scepticism can be useful for rethinking, with less naïveté, many assumptions made by common sense. Nonetheless, if we surrender to the temptation of radicalizing it, it can become an insidious cage.

Danto's position (1989, 137–75), then, is not surprising. He argues that the internalist perspective is spoiled by a concession to scepticism, which is not at all necessary but that, if granted, yields results that are of little benefit and, ultimately, inadmissible. The principle is found in the impossibility of returning to an external world after its reality has been doubted through a double theoretical move: the affirmation of the existence of separate substances (i.e. material and thinking substances) and the argument of natural doubt. Danto warns that this move is without return – unless, of course, we accept the ontological argument which proves the existence of God.[17] This is, after all, the same objection raised suitably by David Hume in the beginning of his *Treatise* and of his first *Enquiry*, when he formulates his theory of mind. Fully aware, Hume adopts the implications of Descartes's inquiry of the boundaries of subjectivity and emphasizes how any Cartesian theory of the mind that wishes to renounce theological guarantees cannot venture beyond its own representations to evaluate its pertinence to the world.

Put simply, an internalist epistemology makes the very possibility of referring to the world difficult, and this cannot be permitted as it would jeopardize the possibility for human beings to formulate beliefs, judgements of truth and judgements of value. The paralysis of pure reason would bring about a corresponding paralysis of practical reason.

For the love of analysis, let us suppose that this is not the case. Let us suppose that Humean analysis produces highly elusive results, and that Descartes was right in warning the world, and advancing the principle of prudence which declares that if something has deceived us once it is impossible to exclude the possibility that it can always deceive us. We shall, then, hyperbolize the reasons of doubt and propose the argument of the evil genius. Let us consider what the consequences of this decision might be. By doubting the existence of an external world, without there being a pressing need to, we may find ourselves in situations of theoretical unease. Let us assume, suggests Danto (1989, 155–7), that an evil genius – a very powerful and clever genius with the same characteristics as the genius recalled by Descartes – decides to orchestrate a distasteful trick. In the history section of an important library, they substitute each book with books that describe single events in history but that, in reality, are simple stories of fiction (and, as we all know, by definition, fiction is not meant to elaborate true representations). Despite not having proof, the new librarian suspects that something is off and that the books do not tell the truth, and so they do their best to contrive a solution that will confirm their suspicion.

What to do? Might it be of use to search for a super-book that is able to confirm the way things really went during, let's say, the French Revolution? Clearly not. The genius could have intervened anywhere and altered the markers that normally attest to the correspondence between a representation and reality. The only option the librarian is left with is to surrender and to 'leave' their library in order to do what historians normally do: go out into the world to look for evidence, documents, objects and, basically, anything that can prove that things went the way someone once told us they did.

Danto formulates a mental experiment that, in many ways, is similar to Descartes's (in both cases there dominates a powerful and evil genius, in both cases someone tries to find a trick to rely upon in order not to doubt something that seems to be certain, but that could eventually prove a colossal deceit) and is formulated in the spirit of the hyperbole that characterizes the Cartesian movement.

As much as Danto's genius might resemble that of Descartes, Danto's librarian and Descartes (the protagonist of his own mental experiment) propose different solutions to a problem that is, fundamentally, one and the same. In order to overcome his predicament, Descartes must turn to the ontological argument whose weakness is found in the fact that it considers existence to be an indispensable attribute to the perfection of the concept of God. The significance of this argument is well known: given that the concept of a most perfect being belongs to us, to consider it without its definition involving existence would be to consider it imperfect (which, by definition, is impossible). Yet, according to Kant, existence does not belong to the definition of a most perfect being; in other words, it is not a predicate, and it does not add anything to the concept of a perfect being – just as the concept of the colour green does not belong to the definition of a triangle. The upsets experienced by the theoretical internalist have the potential to be truly relevant. It is for this very reason that Danto is committed to elaborating a position that avoids making the distinction between the substances.

If we refuse to assume (or to accept) the distinction, then the starting point would clearly have to be material substance and, if we have human beings in mind, their body – the body that houses things with particular appearances, such as the beliefs previously mentioned. It is banally true that a belief is a special type of object when compared to a material object. First, because, as we were saying, it exhibits a rather peculiar ontological status: it is something found in the brain, one of those elements that testify that a body is something different from a person, precisely because people have beliefs and bodies do not. What, then, is a belief? It seems to be a state or a process that, as such, is characterized by a temporal persistence. In other words, it comes into existence at a certain moment, it has a duration and then ends – on its own or simply due to the fact that, eventually, the very subject that possesses it must end. On the other hand, beliefs exhibit propositional content that, as such, is true or false, but that quite certainly is not determined temporally. Beliefs have a semantic connotation.

Representational materialists choose to separate the mental state (of who formulates the belief) from the content of that state. This move allows them to resolve certain important problems. Furthermore, it emphasizes how belief has an intentional nature; it relies on our representation of the object, not on the object itself, which explains why different people can formulate different beliefs about the same object.

Let us consider certain beliefs about Ulysses:

1. Polyphemus believes that his name is 'No One'.
2. The Cyclopes believe that no one is there.
3. Penelope believes that he is her husband.

These beliefs are possible due to the fact that they are in reference to the representations that Polyphemus, the Cyclopes and Penelope have of Ulysses, and not to Ulysses himself, who remains who he is. Different subjects, therefore, can have different representations of a single object (a Christian believes that Jesus is the son of God, an atheist believes that he is an ordinary man – just with more charisma, perhaps – and a Jew believes that he is simply a Jew). Yet, one subject can also have various representations of the same object (all of the residents of Metropolis believe that Superman is extremely courageous, while the residents of Metropolis who know Clark Kent think that he is a docile man). For the most part, the object 'Superman-Kent' remains what it is; the representations of the residents of Metropolis are what change. Jocasta remains what she is – the wife of Laius, the queen of Thebes and the mother of Oedipus. The representations of the Thebans, of Laius, Creon, Tiresias and, finally, of Oedipus are what differ from each other.

The fundamental point, then, is this: human beings elaborate representations that are inscribed upon a brain that is housed within a body. As far as we are concerned, a plant coincides entirely with its body insofar as nothing exists beyond the *res extensa* that defines its boundaries; the plant, in other words, is not able to represent reality. An animal, on the other hand, is capable of thoughts and, therefore, representations (although it is most likely incapable of metarepresentation, leading Descartes to conclude that animals are autonomous). Thoughts and representations, therefore, are embodied or, better yet, inscribed upon nervous tissue and are housed in bodies.

In trying to avoid the consequences of Cartesian dualism, reductionist theories consider thoughts as simple alterations of the chemistry of bodies. The matter, however, remains unsolved: the content and the material of a representation do not coincide, if for no other reason than the fact that the same representational content can be carried by the most disparate of things, or it can assume the most diverse of forms. I can 'think' 'Giacomo is a child whose head is made of glass', or I can 'write' 'Giacomo is a child whose head is made of glass' or I can 'say' 'Giacomo is a child whose head is made of glass' to a friend of mine. In the first example, the representation of Giacomo is inscribed in my brain; in the second example, it is found in a stroke of ink; while in the third example, it is contained in a sound wave. And when I write 'Giacomo is a child whose head is made of glass', I can do so in different ways. This is because while representational content is the same, the form of its expression changes.[18] And so, we have:

Giacomo is a child whose head is made of glass;

GIACOMO IS A CHILD WHOSE HEAD IS MADE OF GLASS;

Giacomo is a child whose head is made of glass;

and even with a mistake:

Giacomo is a chid whose head is made of glass.

In other words, while a thought is chemically modified nervous tissue, it is also representational content that is housed in that nervous tissue and, as we were saying, it can be inscribed in different places and in different forms.

Acting, perceiving, inferring all involve representations: one believes that P, one infers that Q if P, ones sets out to test if Q is true, one observes that it is false, in which case one modifies one's belief that P, or one finds out that it is true, in which case one regards one's belief that P as confirmed. All these processes have a common propositional content, we might say: One believes that P, infers Q from P, tests in order to see if P is true, and so on. And the questions that then face the philosopher are what to do with this content and where these representations are to be housed. (Danto, 1989, 243)

Danto's idea, then, is that, for the most part, the content of the beliefs of our representations of the world are housed within the mind – or in the nervous tissue of the brain – a bit like a form houses a certain content.

Self-awareness – the ability to reflect upon our thoughts – is, then, the element that truly describes the ontological specificity of a human being. Mountains have neither thoughts nor a conscience; bats have thoughts, but not necessarily self-awareness; humans have thoughts, they are aware of them and they treat them reflectively. They are, in other words, able to direct their conscious thinking towards the most disparate of objects and, at times, they are aware of doing so in the precise moment in which they do so. This is a small detail that, nonetheless, makes a significant difference.

Let us consider the following diagram:

natural objects → do not have thoughts;
living beings → have thoughts, but do not think about thinking;
human beings → have thoughts and are capable of thinking about thinking.

For our purposes, the final line is the most interesting: human beings are objects that embody meanings (thoughts, beliefs, desires) and that are aware of this uniqueness. They do not need another living being to recognize them as semantic vehicles.

The ball of fire that rapidly runs through Giacomo's head has propositional content – when his mother asks him 'what grade did you receive on your math project?', Giacomo replies: 'the teacher gave me a C', knowing very well that he had really only earned a low D. Giacomo's specific answer can or cannot coincide with the world: the teacher kept the stack of projects in a drawer at school, which includes the boy's low grade. That ball of fire, therefore, is a symbol of the fact that the representation that Giacomo communicates intentionally to his mother 'does not' coincide with the world – it does not correspond to it. In this case, then, Giacomo's statement (that should describe a state of things) intentionally fails to capture that state. In short, statements can either be true or false, just as the thoughts that Giacomo formulates with regard to the world.

Clearly, not all statements exhibit this same structure. Let us suppose that Giacomo is the student representative of his class and that, during an assembly, he tells his classmates that 'in order to improve our performance in Greek we must ask the teacher to dedicate more class time to grammar'. This type of statement does not offer the representation of a state of things (as it appears to be a request for something that does not yet exist – additional hours of grammar) but, rather, it intends to 'intervene' in a state of things in order to modify it. This typology of statements, however, affirms something about the world; in particular, it describes how reality should be considered in the best way possible – Giacomo's sentence, in particular, asserts that a certain academic program should include a greater number of hours dedicated to grammar. There obviously exists a third group of statements that express another peculiarity: that of performatives which, in suitable conditions, have the property of making something happen in the world.

Statements which function as models, and that interest representational theorists, belong to neither the second nor the third type but, rather, to the first type: the statements that describe reality and that help us understand it. Knowledge and understanding are two distinct activities and, yet, at times they can be confused. Knowledge cannot prescind from reality; in fact, it takes it upon itself to verify the correspondence between statements and the world. For the most part, in order to answer the question of whether Manhattan is really an island, it is assumed that one would have to go to that part of the world and verify if an island called Manhattan exists or not; just as one would have to go out into the world to know if Michelangelo truly painted *The Last Judgment*. Yet, something different occurs when we are dealing with the understanding of an artwork: in this case the world is useful to us to contextualize the work and to better determine its historical and relational properties, but not to verify if the work's connections to the world are true. Nothing would change if they were absolutely false, and, most of the time, they are.

2.4 What, therefore, is a work of art?

We have reached a fundamental junction: human beings, just as statements, just as works of art, are types of semantic vehicles. In other words, they are things that embody meanings; they are things that 'transport' other things. There is, naturally, a difference and it is a difference of substance. If the statements that we need to formulate our understandings are founded upon representations that are extensional, then works of art (along with our beliefs) carry representations that are intentional. In one instance – the first – we are dealing with truth, while in the second instance we are not (or at least not necessarily). I do not need to carry out any sort of inquiry 'into the world' in order to understand *Don Quixote*; abiding by the text and following the development of the plot is sufficient, as well as convenient. Certainly, if we were to possess subsidiary knowledge of the life of knights errant, our understanding of the novel would improve, but we would have not an additional ounce of knowledge.

Works do not say anything about the world if not incidentally and, as is often said, accidentally. In other words, a tourist is not likely to choose to walk the streets of Manhattan by using Aner Shalev's novel *Ha-Chomer Ha-Afel (Where New York Ends)* instead of a Lonely Planet travel guide. The novel could, perchance, be extremely accurate in its representations of the city, but whether it truly is is a question that concerns the choice of the author. Salgari, for instance, set the adventures of his characters in India without having ever been there, precisely because the worlds of fiction have ample authority with regard to reality, and they are not required in any way to develop extensional representations, not even when dealing with something that actually exists.

Salgari, then, can give the name 'India' to the representation of something that only resembles the real India, just as Dante can represent Charon in the act of ferrying the souls of the dead without the expectation that the indomitable coxswain really lives in one of the subterranean rivers. Similarly, no one expects Masaccio's 'Trinities' to have a certain correspondence with 'something', an individual who is both one and triune, that is found somewhere in space-time. We might also conjecture that India and the Trinities caused the works of Salgari and Masaccio; yet, if there is causation, then it must be a different type in comparison to traditional causation, which – for instance – allows heat to boil water at 212°.

It is for this reason that we can understand an image – let's say, a representation of the Sphinx – without having to ask ourselves if a lion with the head of a man really exists in an Egyptian desert. In general, then, we understand an image (that is to say, we classify it adequately, or we identify its representational content) without knowing if what it depicts actually exists; we understand its meaning and this is enough.

This is our first point. When dealing with vehicles of representations that are works of art, it makes no difference if the object that is represented exists or not. To affirm that we understand 'Pinocchio' means that we have formulated a certain idea about how the world would be if wooden puppets who talk or blue fairies who protect us were to exist. Since nothing of the sort exists – though we see numerous Pinocchio figurines, but not the slightest hint of Pinocchio's world – our representations are literally false (which is of little importance).

At this point, we shall use the necessary theoretical tools in order to understand Danto's definition of works of art as semantic vehicles. These are objects which we use to embody our representations, which do not necessarily have a dependent connection to reality.

Therefore:

x is a work of art only if it *embodies a meaning*; that is, if it carries a specific representation of the world.

Clearly, this condition alone is not sufficient if we consider that, as has already been disclosed, semantic vehicles exist (i.e. objects that carry representations that are not works of art). What might we say, then, about things like street signs, *emoticons* and symbols in general? If there were no way to distinguish a symbol that is a work of art from the myriad of symbols that surround us that are not, we would be fortunate enough to live in an open-air museum or, in contrast, everything would be a work of art.

What might we say about a cross, for instance? It is an age-old semantic vehicle that boasts a history that predates its use throughout Christianity. If we consider its modern-day meanings, those which we are able to decipher without the help of certain reading guides, the following come to mind: the death of Jesus, the presence of a church, a hospital, a cemetery or a tomb, a pharmacy, a street intersection or a dead-end street. The matter is quite simple, and can be formulated in these terms: for what reason is the first cross, depicted in Figure 4.1, not a work of art, while the second and the third, depicted in Figures 4.2 and 4.3, are?

The cross in Figure 4.1 represents a dead end on a street sign, while Figures 4.2 and 4.3 depict two works by imaginative and polyvalent French artist, Clet Abraham. In his cross, the artist evidently embodies new meanings. In Abraham's work, the road sign in the shape of a cross becomes a real cross. From it arises Figure 4.2, which displays a stylized body hanging from a pole without an outlet, just as the dead-end street depicted on the street sign, and Figure 4.3, which cites the most classic and widely known deposition.

An ordinary object, a sign that regulates the flow of traffic on a street, 'can', therefore, become a work of art.

But if this is so, then what is the difference between normal signs that also have representative content? Abraham's representations are contained in a

Figure 4.1 Street sign: dead-end-street

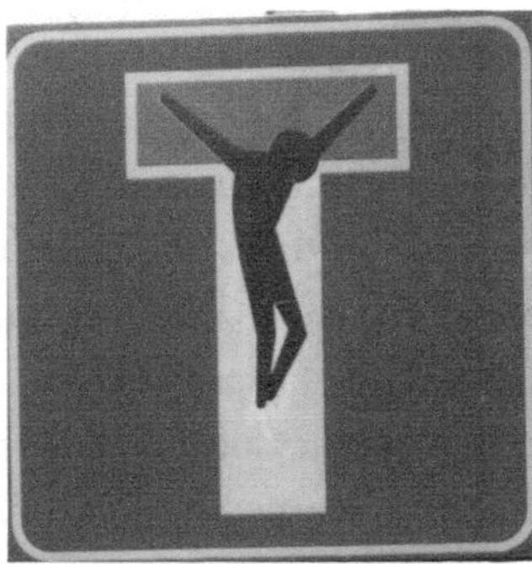

Figure 4.2 Clet Abraham: *Dead-End-Street*

Figure 4.3 Clet Abraham: *Pietà*

medium, a body, that is not transparent[19]: hanging on walls and found along the streets of Florence, the signs are looked at because of what they are and not only because of the classic meaning that they embody (the warning of a dead-end street).

Here, then, is the second condition:

x is a work of art only if the medium of *x* is not transparent.

Abraham's signage (along with many other works in contemporary art) is particularly rich as it presents a stratified plurality of meanings. There are the meanings exemplified by the street sign and those implemented by the artist which, as evident as it may be, are greatly akin. The cross is a dead-end road: a man who has been hung on a cross or who is taken down from a cross, and lies in the arms of a grieving mother, represents the expression of that which is, in the most definitive of ways, without outlet. There is no trace of transcendence in the representation of a man hanging from a cross depicted on a street sign, nor is there in its exposition to the distracted passers-by. It is not a sacred place that conserves and protects the power of that symbol. Rather, the symbol is injured both by the distractions of the bystanders who will confuse it with a banal road marking, and by the exhaust pipes of the passing cars.

In order to bypass the transparency of the medium, artists, poets, writers, musicians and composers have learned to implement complex rhetorical strategies that trace a sort of marker around a work of art, allowing it to be recognized as such by rescuing it from the flux of the ordinary. Words, sounds and drawings belong to our lives without being works of art, and yet, the appropriate use of those mediums can allow a work to become the most diverse and trivial of things.

Let us now consider the explicitly reactional and historical character of artworks. As we were saying, artworks are social objects; they are, in other words, objects that depend on human beings, on their intensionality and on their way of reading the world, reconstructing history and envisioning traits and characters. Clearly, even from this perspective, neither eyes nor ears alone are sufficient for allowing for a good understanding of a work of art: the history of the relationships from which artworks emerge is an inescapable element as, oftentimes, those very relationships determine, at least partially, the meanings expressed by works of art. Similarly, it is equally necessary to read works of art keeping in mind the history of the effects determined by their reception.

The social world, along with its objects, is a world that exhibits properties that are connected to history. In other words, while the properties that determine the series of prime numbers are not determined historically (i.e. they do not depend on human beings), certain properties that determine *The Adventures of Pinocchio* are. Pinocchio is an exceptionally human puppet, and the traits of his character are typically infantile: selfish, narcissistic, domineering, arrogant, ingenuous, credulous, generous at times but, most of all, untruthful. And what can we say about Pinocchio's world? As Benedetto Croce observed in his brief essay in *La letteratura della nuova Italia: saggi critici* (1903), Pinocchio is a 'human book', a book that represents all of the salient characteristics of the human world. And how are we to blame him? In Pinocchio's world, there is loyalty, falsehood, friendship, the sense of guilt, love, and then there are things like promises – the types of acts that, par excellence, exemplify a social relationship.

Therefore, on the one hand, the represented world is a social and historical world, while, on the other, certain properties that comprise works of art express historical associations and relationships. As we were saying, in order to understand the narration of a novel, or the meaning of a painting, it is not necessary to go out into the world, in the sense that it is not necessary to search for Othello, Funes, Mona Lisa or Juliet and Romeo. And yet, it is not entirely accurate to say that we can prescind from the world all together; we will need to, but in a different way compared to when we make a judgement of truth. The world that we are in need of is a world that allows for a contextualized understanding of a work of art, and that allows us to focus on the invisible, but fundamental, relationships that connect artworks to the world that produced them, and to the other worlds that have received, reread and interpreted them.

Let us turn to a recent case that has emerged from a fusion of architecture, video-art, music and dance: *You Tube Play. A Biennal of Creative Video* (2010). This is a project that showcases a typically Pop spirit: revisiting – by violating – one of the new barriers of the contemporary world, which separates the system of art, and the open and fluid world, from *user-generated content*. In *You Tube Play*, video-art enthusiasts were given the possibility to shoot a video and to present it to an international jury.[20] The 20 videos that were selected were presented simultaneously at the Guggenheim museums in Berlin, Bilbao and Venice, and were the protagonists of a large closing function for a four-day-long event at the Guggenheim in New York.

This brings us to our main point. In order to understand what certainly is a work of art – the Guggenheim Museum designed by Lloyd Wright – as well as the transformations that it endured during the days of *You Tube Play*, we can prescind neither from the knowledge of New York and of its metropolitan reality, nor from American art of the second half of the twentieth century. Nor can we ignore what it means to live in a globalized world; we must know the expressive possibilities of digital media, and it is also a good idea to know what it means to speak of a total work of art, an idea presented by Richard Wagner that was exemplified at the Guggenheim during *You Tube Play*.

Now, let us suppose that a native of a remote African region finds themself in New York, on Fifth Avenue and Eighty-Ninth Street, when they catch sight of the Guggenheim illuminated by millions of videos. What would they think? Most likely that they are the same ads that cover Midtown Manhattan, or that New Yorkers find a strange enjoyment in transforming the city's buildings into curious Christmas trees. The majority of properties that make that work a social object have to do with our capacity to historically and culturally situate the building, as well as its history, and ours. Some of those properties can then change throughout the course of time, because what surrounds the work changes.

What, then, is a work of art?

It is a social object, an artefact, that embodies a representation, in the form of an inscribed trace upon a medium that is not transparent.

Oftentimes, though not always, artists are able to create works whose representational content means something for our mind and, at the same time, for our emotions. This is the reason for which, as Nietzsche had already observed, artworks can inscribe upon our lives more than a well-formulated argument can.

Evidence of this can be found in Christian Marclay's *The Clock*, a film with an impressive duration of 24 hours. Cinematography boasts more than a few examples of long (and extremely long) films. Nonetheless, *The Clock* is a true gem of cinematographic assemblage in which the separation between reality and the worlds of fiction marks the almost absolute consummation of the boundaries of temporality. Time, which is measured and indicated with obsessive constancy throughout the entire film, coincides with that of our lives in an astonishing way. The spectator realizes this immediately – at first with surprise and then by experiencing mounting unease combined with authentic enjoyment. Time passes and is measured; it is spoken of and is considered throughout the whole of the film, for 24 extraordinary hours. It is measured not only by clocks that capture its rhythm, but also by memory that travels through Marclay's excerpts, contextualizes them, experiences the irony of scenes that belong to a past in black and white, only to open itself to a world of colours. Across time, the answers to some of the most challenging questions are dealt with, some of which, after having been brought up in one scene, are answered in a different one, almost in a new temporal dimension.

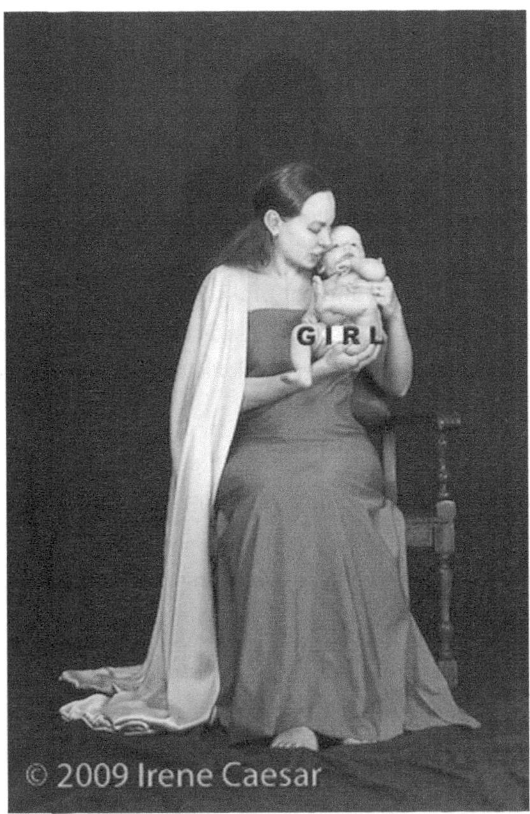

Figure 4.4   Irene Caesar, *Madonna Liberated* (2009)

The medium is never transparent; in fact, we do not watch the kaleidoscopic collage as a collection of images but, rather, as a revisiting of the history of cinematography and, at the same time, of our memory. In art, the medium must be watched, observed, heard, studied, dissected and contextualized. The medium is always the begin-all for constructing or reconstructing meanings endowed by the artist.

Irene Caesar is not an ordinary photographer. She considers herself to be provocative, an artist who loves to provoke in order to test the validity of ideas; that is, the conceptual structures that allow us to interact with the world. As a result, she requires something very simple of her subjects: to incarnate a particular idea before the lens, to experience it and to represent it. *Madonna Liberated* (Figure 4.4) encompasses all of these dimensions.

First and foremost, she cites the grand art of the *Cinquecento*: the Madonnas of Titian, Tintoretto, Raphael, along with the countless iconographic representations of that maternity scene. Caesar places a woman before her lens, a mother with her child who is loved but also displayed as a symbol. Only, in Caesar's depiction, that symbol is female.

Christian theology tells us that God is male, tradition tells us that God is male, Western art has repeated to us for centuries that God is male. And, yet, whatever God may be, God does not fall under a particular gender distinction; to think of God 'also' as a woman can only help to liberate ourselves from the crystallization of our personal and cultural schemes. It is on these grounds that Caesar cites tradition and, by doing so, indicates its weaknesses and shatters them, demonstrating how one of art's tasks is to call consolidated visions into question.

As Nietzsche put it:

Artists, an intermediary species: they at least fix an image of that which ought to be; they are productive, to the extent that they actually alter and transform; unlike men of knowledge, who leave everything as it is. (Nietzsche, 1901, Eng. trans., 318)

Notes

Introduction

1 This is a case that includes recent examples. The sculptures created by John Baldessari for the 'Giacometti Variations' at the Prada Foundation in Milan were seized by law enforcement and the exhibit was closed nearly two weeks prematurely, on 17 December 2010. The dispute was prompted by Véronique Wiesinger, director of the Giacometti Foundation in Switzerland, who sustained that 'no artistic practice can cover up forgery'. The director asked and was granted that the catalogues of nine sculptures be seized and that the images found on the Prada Foundation site be taken down. Both the Foundation and Baldessari were astonished by the legal actions, appealing, on the one hand, to the creative liberty of the artist and, on the other hand, to the right to render homage to the Swiss maestro. And despite Baldessari's lawyer mentioning former instances of 'artistic plagiarism' throughout the history of art in an attempt to defend himself, Wiesenger argued that in other cases, artists reproduced the artworks of someone else – we might mention Marcel Duchamp and his Mona Lisa with a moustache or the numerous replicas of Picasso, Matisse, Duchamp, Warhol and Brâncuşi by Mike Bidlo – but 'appropriation' in art is a practice that must be legally approved by who holds the creative rights of the reproduced author; and Baldessari was never afforded such permission.

2 Cf. D'Angelo (2011, 13 ff.), for an elaboration of these arguments.

3 Cf. D'Angelo (2008, 3–35, 2011, 48 ff.).

4 Details of the trial can be read in AA.VV (2003).

5 A general introduction to the questions of the philosophy of art and the problems concerning the definition of art, with a focus on research in the Anglo-American field, can be found in Davies (1991).

6 A similar position is argued by Danto (2003, 25–30).

7 For an elaboration, see Carroll (1999, 8).

8 For a closer look at Baumgarten's aesthetics, see Kobau (2001, 2008, 2010).

9 In cases like this one where a reference is not explicitly made, the English translation has been made by the translator.

10 Tatarkiewicz (1975).

11 Refer to Ferraris (1997, 2001, 2003).

12 Cf., for example, Zangwill (2007, 387–95). For the importance of the avant-garde in
    the philosophy of art, cf. pp. 388–9.
13 For more on this subject, cf. Andina (2011, 84–108).
14 Cf., for instance, the work of economist Donald Thompson (1999).
15 For more on the topic, cf. *The Sophist* (235d–236d) and, particularly, the distinction
    between two types of mimesis: one is good – the art of representing – that
    reproduces copies that are congruent with things without paying attention to
    perspective, while the other is bad – the art of appearances – which renders objects
    in the form of illusory images.
16 Vincent Van Gogh, *A Pair of Shoes* (1886, oil on canvas, 37.5 x 45.5, Van Gogh
    Museum).
17 Jacques Derrida will return to the Heidegger-Shapiro dispute (1978, Eng. trans.,
    256–382): while Shapiro accuses Heidegger's interpretation of making a referent
    error (the shoes depicted by Van Gogh are in fact Van Gogh's own rather than a
    farmer's), Derrida equally accuses Shapiro of presuming that he is able to assume
    the point of view of the artist better than the artist himself.

Chapter 1

1 This intuition dates all the way back to Plato who in *Phaedrus* (275c) wrote:
   'Writing, Phaedrus, has this strange quality, and is very like painting; for the
   creatures of painting stand like living beings, but if one asks them a question, they
   preserve a solemn silence. And so it is with written words; you might think they
   spoke as if they had intelligence, but if you question them, wishing to know about
   their sayings, they always say only one and the same thing.'
2 For a closer look into these questions, cf. Goodman (1969, ch. 1, 3–45).
3 I am referring to the well-known cartoon series, *The Simpsons*; specifically, the
   episode *Mom and Pop Art* (season 10, from 1999).
4 An efficacious critique on art as imitation of reality is exhibited in Goodman
   (1969), when the American philosopher constructs his argument through the
   parallelism between visual depiction and language. His point is similar to that
   expressed by Gorgia, and the obvious conclusion is that art does not imitate reality
   (perhaps it represents it), and that each representation is but the selection of a
   subject and the expression of a certain point of view. For more on this last point, cf.
   Goodman (1960, 48–56) as well as Ryle (1954, 81).
5 For more on this point, cf. the beginning of *The Transfiguration of the
   Commonplace* by Arthur Danto (1981, 3–8).
6 For more on this matter, cf. Danto (1999a, 205–32). On a related note, Adorno
   (2005, Eng. trans., 142) writes: 'the less dense reproduction of reality in naturalist

literature left room for intentions: in the unbroken duplication achieved by the technical apparatus of film every intention, even that of truth, becomes a lie.'

7 I am adopting the periodization formulated by Clement Greenberg in his work *Modernist Painting* (1986–95).

8 It would be worthwhile to mention that neurological research regarding art seems to confirm this theory. As noted, for example, by H. Gardner (1982, xi), the artistic impulse in children is not a representational impulse per se. Children play with bread crumbs and mould them without intending to represent something. This is also because, until they reach adolescence, they are unaware of the fact that artworks can be of representational character. Similar conclusions are made by Lorna Selfe and Donald Sanders (1979) who, while studying the progress of Nadia, a severely autistic child with extraordinary artistic ability who at the age of three and a half was able to draw a horse in very little time, without ever having learned to draw and without using a model, notice how the ability to draw is not developed parallel to the ability to mimetically depict objects.

9 *Republic*, I, 386a–387b; XII, 401a–403c.

10 For a closer look at the logic and dynamics of fictional worlds, cf. Voltolini (2010, 12 ff.) and Kroon and Voltolini (2011).

11 Cf. mainly Danto (1981, 1986, 1997).

12 Cf. Whitehead and Russell (1910–13, vol. 1, 51): 'It should be observed that by "indiscernibles" he [Leibniz] cannot have meant two objects which agree as to *all* their properties, for one of the properties of x is to be identical with x, and therefore this property would necessarily belong to y if x and y agreed in *all* their properties. Some limitation of the common properties necessary to make things indiscernible is therefore implied by the necessity of an axiom.'

13 Black (1952, 11): 'if two things, a and b, are given, the first has the property of being identical with a. Now b cannot have this property, for else b would be a, and we should have only one thing, not two as assumed. Hence a has at least one property, which b does not have, that is to say the property of being identical with a.'

14 Cf. Danto (2003).

Chapter 2

1 Cf, endnote 12, Chapter 1.

2 Richard Wollheim groups together any theory of art that is in 'reference to what is said or done by persons or bodies of persons whose roles are social facts' (Wollheim, 1968, 157), and labels them 'institutional theories', a decision I believe to be reasonable.

3 Cf., in particular, Dickie (1969, 1984).

4 Cf. Davies (2006, 38 ff.).

5   For similar considerations, cf. Thomasson (1999, 13 ff.).

6   Danto (1964, 571–84) and id. (1973a, 1–17), an expanded version of the article
    from 1964 was developed in Danto (1992, 33–55).

7   For more on this point, cf. Wieand (1981a, 151).

8   For an examination of the topics of criticism of Dickie's theory cf. Beardsley (1976,
    200), who argues that Dickie's theory is circular, and, even if it were not, it would
    still not be convincing. For more on this matter, cf. also Diffey (1969, 145–56);
    Dipert (1986) and id. (1993, 110).

9   The detailed story of 'tulipomania' can be found in Dash (1999).

10 Danto is of the same opinion (2003, 39) and offers the example of the case of
    Charles Comfort, director of the National Gallery of Canada. Comfort supported
    and endorsed the opinion of Canadian customs when they decided to impose a tax
    on the *Brillo Boxes*, classifying them not as works of art, but as store merchandise.
    This observation permits Danto to emphasize how it is factually impossible to
    consider the art world as a single body, considering the heterogeneity of the
    judgements expressed by its members.

11 Opposite conclusions can be found in Becker (1982, 2–20).

12 Cf. especially Dipert (1993, 110 ff.).

13 For more on this point, cf. Varzi (2007, 17–39). Varzi delineates a parallel between
    work of art and money, maintaining that in both cases it is necessary to resist
    the dualist temptation of multiplying the entity (metal and money, just as the
    physical object and artwork). Money, just like a work of art, is not a new entity
    that is populating our world, but, rather, an object that enjoys particular extrinsic
    properties. In this sense, Nelson Goodman's intuition is correct in changing the
    way in which we ask the question (it is no longer *what is* a work of art?' but, rather,
    '*when* is something art?'). It becomes of utmost importance to establish under
    what conditions something *counts as art* in a certain cultural and social context.
    Varzi openly positions himself in a descriptivist perspective: art is that which is
    established by society (in our case by the *art world*), so that everything that is
    decreed to be a work of art is, in fact, a work of art, just like in the case of money.
    There is no difference between a coin, a bill, a debit card or even a cheque; all can
    be used as money without there being necessary particular conditions beyond
    those established by society. Varzi (and this applies to all conventionalist positions
    in general) disproportionately expands the category, thereby making the concept
    of classes of artworks unnecessary. In Varzi's definition, anything can truly be a
    work of art, under the sole condition that, through an act of stipulation, the context
    decides it.

14 For more on this point, see Andina (2011, 67–104).

15 Wollheim (1968, 20).

16 Cf. Ibid. (6–8, 5–10) and (9–19, 10–34).

17 Dickie (1974, 44–5) and id. (1969, 253–6).

18 For more on this point, see Ryckman (1989, 176).

19 As an example, cf. Heidegger (1927, 15, Eng. trans., 98 ff.).

20 For more on the 'RIF intention', cf. Dipert (1993, 113): this is an intentional act in which recognition implies a form of recognition that brings about fulfilment.

21 For more on the notion of aesthetics and its relationship with the philosophy of art, refer to, among others, Abercrombie 1922; Leon, 1931; Beiswanger, 1939; Dickie, 1974; Osborne, 1981, 1–11; Beardsley, 1983a, 15–29; Dziemidok, 1988, 1–17; Carroll, 1991, 307–34; Ferraris, 1997, 2007; Lamarque, 2010.

22 Among the numerous exemplifications of this theoretical discourse, cf. in particular Dewey, 1925, 1934; Gilson, 1957; Kupfer, 1983; Sartwell, 1995; Shusterman, 1992, 1997, 2000; D'Angelo, 2011; Velotti, 2012.

23 For a closer examination of these matters in particular, cf. Margolis (1980, 1999, 15–40). The specific meaning of Margolis's definition may be summarized as the following: 'artworks are physically embodied and culturally emergent entities' (id., 1999, 68).

24 It is not by chance that studies in neuroscience tend to favour classic art almost exclusively, since aesthetic pleasure received by contemporary art, if it exists at all, is certainly different.

25 For a general discussion of aesthetic experience in the realm of the philosophy of art, see Stolnitz, 1960; Beardsley, 1983a, especially sec. 1.

26 For an introduction to the philosophical questions concerning aesthetic qualities, see Pepper 1937; Siebley, 1959, 1965; Pettit, 1983, 17–38; Hermerén, 1988; Goldman, 1993; Zemach, 1997.

27 This is the rather uncultured, simpleton protagonist from *The Artworld*, Arthur Danto's essay published in the *Journal of Philosophy* in 1964. In Danto's narrative, Testadura is unable to distinguish an ordinary material object from a work of art; accordingly, he is unable to distinguish Brillo box from *Brillo Box*.

28 For more on this particular question, see Bell, 1914; Beardsley 1981.

29 Such is suggested, for instance, by studies in cognitive science that deal with these questions. For a useful general introduction and discussions, see Cappelletto, 2009; Skov and Vartanian, 2009; Desideri, 2011.

30 For a critique of the classic concept of disinterest, cf. Dickie (1964, 56–65); further arguments can be found in Carroll (1986, 57–68).

31 "O living creature gracious and benignant / Who visiting goest through the purple air / Us, who have stained the world incarnadine, / If were the King of the Universe our friend, / We would pray unto him to give thee peace, / Since thou hast pity on our woe perverse. / Of what it pleases thee to hear and speak, / That will we hear, and we will speak to you, / While silent is the wind, as it is now. / [. . .] Love, that on gentle heart doth swiftly seize, / Seized this man for the person beautiful / That was

ta'en from me, and still the mode offends me. / Love, that exempts no one beloved from loving, / Seized me with pleasure of this man so strongly, / That, as thou seest, it doth not yet desert me; / Love has conducted us unto one death; / Caina waiteth him who quenched our life! [...] And all the while one spirit uttered this, / The other one did weep so, that, for pity, / I swooned away as if I had been dying, / And fell, as a dead body falls" (Dante, *Inferno*, Canto V, 88–142).

32 For a closer examination of these topics, cf. Goodman (1969, 241–52), who openly critiques the theories that unite art and the expression of emotions. In fact, Goodman rejects the separation of science and art by arguing that such a separation conveys a fictitious partition that is not confirmed by the architecture of the human mind.

33 Various examples of this position may be found in the writings of: Collingwood, 1938; Langer, 1953; Goodman, 1969; Stecker, 1984; Barwell, 1986; Hjort and Laver, 1997; Matravers, 2001; Nussbaum, 2001.

Chapter 3

1 References for the formulation of the neo-Wittgensteinian perspective are: Weitz, 1956, 1977; Ziff, 1951; Kennick, 1958.

2 Cf. Wittgenstein (1953, 66–7). As we shall see in detail, this is a position from which the general theory of Ludwig Wittgenstein stands by applying it to the specific field of philosophy of art.

3 Kennick alludes to the formalist theory, established by Clive Bell (1914) and Roger Fry (1926), that theorized that the necessary and sufficient condition for an object to be considered a work of art was the exhibition of a significant form.

4 In addition to Weitz, this position is discussed and explained by Ziff (1953, 466–80) and Gallie (1956).

5 This theoretical model is developed in: Carroll, 1988, 1993, 1994; Kivy, 1997, especially ch. 1.

6 For an example, cf. Dilthey (1959).

7 An excellent application of this theoretical model, which also includes an in-depth analysis of non-Western arts, can be found in Carrier (2008, 21 ff.).

8 For more on this point, cf. especially Danto (1997). For a critical discussion of the Dantian model, see Margolis (1999, 37 ff.).

9 Naturally, the point of reference here is Vasari (1550).

10 For the details of this theory, cf. Ferraris (2007) and id. (2009, Eng. trans., 271 ff.).

11 This theory is developed in Ferraris (2005, 2009).

12 Cf. Plato, Republic, X, vii 605c–607a, viii 607b–608b.

13　In 1844, American psychiatrist Amariah Bringham, founder of the *American Journal of Insanity*, was already finding a connection between certain types of suicides and news stories, and considered them to be the result of imitative behaviours. This consideration was taken up by sociologist David Philips who spoke explicitly of the 'Werther effect'. The importance of the imitation factor was partially questioned by an artwork dedicated to suicide by Émile Durkeim, which contextualizes the issue from a social perspective. During the 1970s, the Werther effect was revisited by psychiatrist Jerome A. Motto who, in light of a 40 per cent increase in suicides in Los Angeles in the month following Marilyn Monroe's death, reflects not only upon the imitative factor, but also on the narrative structure through which the story is transmitted.

14　For a discussion of this point, refer to Terrone (2008, 274–8), who suggests a helpful path to complete Ferraris's theory.

15　Cf. the formulations and related applications in Ferraris (2009).

16　For examples, see Dissanayake, 1990; Gaut, 2000; Dutton, 2006.

Chapter 4

1　This is a work from the Surrealist movement. The artist first conceived of the idea while conversing with Pablo Picasso and photographer Dora Maar in a Parisian café. As Picasso admired Oppenheim's bracelet, covered entirely with fur, he proposed that one could cover anything with fur, to which Oppenheim responded, 'even this cup and saucer'.

2　In addition to Carroll (1988, 140–56), cf. also Collingwood (1938) and Carney (1991, 272–89).

3　This is the essay entitled *Supplementary Essay I*, contained in the re-edition of *Art and Its Objects* from 1980.

4　Cf. the *lectio magistralis* given by Levinson on 20 May 2010 in Siracusa, Italy, in occasion of the conference 'Estetica Diffusa' sponsored by the Società Italiana di Estetica (www.siestetica.it/).

5　Upon closer examination, the confusion that Sartwell runs into was already encountered by Walter Benjamin (1955), who identifies unlimited technical reproducibility as the fundamental trait of twentieth-century art. It is the possibility to produce, reproduce and spread any artwork at a staggering rate, in virtually unlimited quantities, that causes the loss of 'aura', the element that characterized the art of the pre-industrial periods, and that associated it with the sacred realm. In essence, throughout the course of the twentieth century, artworks are no longer peculiar and irreproducible objects (*ivi*, 8), but, rather, are considered merchandise. In other words, artworks become considered low-cost, easily marketable objects and, accordingly, they lose their singularity. This transformation clearly relates to the economic value of artworks but, as opposed to what is hypothesized by Benjamin, it does not alter the object 'work of art' from an ontological perspective.

6 See Andina (2011, 5–6).

7 The expression 'homeless objects' is borrowed from Roderick M. Chisholm (1982, 37) who, in turn, takes it from Alexius con Meinong, who talks of 'heimatlose Gegestände' in the work entitled *Über die Stellung der Gegenstandstheorie im System der Wissenshaften* (1907).

8 For an in-depth examination of this point, see the Danto-Margolis dispute: Margolis, 1998, 353–74; Danto, 1999b, 321–9; Margolis, 2000, 326–39.

9 The bases of this theory can be found in Meinong (1904).

10 Meinong (1904, 485–6).

11 Cf. Meinong's retort to Russell. Meinong (1906–7, 83–4).

12 Florenskij's position (1922) is rich and highly articulate and ought to be examined in detail. For our purposes, we should simply note how it relates to positions (Heidegger's above all) that consider works of art as a sign of something else – as, for instance, transcendence in the world.

13 Meinong (1899, 387–92). Cf. also the Meinongian principle: 'Where complexion, there relation and vice versa' (*ivi*, 389).

14 For an in-depth examination of these matters, cf. Andina (2011).

15 For an elaboration on these two positions, cf. Collins (1979, 225–43).

16 References from these authors are: Danto, 1968, especially 89–93; Fodor, 1975, especially ch. 1; and Harman, 1973, with particular attention to ch. 4.

17 For a closer examination of these matters, see Andina (2011, 36 ff.).

18 For more on this particular point, cf. Danto (1989, 248).

19 Roman Ingarden (1965, Eng. trans., 245 ff.) refers to this very idea when he makes the distinction between literary works of historical nature (an historical novel, for instance) and historical works. The difference is found in the transparency of the *medium*: 'In *literary* "historical" works, therefore, the situation is the direct opposite of what is true for *scholarly* historical works. In the latter, the purely intentional objectivities are matched, in accordance with their content, with their corresponding real objects and are identified with them; as a result they become [...] transparent, so that the meaning intentions strike directly what is real, and what is purely intentional disappears from view. In the literary work, on the contrary, the purely intentional object – being supposedly "real" – appears in the foreground and attempts, as it were, to conceal the corresponding, real, Represented object by passing itself off for it' (245).

20 For more details, cf. http://www.guggenheim.org/new-york/interact/participate/youtube-play.

Bibliography

This bibliography includes only the works that were explicitly referred to throughout the text. The bibliography includes the works cited throughout the text according to the Anglo-Saxon system (with first the indication of the author, followed by the year of publication and the page number), with the exclusion of the ancient classics whose citation origins are found directly within the text.

AA.VV. (2003), *Brancusi contre états-Unis. Un procès historique,* 1928. Adam Biro, Paris.

Abercrombie, L. (1922), *An Essay towards a Theory of Art.* Martin Secker, London.

Adajian, T. (2007), *The Definition of Art.* Heardword from Stanford Encyclopedia of Philosophy (http://plato.stanford.edu/entries/art-definition).

Adorno, T. (1951), *Minima moralia. Reflexionen aus dem beschädigten Leben.* Suhrkamp, Frankfurt am Main. (Eng. trans.: *Minima Moralia: Reflections From Damaged Life.* Verso, New York, 2005.)

Andina, T. (2011), *Arthur Danto: Philosopher of Pop.* Cambridge Scholars Publishing, Newcastle.

Ast, F. (1805), *System der Kunstlehre.* J.C. Hinrichs, Leipzig.

Austin, J. L. (1962), *How to Do Things with Words, The William James Lectures delivered at Harvard University in 1955.* Clarendon Press, Oxford.

Barkow, H., Cosmides, L. and Tooby, J. (1992), *The Adapted Mind: Evolutionary Psychology and the Generation of Culture.* Oxford University Press, New York.

Barwell, I. (1986), 'How does art express the emotions?' *Journal of Aesthetics and Art Criticism,* XLV(2), 175–81.

Batteux, C. (1746), *Les Beaux Arts réduits à un même principe.* Durand, Paris.

Baumgarten, A. G. (1750–8), *Aesthetica.* Frankfurt/O., Kleyb.

Beardsley, M. (1958), *Aesthetics. Problem in the Philosophy of Criticism.* Harcourt, New York-Burlingame.

— (1976), 'Is art essentially institutional', in M. Beardsley (ed.), *Culture and Art.* Lars Aagaard-Mogensen, Humanities Press, Atlantic Highlands (NJ), pp. 194–209.

— (1981), *Aesthetics: Problems in the Philosophy of Criticism.* Hackett Publishing Company, Indianapolis.

— (1983a), 'An aesthetic definition of art', in H. Curtler (ed.), *What Is Art.* Havens Publishers, New York, pp. 15–29.

— (1983b), *The Aesthetic Point of View. Selected Essays,* M. Wreen and D. M. Callen (ed.). Cornell University Press, New York.

Becker, H. S. (1982), *Art Worlds.* University of Calfornia, Berkeley.

Beiswanger, G. W. (1939), 'The aesthetic object and the work of art'. *Philosophical Review,* 48(6), 587–605.

Bell, C. (1914), *Art.* Chatto & Windus, London.

Benjamin, W. (1955), *Das Kunstwerk im Zeitalter seiner technischen Reproduzierbarkeit.* Suhrkamp, Frankfurt am Main. (Eng. trans.: *The Work of Art in the Age of Mechanical Reproduction.* Penguin Books, London, England, 2008.)

Black, M. (1952), 'The identity of indiscernibles'. *Mind,* 61, 11–164.

Cappelletto, C. (2009), *Neuroestetica.* Laterza, Roma-Bari.

Carney, J. (1991), 'Style theory of art'. *Pacific Philosophical Quarterly,* 72, 272–89.

Carrier, D. (2008), *A World Art History and Its Objects.* The Pennsylvania State University Press, Pennsylvania.

Carroll, N. (1986), 'Art and interaction'. *The Journal of Aesthetics and Art Criticism,* XLV(1), 57–68.

— (1988), 'Art, practice and narrative'. *The Monist,* 71, 140–56.

— (1991), 'Beauty and the genealogy of art theory'. *Philosophical Forum,* XXII(4), 307–34.

— (1993), 'Historical narratives and the philosophy of art'. *Journal of Aesthetics and Art Criticism,* 51, 313–26.

— (1994), 'Identifying art', in R. J. Yanal (ed.), *Institutions of Art: Reconsiderations of George Dickie's Philosophy.* The Pennsylvania State University Press, University Park (PA), pp. 3–38.

— (1999), *Philosophy of Art. A Contemporary Introduction.* Routledge, New York.

Chisholm, R. M. (1982), *Brentano and Meinong Studies.* Rodpoi, Amsterdam.

Collingwood, R. G. (1938), *Principles of Art.* Clarendon Press, Oxford.

Collins, A. W. (1979), 'Could our beliefs be representations in our mind?' *The Journal of Philosophy,* 76(5), 225–43.

Croce, B. (1914), *La letteratura della nuova Italia.* Laterza, Roma-Bari.

D'Angelo, P. (2008), *Introduzione all'estetica analitica.* Laterza, Roma-Bari.

— (2011), *Estetica.* Laterza, Roma-Bari.

Danto, A. C. (1964), 'The artworld'. *Journal of Philosophy,* 61(19), 571–84.

— (1965), *Analytical Philosophy of History.* Cambridge University Press, Cambridge.

— (1968), *Analytical Philosophy of Knowledge.* Cambridge University Press, Cambridge.

— (1973a), 'Artworks and real things'. *Theoria,* 39, 1–17.

— (1973b), *Analytical Philosophy of Action.* Cambridge University Press, Cambridge.

— (1981), *The Transfiguration of the Commonplace. A Philosophy of Art.* Harvard University Press, Cambridge (MA).

— (1986), *The Philosophical Disenfranchisement of Art.* Columbia University Press, New York.

— (1989), *Connections to the World. The Basic Concepts of Philosophy.* Harper & Row, New York.

— (1992), *Beyond the Brillo Box: The Visual Arts in Post-Historical Perspective.* Farrar, Straus & Giroux, New York.

— (1997), *After the End of Art, Contemporary Art and the Pale of History.* Princeton University Press, Princeton.

— (1999a), *Philosophizing Art.* University of California Press, Berkeley-Los Angeles.

— (1999b), *The Body / Body Problem.* University of California Press, Berkeley-Los Angeles-London.

— (1999c), 'Indiscernibility and perception'. *British Journal of Aesthetics*, 39, 321–9.

— (2003), *The Abuse of Beauty: Aesthetics and the Concept of Art.* Open Court, Chicago-La Salle (IL).

— (2008), 'Lectio magistralis', in T. Andina and P. Kobau (eds), *Il futuro dell'estetica*, in *Rivista di estetica*, 38(2), 11–19.

— (2009), *Andy Warhol.* Yale University Press, Yale.

— (2011), *Kallifobia nell'arte contemporanea.* Supplementa, Palermo, pp. 51–62.

Dash, M. (1999), *Tulipomania: The Story of the World's Most Coveted Flower & the Extraordinary Passions It Aroused.* Crown, New York, 2000.

Davidson, D. (1971), 'Agency', in R. Binkley, R. Bronaugh and A. Marras (eds), *Agent, Action and Reason.* University of Toronto Press, Toronto.

Davies, S. (1991), *Definitions of Art.* Cornell University Press, Ithaca.

— (2006), *The Philosophy of Art.* Blackwell, Malden-Oxford-Victoria.

Derrida, J. (1978), *La verité en peinture.* Flammarion, Paris (Eng. trans.: *The Truth in Painting.* The University of Chicago Press, Chicago, 1987.)

Descartes, R. (1641), 'Meditationes de prima philosophia', in Ch. Adam and P. Tannery (eds), *Oeuvres de Descartes*, vol. VII. Vrin, Paris, 1983. (Eng. trans.: *Meditations on First Philosophy.* Hackett Publishing Company, Cambridge, 1993.)

Desideri, F. (2011), *La percezione riflessa. Estetica e filosofia della mente.* Cortina, Milano.

Dewey, J. (1925), *Experience and Nature.* Dover Publications, Inc., New York.

— (1934), *Art as Experience*, J. Boydston (ed.). Southern Illinois University Press, Carbondale.

Dickie, G. (1964), 'The myth of aesthetic attitude'. *American Philosophical Quarterly*, 1, 56–65.

— (1969), 'Defining art'. *American Philosophical Quarterly*, 6(3), 253–6.

— (1974), *Art and the Aesthetic: An Institutional Analysis.* Cornell University Press, Ithaca-London.

— (1977), 'A response to Cohen: the actuality of art', in G. Dickie and R. J. Sclafani (eds), *Aesthetics a Critical Anthology.* St. Martin's Press, New York.

— (1984), *The Art Circle: A Theory of Art.* Haven Publications, New York.

Diffey, T. J. (1969), 'The republic of art'. *British Journal of Aesthetics*, IX, 145–56.

Dilthey, W. (1959), *Einleitung in die Geisteswissenschaften.* Teubner, Stuttgart. (Eng. trans.: *Introduction to the Human Sciences.* Princeton University Press, Princeton, 1991.)

Dipert, R. (1986), 'Art, artifacts and regarded intentions'. *American Philosophical Quarterly*, 23, 401–8.

— (1993), *Artifacts, Art Works, and Agency.* Temple University Press, Philadelphia.

Dissanayake, E. (1990), *What Is Art For?* University of Washington Press, Bellingham.

Dutton, D. (2006), 'A naturalist definition of art'. *Journal of Aesthetics and Art Criticism*, 64, 367–77.

Dziemidok, B. (1988), 'Controversy about the aesthetic nature of art'. *British Journal of Aesthetics*, 28, 1–17.

Eco, U. (1968), *La definizione dell'arte.* Mursia, Milano.

Eder, G. J. (ed.) (1995), *Alexius Meinong und Guido Adler. Eine Freundschaft in Briefen.* Rodopoi, Amsterdam/Atlanta (GA).

Fechner, G. (1879), *Vorschule der Aesthetik.* Breitkopf & Härtel, Leipzig.

Ferraris, M. (1997), *Estetica razionale.* Cortina, Milano.

— (2001), *Il mondo esterno.* Bompiani, Milano.

— (2003), *Ontologia.* Guida, Napoli.

— (2005), *Dove sei? Ontologia del telefonino.* Bompiani, Milano. (French trans.: *T'es où? Ontologie du téléphone mobile.* Albin Michel, Paris, 2006.)

— (2007), *La fidanzata automatica.* Bompiani, Milano.

— (2009), *Documentalità. Ontologia del mondo sociale.* Laterza, Roma-Bari. (Eng. trans.: *Documentality. Why It Is Necessary to Leave Traces.* Fordham University Press, New York, 2012.)

Florenskij, P. (1922), *Ikonostas.* Mir Knigi, Moskva, 2007. (Eng. trans.: *Iconostasis.* St. Vladimir's Seminary Press, Crestwood, New York, 1996.)

Fodor, J. (1975), *The Language of Thought.* Harvard University Press, Cambridge (MA), London.

Foucault, M. (1973), *Ceci n'est pas une pipe.* éditions Fata Morgana, Paris. (Eng. trans.: *This Is Not a Pipe.* University of California Press, Berkley,1983.)

Fry, R. (1926), *Transformations: Critical and Speculative Essays on Art.* Chatto & Windus, London.

Gadamer, H. G. (1960), *Wahrheit und Methode.* J.C.B. Mohr, Tübingen. (Eng. trans.: *Truth and Method.* Continuum, London, New York, 1975.)

Gallie, W. B. (1956), 'Art as an essentially contested concept'. *Philosophical Quarterly*, VI, 97–114.

Gardner, H. (1982), *Art, Mind, and Brain: A Cognitive Approach to Creativity.* Basic Books, New York.

Gaut, B. (2000), '"Art" as a cluster concept', in Noël Carroll (ed.), *Theories of Art.* University of Wisconsin Press, Madison, pp. 25–44.

Gilson, É. (1957), *Painting and Reality.* Princeton University Press, Princeton.

Goldman, A. H. (1993), 'Realism about aesthetics proprieties'. *The Journal of Aesthetics and Art Criticism*, 51(1), 31–8.

Gombay, A. (2007), *Descartes*. Blackwell Publishing, Oxford.

Goodman, N. (1960), 'The way the world is'. *Review of Metaphysics*, 14, 48–56.

— (1969), *Languages of Art*. Hackett Publishing, Indianapolis.

— (1978), *Ways of Worldmaking*. Hackett Publishing, Indianapolis.

Greenberg, C. (1986–95), *Collected Essays and Criticism*. The University of Chicago Press, Chicago-London.

Harman, G. (1973), *Thought*. Princeton University Press, Princeton.

Hegel, G. W. F. (1935–8), *Vorlesungen über die Ästhetik*. Suhrkam, Frankfurt am Main, 1970. (Eng. trans.: *Aesthetics*. Oxford University Press, Oxford, 1975.)

Heidegger, M. (1927), *Sein und Zeit*. Tübingen, Max Niemeyer Verlag. (Eng. trans.: *Being and Time*. Harper & Row, New York, 1962.)

— (1950), *Holzwege*. Klostermann, Frankfurt am Main. (Eng. trans.: *Off the Beaten Track*. Cambridge University Press, Cambridge, 2002.)

Hermerén, G. (1988), *The Nature of Aesthetics Qualities*. Lund University Press, Lund.

Hilpinen, R. (1993), 'Authors and artifacts'. *Proceedings of the Aristotelian Society, New Series*, 93, 155–78.

Hjort, M. and Laver, S. (eds) (1997), *Emotions and the Arts*. Oxford University Press, Oxford-New York.

Hume, D. (1748), *An Enquiry Concerning Human Understanding*. Dover Publications, New York, 2004.

Ingarden, R. (1965), *Das literarische Kunstwerk*. M. Niemeyer, Tübingen. (Eng. trans.: *The Literary Work of Art*. Northwestern University Press, Chicago, 1973.)

James, W. (1909), *The Meaning of Truth. A Sequel to Pragmatism*. Longmans, Green, & Co., New York.

Kelley, M. (2007), *Online Conference in Aesthetics* (http://artmind.typepad.com/onlineconference/).

Kennick, W. E. (1958), 'Does traditional aesthetics rest on a mistake?' *Mind*, 67, 267, 317–34.

Kivy, P. (1997), *Philosophies of Art*. Cambridge University Press, Cambridge.

Kobau, P. (2001), 'Estetica e logica', in *L'altra estetica* (with M. Ferraris). Einaudi, Torino, pp. 209–26.

— (2008), 'Wolffs Lehre von der lust an der Ähnlichkeit zwischen abbildung und original', in J. Stolzenberg and O. P. Rudolph (eds), *Christian Wolff und die Europäische Aufklärung. Akten des 1. Internationalen Christian-Wolff-Kongresses in Halle 4.-8. April 2004*, 5 vol. Hildesheim, Olms, vol. 4, pp. 179–92.

— (2010), 'A. G. Baumgarten', in M. Kuehn and H. F. Klemme (eds), *Dictionary of Eighteenth-Century German Philosophers*. Thoemmes, Bristol.

Kroon, F. and Voltolini, A. (2011), 'Fiction', in Edward N. Zalta (ed.), *The Stanford Encyclopedia of Philosophy* (Fall 2011 edn) (http://plato.stanford.edu/archives/fall2011/entries/fiction/).

Kupfer, J. (1983), *Experience as Art: Aesthetics in Everyday Life*. State University of New York, Albany.

Lamarque, P. (2010), *Work and Object*. Oxford University Press, Oxford.

Langer, S. (1953), *Feeling and Form*. Scribner, New York.

Leon, P. (1931), 'The work of art and the aesthetic object'. *Mind*, 40(159), 285–96.

Levinson, J. (1979), 'Defining art historically'. *British Journal of Aesthetics*, 19, 232–50.

— (1989), 'Refining art historically'. *The Journal of Aesthetics and Art Criticism*, 47(1), 21–33.

— (1993), 'Extending art historically'. *The Journal of Aesthetics and Art Criticism*, 51(3), 411–23.

Lewis, C. I. (1946), *An Analysis of Knowledge and Valuation*. Open Court, La Salle.

— (1947), *Analysis of Knowledge and Valuation*. Open Court, La Salle.

Mandelbaum, M. (1965), 'Family resemblances and generalizations concerning the arts'. *The American Philosophical Quarterly*, 2(3), 219–28.

Margolis, J. (1979), 'A strategy for a philosophy of art'. *The Journal of Aesthetics and Art Criticism*, 37(4), 445–54.

— (1980), *Art and Philosophy*. The Harvester Press, Brighton, Sussex.

— (1998), 'Farewell to Danto and Goodman'. *British Journal of Aesthetics*, 38, 353–74.

— (1999), *What, After All, Is a Work of Art? Lectures in the Philosophy of Art*. Pennsylvania State University Press, University Park.

— (2000), 'A closer look at Danto's account of art and perception'. *British Journal of Aesthetics*, 40(3), 326–39.

Matravers, D. (2001), *Art and Emotions*. Oxford University Press, Oxford, New York.

Meinong, A. von (1899), *Über Gegenstände höherer Ordnung und deren Verhältnis zur inneren Wahrnehmung; Gesamtausgabe*, II. Akademische Druck und Verlagsanstalt, Graz, 1971, 377–471.

— (1904), 'Über gegenstandstheorie', in A. Meinong, R. Ameseder and E. Mally (eds), *Untersuchungen zur Gegenstandstheorie und Psychologie*. Barth, Leipzig, pp. 1–50.

— (1907), *Über di Stellung der Gegenstandstheorie im System der Wissenschaften*, R. Leipzig, Voigtländer, indi Roderick M. Chisholm (eds). Akademische Druck, Graz, 1973.

— (1923), 'Zur grundlegung der allgemeinen werttheorie', in *Über Gegenstände höherer Ordnung und deren Verhältnis zur inneren Wahrnehmung; Gesamtausgabe*. Akademische Druck und Verlagsanstalt, Graz, 1971, vol. III.

Nietzsche, F. (1901), *Der Wille zur Macht. Versuch einer Umverthung aller Werthe*. Naumann, Leipzig. (Eng. trans.: *The Will to Power*. Random House, Inc., New York, 1967.)

Nussbaum, M. (2001), *Upheavals of Thought: The Intelligence of Emotions*. Cambridge University Press, Cambridge.

Osborne, H. (1981), 'What is a work of art?' *British Journal of Aesthetics*, 23, 1–11.

Peirce, Ch. S. (1953), *Charles Peirce's Letters to Lady Welby*, I. Lieb (ed.). Whitlock's, New Haven.

Pepper, S. (1937), *Aesthetic Quality: A Contextualist Theory of Beauty*. Charles Scribners' Sons, New York.

Pettit, P. (1983), 'The Possibility of Aesthetic Realism', in E. Sharper (ed.), *Pleasure, Preference and Value*. Cambridge University Press, Cambridge, pp. 17–38.

Quine, W. V. O. (1948), 'On what there is'. *Review of Metaphysics*, 2, 21–38.

Rodari, G. (1962), *Favole al telefono*. Einaudi, Torino. (Eng. trans. by Bart Anderson, www.energybulletin.net/stories/2010-08-20/giacomo-crystal.)

Rosenkranz, K. (1853), *Aesthetik des Hasslichen*. Verlag der Gebruder Bomtrager, Konigsberg.

Russell, B. (1903), *The Principles of Mathematics*. Cambridge University Press, Cambridge.

— (1905), 'On denoting'. *Mind*, 14, 479–93.

Ryckman, Th. C. (1989), 'Dickie on artifactuality'. *The Journal of Aesthetics and Art Criticism*, 47(2), 175–7.

Ryle, G. (1954), *Dilemmas*. Cambridge University Press, Cambridge.

Sartwell, C. (1990), 'A counter-example to Levinson's historical theory of art'. *Journal of Aesthetics and Art Criticism*, 48(2), 157–8.

— (1995), *The Art of Living: Aesthetics of the Ordinary in World Spiritual Traditions*. SUNY Press, Albany.

Schelling, F. W. (1802–4), *Philosophie der Kunst*, Wissenschaftliche Buchgesellschaft, Darmstad. (Eng. trans.: *The Philosophy of Art*. University of Minnesota, Minneapolis, 1989.)

Schlegel, A. (1801), *Die Kunstlehre*, in E. Lohner (ed.), *Kritische Schriften und Briefe*. Kohlhammer, Stuttgart, 1963, vol II.

Searle, J. (1995), *The Construction of Social Reality*. The Free Press, New York.

Selfe, L. and Sanders, D. (1979), *Nadia. A Case of Extraordinary Drawing Ability*. Houghton Mifflin Harcourt Publishing, Orlando.

Shurman, K. (2004), 'Selected papers on phenomenology', in C. Leijenhorst and P. Steenbakkers (eds), *Selected Papers on Phenomenology*. Kluwer Academic Publishers, Dordrecht.

Shusterman, R. (1992), *Pragmatist Aesthetics: Living Beauty, Rethinking Art*. Blackwell, Oxford, Cambridge (MA).

— (1997), 'The end of aesthetic experience'. *Journal of Aesthetics and Art Criticism*, 55, 29–41.

— (2000), *Performing Live: Aesthetic Alternatives for the Ends of Art*. Cornell University Press, Ithaca.

Siebley, F. (1959), 'Aesthetics concepts'. *Philosophical Review*, 68, 421–50.

— (1965), 'Aesthetics and non-aesthetics'. *Philosophical Review*, 74, 135–59.

Skov, M. and Vartanian, O. (2009), *Neuroaesthetics*. Baywood Publishing Company, Amityville.

Sloutsky, V. M. (2003), 'The role of similarity in the development of categorization'. *Trends in Cognitive Sciences*, 7(6), 246–61.

Sloutsky, V. M., Lo, Y. F. and Fisher, A. V. (2001), 'How much does a shared name make things similar? Linguistic labels, similarity, and the development of inductive inference'. *Children Development*, 72(6), 1695–1709.

Stecker, R. (1984), 'Expression of emotion (in some of) the arts'. *Journal of Aesthetics and Art Criticism*, XLII(4), 409–18.

Stieglitz, A. (1917), 'The Richard Mutt case'. *The Blind Man*, 2, 5–7.

Stolnitz, J. (1960), *Aesthetics and the Philosophy of Art Criticism*. Houghton Mifflin Co., New York, 32–42.

Strawson, P. (1950), 'On referring'. *Mind*, 59(235), 320–44.

— (1959), *Individuals. An Essay in Descriptive Metaphysics.* Routledge, London, New York.

Tatarkiewicz, W. (1975), *Dzieje szésciu pojęć*, Warszawa, PWN, 1975. (Eng. trans.: *A History of Six Ideas*. The Hague, Boston, 1980.)

Terrone, E. (2008), *Fidanzate in esubero. L'opera d'arte come oggetto metasociale*, in *Rivista di Estetica*, 37(1), 274–8.

Thomasson, A. L. (1999), *Fiction and Metaphysics*. Cambridge University Press, Cambridge.

Thompson, D. (1999), *The \$12 Million Stuffed Shark*. Palgrave Macmillan, London.

Tversky, A. (1977), 'Features of similarity'. *Psychological Review*, 84, 327–52.

Twardowski, K. (1894), *Zur Lehre vom Inhalt und Gegenstand der Vorstellungen.* A. Hölder, Wien. (Eng. trans.: *On the Content and Object of Presentations*. Martinus Nijhoff, The Hague, Netherlands, 1977.)

Varzi, A. (2007), *Il denaro è un'opera d'arte (o quasi)*, in *Quaderni dell'Associazione per lo Sviluppo degli Studi di Banca e Borsa*, 24, 17–39.

Vasari, G. (1550), *Le vite de' più eccellenti architetti, pittori et scultori italiani, da Cimabue insino ai tempi nostri.* Einaudi, Torino, 2005. (Eng. trans.: *The Lives of the Artists*, Oxford University Press, New York, 1991.)

Velotti, S. (2012), *La filosofia e le arti. Sentire, pensare, immaginare.* Laterza, Roma-Bari.

Voltolini, A. (2010), *Finzioni. Il far finta e i suoi oggetti.* Laterza, Roma-Bari.

Weitz, M. (1956), 'The role of theory in aesthetics'. *The Journal of Aesthetics and Art Criticism*, 15(1), 27–35.

— (1977), *The Opening Mind.* University of Chicago Press, Chicago.

Whitehead, A. N. and Russell, B. (1910–13), *Principia Mathematica*. Cambridge University Press, London, 3, 1925–7.

Wieand, J. (1981a), 'Duchamp and the artworld'. *Critical Inquiry*, 8(1), 151–7.

— (1981b), 'Can there be an institutional theory of art?' *The Journal of Aesthetics and Art Criticism*, 39(4), 409–17.

Witasek, S. (1904), *Grundzüge der allgemeinen Ästhetik*. Leipzig, Barth.

Wittgenstein, L. (1953), *Philosophische Untersuchungen*. Akademie Verlag, Berlin. (Eng. trans.: *Philosophical Investigations*. Blackwell Publishing Ltd., Oxford, 2009.)

Wölfflin, H. (1886), *Prolegomena zu einer Psychologie der Architektur*. Mann, Berlin.

Wollheim, R. (1968), *Art and Its Objects: An Introduction to Aesthetics*. Harper & Row, New York.

— (1980), *Art and Its Objects: With Six Supplementary Essays*. Cambridge University Press, Cambridge.

Zangwill, N. (2007), 'L'irrilevanza dell'avanguardia'. *Rivista di estetica*, 35(2), 387–95.

Zemach, M. (1997), *The Real Beauty*. The Pennsylvania University Press, Pennsylvania.

Ziff, P. (1951), 'Art and the object of art'. *Mind*, LX, 466–80.

— (1953), 'The task of defining a work of art'. *Philosophical Review*, 62, 466–80.

Index

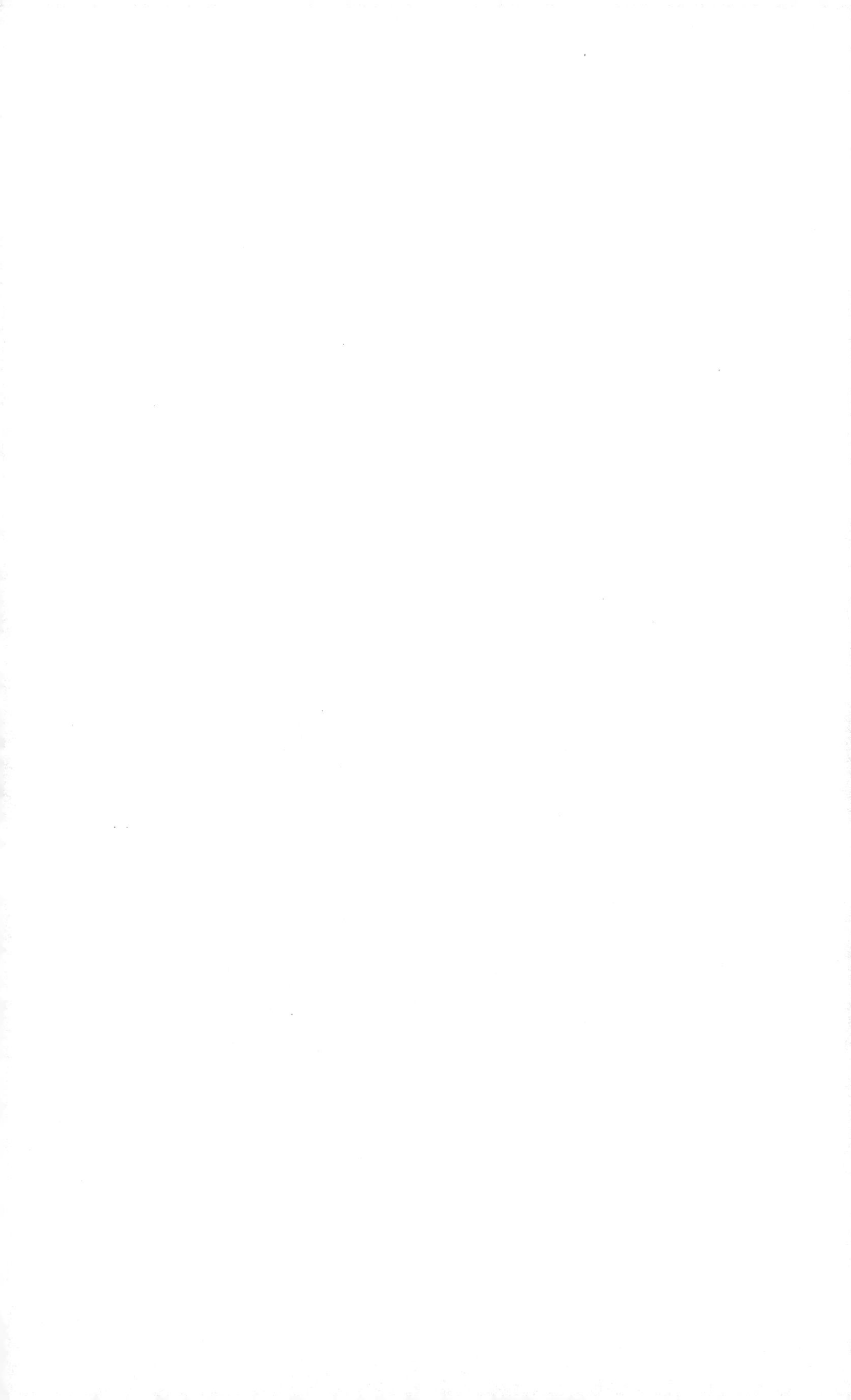